FROM LIVERPOOL TO ISTANBUL

First published in 2007 by

WOODFIELD PUBLISHING LTD
Bognor Regis ~ West Sussex ~ England ~ PO21 5EL
www.woodfieldpublishing.com

ISBN 1-84683-045-1

From Liverpool to Istanbul

A Scouse Odyssey

M‌ICHAEL B‌AILEY

Woodfield

Woodfield Publishing Ltd

Woodfield House ~ Babsham Lane ~ Bognor Regis ~ West Sussex ~ PO21 5EL
telephone 01243 821234 ~ **e-mail** enquiries@woodfieldpublishing.com

Interesting and informative books on a variety of subjects

For full details of all our published titles, visit our website at
www.woodfieldpublishing.com

For my Dad, who gave me Liverpool FC

~ Contents ~

Introduction

During the months of March and April 2005, three friends of mine lost their fathers. One of these friends, Steve, had been a close friend since I was 18 years old. Steve's dad, Arthur, was a few years older than my own father and I did not know him very well, but I could see similarities between them. Arthur was strong, proud, fiercely loyal and extremely generous. He hailed from old Swan in Liverpool and was a member of Saint Anne's Church, only a hundred yards away from the first home bought by my dad for his young family. At Arthur's funeral his sister-in-law recalled a life of loyalty and generosity that I know made Steve and his family very proud. Arthur's funeral made me feel very lucky to still have my own dad with me.

On 3rd May 2005 Liverpool beat Chelsea 1-0 at Anfield to secure a place in the European Cup Final for the first time in 21 years. In the days after the match it became apparent that my dad and I might be able to get tickets for the final, to be held at the Ataturk Stadium in Istanbul.

Financially, the timing could not have been worse, but the opportunity was too good to pass up. I thought about Steve and his Dad and decided that we had to go. Five days before the final we got our tickets. I spent most of those five days shaking my head in disbelief. We were going to the European cup final.

And what a final it turned out to be...

Preface

When you have experienced something as exciting and eventful as Istanbul was for me, it's hard to keep it to yourself. I wanted to write it down so I would never forget what it was like. This book is about my love of Liverpool Football Club and how much it means to me. It's also about how much I love my family and my Dad. And it's about how a journey to Istanbul to see a football match somehow highlighted the importance of all these things.

I also wanted to write this book for other Liverpool fans, who must have experienced similar emotions as a consequence of Liverpool's victory. It would be nice if a few of the fans who were present at that incredible game could read these pages and relive the overwhelming emotions of the experience. And for the devoted fans who watched the game on their TV screens back in England, it would be wonderful if I could provide some idea of what the trip was like.

To anyone about to turn the next page with the intention of reading my book, I'd like to request your patience and forgiveness for my lack of authoring expertise. A few years back I spent four years as a Technical Author working for a US software monolith. It didn't help me become a better writer. I hated the job and I was crap at it. And I mean that, I really was crap at it. I consider it one of my smaller, yet significant, achievements in life that I managed to hold onto that job for as long as I did. The inflated salary kept me content with being crap for four years longer than it should have done but eventually enough was enough and I had to reclaim my soul.

I'm not a professional writer and this is my first attempt at writing a book. This book is a labour of love and as such I hope you will treat its pages with some sympathy and allow for it's certain deficiencies. On these pages you will find an account of one of the greatest nights of my life. A night that extended beyond football into something much bigger and much more important. Shankly's famous life and death quote *may* have been tongue in cheek but during the Istanbul trip my life gained very real perspective. The most important things in my life crossed over into the dreams and songs that form part of loving Liverpool Football Club. So permit me to ask for your patience. I'm not aiming for a literary prize or critical acclaim. I definitely don't have any pretentious financial ambition. I just had to write this book. And I hope in some small part, these pages can provide you with a flavour of what it was like to be there, and what it meant to me.

Michael Bailey

1. Scouser Tommy

Let me tell you the story of a poor boy
Who was sent far away from his home

Poor Scouser Tommy

Football is a huge part of my life and Liverpool Football Club means a great deal to me. My Dad took me to my first game at Anfield on 2nd September 1978 against a newly promoted Tottenham Hotspur side sporting Osvaldo Ardiles and Ricardo Villa in their line up. Ardiles and Villa were part of the Argentina side that had won the World Cup on home soil just two months earlier. 2nd September 1978 was also my seventh birthday. Liverpool won the game 7-0 and the whole experience had an enormous effect on me. By the time I was seven years old I had already watched Liverpool win successive European Cups on television. Those nights lying sprawled across the living room floor, watching the reds reach the very pinnacle of European football, were literally life-changing events for me. Before Dad took me to Anfield I was already obsessed by the game but watching Liverpool win 7-0 on my seventh birthday took my obsession to another level. I felt as if that particular match had been played entirely for my benefit.

Many of my memories of that day remain crystal clear. My Dad bought me a red and white silk scarf with *Con-*

querors of Europe written on it. He bought it for me from a street vendor on the corner of Anfield Road opposite the Arkles pub. I still treasure that scarf and I took it with me to Istanbul for the 2005 European Cup final. 28 years on, that same spot is still used by street vendors selling flags and scarves in much the same way as it was then. In fact, on match days, lots of things have remained largely unchanged around the streets of Anfield Road. Some of the noises and smells are as familiar today as they were 28 years ago. Apart from the flag sellers on the corner you can still hear the shouts of 'Golden Goal!' up and down Anfield Road on any match day. The Golden Goal tickets give you a time for the first goal scored, a kind of a lottery. I don't think we have ever bought one. To be honest I'm no mathematician but the chances of buying a ticket with the exact time of the first goal, to the second, have always seemed a bit slim. The odds never tempted us, even when the first prize *was* a Hitachi clock radio. The strange combined smell of hotdogs and fresh horse manure, courtesy of the local patrolling cavalry, is a smell I could only ever associate with approaching Anfield on match day. As strange as it might sound it's a smell I quite like. A million other Kopites will probably understand what I mean. To me it's a smell I associate with anticipation, excitement, and most of all, success.

I can remember the sheer exhilaration of seeing the Anfield pitch for the first time. It was immaculate in glorious sunshine. Three of us went to the game, me, my Dad, and my older brother Steve. Dad bought us tickets for the Main Stand about three quarters of the way up and near the Kop end of the ground. It was a ritual in our family that your first game would be viewed from the Main Stand. My older brother watched his first game there and in time my younger sister would too. I could see the whole ground perfectly from my fold down wooden panel seat. Dad proudly introduced me to various parts of the ground, the Paddock, the Kemlyn, and the section of the Kop where Dad he used to stand as a boy, in the boys pen.

In 1978 you were allowed to take a pint out into the seats or the terraces. My Dad stood in front of his seat with a pint of Higson's in a paper cup and he smoked a Hamlet cigar, another smell I associated with Anfield for many years. Steve and me munched through a couple of bags of Bensons crisps. I sat staring at the Kop as it slowly filled. The middle of the Kop filled first and then slowly the whole giant terrace packed out and began to come alive. When the Kop sang You'll Never Walk Alone before the game I didn't know what to do. I just stared in awe. Before the match I loved football. After the match I was completely intoxicated with Liverpool football club. The double European Champions were irresistible that day. Dalglish scored twice and Ray Kennedy made it 3-0 at half time. In the second half substitute David Johnson scored a couple and Phil Neal stuck away a penalty but the best goal of the game was saved until last. With 15 minutes to go Liverpool defended a Spurs corner at the Kop end. The corner was intercepted and Ray Kennedy cleared to Dalglish who fed Johnson. Johnson sent Heighway clear on the left wing and Terry McDermott, who had begun the move defending the far post at the other end of the pitch, headed his pinpoint thirty-yard cross into the top corner. I have seen that goal so many times I can replay it in my mind over and over again. I count myself extremely lucky to have been one of fifty-odd thousand at Anfield to witness a total football exhibition.

I also count myself lucky to be a Liverpudlian. My brother and me have my Dad to thank for that. I believe that the core of a club's fanbase should always be comprised of people born and raised in the immediate area. This is the heart of the club's personality. The strength of any fanbase and therefore the football club is family and tradition. My Dad is a lifelong red and his father was before him. Part of what makes my family what it is resides in that tradition. If my granddad was looking down on us as we stood in the Ataturk Stadium on May 25th 2005 I know he will have been very proud and wishing he was there with us. Of course I'm not saying that all Liverpool fans should come from Liverpool or have been born in the city but I do believe the heart of any club must have those vital connections and I feel part of that. It's the same for any football club. There has to be a core of supporters who know the city or town that the club comes from and understand its people. I count myself lucky to be a Liverpudlian because I could have quite easily have been an Evertonian or even born elsewhere in the country. If my forefathers had settled elsewhere in the country I could quite conceivably have been a Sheffield Wednesday fan or support Crystal Palace. You can't choose where you are born or your parents but if I could have chosen, I'd have chosen Liverpool and as it happens I'm pretty pleased with my parents too. I was born in Liverpool on September 2nd 1971. By this time Bill Shankly's Liverpool team was already well established as a force in English football and was winding itself up for a relentless twenty years of domestic success. European football too was about to fall under the influence of his untamed passion for football dominance. 1971 was a particularly good year to be born into a red family.

I play the game too. I spent most of my youth playing 11 a-side football as a striker or a winger and had a reasonable amount of success. My Dad was always there with me week in week out. He would even come and watch my school matches if he got home from work in time. My school games would usually kick-off well before he got home from work but quite often he would appear on the line for the last 10 or 15 minutes. Those last 10 or 15 minutes would usually be my best of the game. My Dad got fairly heavily involved in the teams I played for. He even managed one of them, Halton Lodge, for a couple of years when I was 11 and 12. This was the only period in my life when I really was head and shoulders above most of the other lads my own age. My Dad gave me enormous confidence and I always wanted to impress him. It was rare for Dad to give me praise or advice on my game. He really didn't say much at all or push me very hard. But the little things he did say meant everything to me. I can remember a game when we were losing 2-0 at half-time but I scored twice in the second half to earn us a draw. After the game my Dad told me my first goal was the best he had ever seen me score. That is precisely why I can still remember that game today some 24 years later. If anyone would like to indulge me I can talk them through that goal too! I am certain he has no idea what affect his words used to have on me. It wasn't always a blessing that my Dad managed the team I played for. Youth football was seriously competitive and I used to get some vicious stick from big fat blokes on the line that thought it would be good to get stuck into the manager's son. When I was 11 I was voted my teams player of the year by opposing managers, and that made things worse for me. Not only did I have to deal with opposing managers and players, I now had jealousy from my own teammates and sometimes their parents too. At 12 years old I used to have 18 stone blokes calling me Daddy's boy as I stood next to them on the wing. When I was 13, Halton Lodge merged with another local boys side, Woodside, and became Runcorn Villa. My Dad decided he no longer wanted to run the team and I got the impression he wasn't terribly welcome in the new set-up. I didn't feel welcome either and left to play for Runcorn Boys Club. Runcorn Boys Club weren't quite as good as the newly formed Runcorn Villa but they were a friendlier club and they played on the best pitch in the league. I loved playing for them. Only one thing felt wrong. Dad started missing some of my games. He would come to one game and then miss a couple. I didn't understand why. At first I thought it was because I wasn't playing as well as when I was 11 or 12 but soon I realised that wasn't the reason. In one of my first games we won 8-0 and I scored six goals. After the game I ran all the way home to tell my Dad. He was really pleased for me but he still didn't come to my next game. I slowly came to realise that he was just letting me grow up and stand up on my own two feet but I still wished he was there. One other thing bothered me. On the football pitch I am an uncontrollable whinger, a kind of poor man's Craig Bellamy. At 35 I now play in a local six a-side league and I whinge now pretty much the same way as I did when I was 12 years old. Perhaps Dad just got sick of my whining! By the time I was 18 and playing open age football my Dad hardly came to watch my matches at all. Out of the blue he came to watch me in a five a-side tournament when I was 19. The tournament lasted all night and I spotted my Dad standing with my Mum during one of the early matches. I played my socks off that night and scored a golden goal winner in the final. It was just like when I was playing for my school team and he would turn up for the last 10 minutes. I ran my heart out.

It's probably fairly obvious by now that some of the inspiration for me writing this book is my love of Liverpool Football Club but mostly this book is about what my Dad means to me. My Dad has Liverpool Football Club running through his veins. My Mum always said that Liverpool Football Club came first in our family and everything queued up behind. That's not exactly true but she wasn't far wrong. My Dad is an archetypal scouser. Not the crap you see stereotyped in the media day in day out, my Dad is the real McCoy. Dad grew up in Norris Green, in a working class family and he had a strict upbringing. He loved his father very much. The day my granddad died of lung cancer in 1993 my devastated father told me that he had thought his Dad was going to live forever. It wasn't until that day that I began to appreciate that my Dad wouldn't live forever either. Dad has worked all of his life and worked extremely hard to build a home for his family. Where he grew up in Norris Green is about four miles from Anfield and later he spent 33 years working at Ford Halewood. He has never been in any kind of trouble with the law and lives to make his family happy, which it is. And yes he does have a brilliant sense of humour. Every scouser in Liverpool will recognise this basic blueprint.

My Dad has been to over a thousand Liverpool matches. He is also my idol. As a boy I tried hard to copy the footballing talents of my hero's Dalglish, Rush, Walsh, and Barnes. As a human being I have only ever wanted to be my Father. My Dad is handsome, strong, gentle, kind, and incredibly modest. Dad took up distance running in his early thirties and proved to be a talented athlete. He has run hundreds of races including 22 marathons. He once ran the Mersey marathon in three hours nine minutes but never quite managed to break three hours, something I know he was capable of and I think he regrets. My Dad would never tell anyone quite how good he was. I remember attending a presentation night with some of the family for Ford Halewood athletics club. There were dozens of awards given out and I was sat talking to my Dad for most of the ceremony. Then whilst we were in mid conversation I thought I heard my Dad's name called out. 'Hang on', I said, 'I think they just called out your name'. We all looked across to the stage to hear the compere repeat 'The award for club over fifties champion is, Tommy Bailey'. Dad got up to receive his award. When he returned from the stage he just plonked his trophy next to his pint of Guinness and carried on our conversation where we had left it. That is a measure of my Dad.

During the months of March and April 2005 three friends of mine lost their fathers. One of these friends Steve Tutte, has been a close friend since we met when I was 18 years old. When I first met Steve he was sitting on someone's shoulders sticking a Panini sticker of Paolo Maldini to a road sign. He is a mildly eccentric football nut and a die-hard Evertonian. Steve's Dad, Arthur, was a few years older than my own father and I didn't know him very well but I could see similarities within their personalities. Arthur was a die-hard Evertonian who passed his blue devotion on to his two sons in much the same way as my Dad gave us Liverpool FC. Arthur was strong, proud, fiercely loyal, and extremely generous. Arthur hailed from Old Swan in Liverpool and was a member of St Anne's church only one hundred yards away from the first home bought by my Dad for his then young family in Gidlow Road. When I met Arthur for the first time he asked me whereabouts in Liverpool my family was from. When I told him Old Swan he beamed. Arthur was extremely proud of his roots. At Arthur's funeral his sister in law recalled a life of loyalty and generosity that I know made Steve and his family very proud. Sadly after Arthur died two other friends lost their fathers too, both somewhat unexpectedly. I didn't know either of the deceased but following Arthur's funeral and the two further bereavements I felt very lucky to still have my Dad with me.

On 3rd May 2005 Liverpool beat Chelsea 1-0 at Anfield to record a 1-0 aggregate win in the semi-final of the Champions League. Liverpool had booked their place in the European Cup Final for the first time in 21 years. In the days after the match it became apparent that my Dad and I might be able to get tickets for the final. Financially the timing was shocking as my wife, Yvonne, and I were saving to move house but emotionally the opportunity seemed too good to pass on. I talked with my wife and she urged me to go. Normally my brother would have come along but he had a holiday in Cyprus booked for him and his girlfriend. If we were going to go it would be expensive and it would be just Dad and me. I thought about Steve Tutte and my other recently bereaved friends and decided I had to go. It wasn't easy getting tickets but we finally got confirmation of our package five days before the final. I spent most of those five days shaking my head in disbelief. We were going to the European Cup Final.

Before the trip I hoped to come home with an experience of a lifetime under my belt. I hoped to come home having watched Liverpool regain the European Cup after 21 years. Most of all I wanted to bring home memories of my Dad and me together that I could cherish for the rest of my life.

2. Early Doors

I fell in to a burning ring of fire
I went down, down, down and the flames went higher.
And it burns, burns, burns the ring of fire
The ring of fire.

Johnny Cash

On the morning of Wednesday 25th May 2005 my alarm
was set for the ungodly time of 3:40am. The itinerary sent
by Lonsdale Travel advised we get to Liverpool John Lennon airport for 4:30am but Dad and I agreed that was too
early. The taxi was booked to pick me up at my house first
at 4:30am and then pick Dad up at around 4:40am. This
meant we would be at the airport for 5:00am in plenty of
time for our 7:30am flight to Istanbul.

The alarm wasn't actually necessary. Through the night I
didn't sleep for more than thirty minutes at a time. After
each thirty-minute nap I raised my head to check the
clock and then fell asleep again for another thirty minutes
or so. When I woke at 3:30am I stared at the clock for 10
minutes until the alarm went off. It's amazing how easy it
is to get out of bed at 3:30 am when there is a European
Cup Final to go to. I got up and peeked through the bedroom blinds at our street. It was a dark and chilly morning
even for the time of year. It was drizzling rain outside, 'that
rain that soaks you through,' as Peter Kay might say. After a

quick shave and shower I crept downstairs. In the living room my bag sat on the couch next to where I had laid out my Liverpool shirts and scarves the night before. I had packed and double-checked my bag over and over the previous night but one last check wouldn't hurt. I decided to wear a gold Liverpool away shirt for the journey and keep my favourite red home shirt for the game. The gold shirt wasn't too popular with fans but I always loved it. It reminded me of a great holiday I'd had in Magaluf in 1994. I'd taken delivery of the shirt the day before we flew out to Majorca and hammered that shirt for the full fortnight. I have always felt it was a lucky shirt but I haven't a clue why. We didn't win anything in it and what's more it nearly cost me dear the first time I wore it one night early on in the Magaluf holiday. I was walking back to the hotel on my own a little worse for wear when I decided to stop to buy a burger. Whilst I was in the queue a group of three blokes started asking me about the shirt. I could tell they weren't enthusing about it. The questions were more along the lines of 'what the bloody hell is that?' rather than 'nice shirt, where did you get it?' One of the lads became aggressive and started pointing to a tattoo in his forearm. I hadn't a clue what he was saying but I recognised the tattoo as a Manchester United badge. I stood my ground for a moment. One of them then asked for the shirt. 'It's too late lads...' I said '... you've been born Mancs'. I tried to pitch it as a joke but I failed very miserably. I decided against the burger and walked out of the burger bar in the direction of my hotel. At first I thought the Manc trio had stayed in the burger queue but I kept looking over my shoulder. About thirty yards up the street

I turned around to see them charging after me. My natural instinct was to run. I'm thankful I was pretty young and fit at the time. They pursued me right into the hotel foyer at which point they thought better of taking on security and retreated.

I chose two scarves for the trip. I took a red, white, and yellow woollen scarf with *Ace of Clubs* written on it along with my treasured white silk scarf with *Conquerors of Europe* written on it. I intended to take the red and white scarf to the game itself but the silk scarf was just along for the trip. To be honest I'm not sure if I took the silk scarf to Istanbul to bring us good luck or just so I could show my Dad I still had it. I'm certainly not superstitious but somehow it felt right to take it along.

I normally enjoy breakfast but this morning I wasn't hungry. I force-fed myself a bowl of bran flakes and went back upstairs to say goodbye to my wife Yvonne. I didn't have the stomach for toast. Yvonne was half-asleep but I think she heard me. I then crept into my little girls' rooms and gave them a kiss goodbye. Hannah was three years old and Jessica just 16 months old. They were both fast asleep. Previously I had been away from them for five days at a time working but this two-day trip was altogether completely different. I felt like I was going to the other end of the earth.

There was a little added apprehension about the trip provided by lots of well meaning friends and family telling me to 'take care' in Istanbul. Istanbul has something of a reputation after several high profile football matches with other English clubs. The most infamous of these clashes was the UEFA Cup semi-final between Leeds and Galatasaray in April 2000. Two Leeds fans were stabbed and murdered the night before the game after trouble flared between the two sets of supporters. The trouble was centred on Taksim Square, the main entertainment district in Istanbul where Liverpool supporters were most likely to gather for the build up to the final. The fans of Galatasaray have established a fearsome reputation for their club stadium the Ali Sami Yen or 'hell' as they like to call it. A famous banner once greeted a visiting Manchester United team with 'Welcome to Hell' emblazoned on it as the Galatasaray fans attempted to enhance the stadiums fearsome reputation. Years later in 2001 Liverpool fans took a banner of their own to the much feared Ali Sami Yen it read, 'If you think this is hell you want to try The Grafton on a Friday night'. I read somewhere that the owner of the infamous Grafton nightclub bought that banner for the club. Not sure if that's true. There were plenty of friends and family that worried for our safety but rightly or wrongly I felt we would be fine. Besides this final wasn't featuring Galatasaray, and wasn't being played in the Ali Sami Yen. I always felt the Turkish people would be bending over backwards to help and to provide their premier city with a more welcoming reputation. I didn't feel like I was travelling anywhere where we wouldn't be safe.

I went back downstairs and took up a position at the kitchen window waiting for a sign of our cab. The rain still drizzled and it was still dark. I stood in the kitchen with the light off so I could see clearly through the window. It was now 4:20am and my stomach turned nervously. Perhaps my regular breakfast fayre of bran flakes wasn't such a good choice. I'm a slave to my bowel. I'm a really confident person but I've always suffered from nerves where football is concerned. Whether I'm getting ready to play or going to watch the reds my preparation always involves a few trips to the toilet. After a particularly productive trip to the downstairs toilet I resumed my position at the window. The minutes passed and my stomach turned. I took a couple of paracetamol and stuffed the rest of the packet into my bag. At 4:40am I rang the taxi firm. I was told that our taxi driver had fallen asleep at home and would be another five minutes. At 4:55am the taxi finally arrived and we set off for my Dad's place. The taxi driver wasn't particularly apologetic, which pissed me off a bit. It's only 10 minutes drive to my Mum and Dad's house and I managed to field some fairly stupid football related questions from the taxi driver. To be fair, he immediately confessed he didn't understand much about football when I got into the cab. 'I only really watch the big games on Sky,' he said. Perhaps if he had understood a bit more he would have been on time.

As soon as the taxi pulled up outside my Dad's place he was out like a shot. He had a rucksack over his arm with his Liverpool scarf tied to it. For as long as I can remember my Dad has taken the same scarf to the games. It's a very traditional red and white striped one, no words, no badges, just thick red and white stripes.

The roads were empty and the journey to John Lennon airport was smooth. I checked the contents of my bag for a final time before I got out of the cab. We arrived at John Lennon at 5:30am. The rain had stopped and it was light now. Liverpool fans were converging on the airport from all directions, jumping out of cabs, and marching across from the car parks. There was a great atmosphere inside the airport building and the cheque-in area was packed. The reality that I was actually going to be part of this was only just starting to sink in. We found our check-in queue quickly. There were about two-dozen check-in queues but luckily our queue was just about the shortest. Our queue was on the far right of the check-in desks just beneath a walkway. The walkway had a number of huge banners hanging from it. The most memorable one was a tribute to Jamie Carragher referring to the words of his Kop chant. Sung to the tune of 'We all live in a yellow submarine', Jamie's song is 'We all dream of a team of Carraghers'. The banner read like a team sheet:

1. Carra
2. Carra
3. Carra
4. Carra
5. Carra
6. Carra
7. Carra
8. Carra
9. Carra
10. Carra
11. Carra

'We all dream' was written along the bottom.

It dominated the whole check-in area and it was the first time I can recall a banner giving me goosebumps. I had a feeling that I was looking up at a very small part of Liverpool history in the making. Liverpool fans have a history of making great banners. Perhaps one day in the future this banner would one day sit alongside the 'Joey ate the frogs legs' banner of Rome 1977.

My Dad knows Karl, the bloke in charge of security at John Lennon airport. Karl appeared on the walkway just next to the Carragher banner. He spotted us and came down for a chat. He seemed relaxed, which had to be a good sign. Check-in was quick and we made our way up to departures.

Unsurprisingly departures was hammered with reds. I began to wish I'd put on one of my red Liverpool shirts instead of the gold one I had on, as most people were in red. I realised that this wasn't a time to be different. If ever there was a crowd I was happy to be part of, it was this one. The bar areas were already full and plenty of people were enjoying an early morning beer. Had my brother Steve been there he would have fancied a beer, no doubt, but Dad and me never really contemplated it. There would be plenty of time for a bevvy over the next two days.

Our Steve would certainly have been with us if he hadn't been on holiday in Cyprus. I know he was gutted to miss out on the Istanbul trip but at least he would get to see the game within a great atmosphere on holiday. There was bound to be a huge gathering of reds at all the popular British holiday destinations and I knew he would have a great time. Apart from Istanbul or Liverpool city centre, being away on holiday was probably the best place to be. In my twenties I used to go away on holiday every year with my mates. We would always book to go during the closed season so I hadn't watched many Liverpool games whilst away with the lads. The only time I'd watched an important game whilst on holiday was when England played Germany in the 1990 World Cup semi-final. I was 19 at the time and on holiday with six mates on the Costa Brava. There was an incredible atmosphere in the bar where we watched the game and I guessed that's what Steve had to look forward to. In terms of importance, the European Cup Final is light years ahead of anything the World Cup has to offer, at least to a kopite. Our Steve would have a great time watching the match in Aya Napa, much better than my memories of the Costa Brava.

Dad bought a newspaper and I bought a Champions League Magazine and some water. We were lucky enough to get a couple of seats in a busy café and sat down for a coffee. There was no milk so I had my coffee black. It was steaming hot and like treacle. I couldn't stomach anything to eat. Dad was visibly far more relaxed than I was. We sat for half an hour or so and had our first long chat of the day about the game. We talked about who might be in the team and we pretty much agreed on every position. This was fairly unusual, as we would normally have at least one or two differences of opinion. In particular we both agreed Didi Hamman should start but also agreed he probably wouldn't. We didn't think Rafa would play Didi and Xavi Alonso in the same starting line up and it was easy to understand why. Didi gives Stevie Gerrard the freedom to get forward but then again there was probably no better passer of the ball in Europe than Xavi Alonso on a good day. We hoped that Rafa could find a place in the team for all three. Didi Hamman has always been a particular favourite of mine. Within the squad for the final he stood out as one of four or perhaps five world-class players we had.

Along with Didi Liverpool had Alonso, Carragher, Gerrard, and Hyypia, who could arguably boast world-class ability. Didi is a player who can sometimes go long periods without receiving due credit. In some respects he reminded me of Ronnie Whelan. During the 80s and early 90s Ronnie Whelan was often an unsung hero at Anfield. The vital difference with Ronnie was that he had a knack of scoring valuable goals that bought him his own share of the limelight. His goals that beat Tottenham and Manchester United in successive League Cup Finals, and a last minute equaliser in the FA Cup semi-final against Portsmouth are good examples. He also scored the goal of the tournament for the Republic of Ireland during the 1988 European Championships in Germany. A wonderful scissor-kick volley from outside the area against Russia. Ronnie kept Liverpool's midfield tidy and won countless second balls in the centre of the pitch. He would endlessly retrieve all the bits and pieces breaking from centre midfield and Didi did something similar for us now.

After the coffee my guts ordered me to the toilets for a lengthy visit. As I came out of the toilets a large queue leading from the departure gates started to form and within minutes hundreds of people had joined. By 6:30am the whole of departures formed a single queue snaking all the way from the departure gates and down the stairs to the check-in desks. The cafés emptied as everyone instinctively joined the queue. There was no panicking but you could feel that people were getting edgy. All along the queue people were checking their watches and standing on tiptoes trying to work out how long the queue was. My stomach took note. Half an hour later we had only moved about 10 feet down the queue. My stomach ordered me back to the toilet. On my return Dad hadn't moved an inch. It was now 7:10am. With our flight due to depart at 7:30am it came as some relief that an announcement was made to say our flight would be delayed for thirty minutes.

A remarkably quiet and orderly queue eventually made its way through security. Dad warned me that he always gets stopped for a random search. He was dead right. The security guy looked through everything my Dad had with him. And when I say everything I mean *everything*. The security guy even looked through his tin-foiled wrapped butties. He found turkey and ploughman's pickle. Dad looked flustered after his five minutes of being interfered with. He stumbled through the next set of security gates whilst reloading his rucksack and putting his belt back through his jeans. The security guard insisted Dad took his belt off to come through the metal detector, but I didn't see anyone else having to do the same.

The departure gates were really busy with reds sprawled out on the floor as if they had been there some time. The departure gate on our boarding passes stated gate five. Gate five was at the very end of the airport and we waded through hundreds of reds before we got there. When we eventually reached gate five we were greeted by an announcement that our flight would be delayed until 9:30am. During the next hour other flights left through the adjoining gates. My stomach was not impressed and sent me to the toilet once again. It hadn't taken long for the toilets to become almost unusable. The cubicle available to me was something like the scene from *Trainspotting* when Renton goes into the worst toilet in Scotland. I resisted the temptation to dive in.

'Have you got any paper in there mate?' asked the bloke in the next cubicle in a strong scouse accent. I was born in Liverpool but my parents brought me to Runcorn when I was 18 months old. Apart from a couple of years living in Sheffield I have spent my whole life living in Runcorn. My parents and my family have scouse accents so mine is inherited from them. My accent is noticeably softer than the real thing but it's strange how strong it suddenly becomes when I talk to a born and bred scouser. I honestly can't help it but at least I'm not one of those people who suddenly adopted it when they left school. I know plenty of people like that.

'Sorry lad, it's cardboard tube time in ere and I'm not sharing,' I replied. The bloke laughed.

'Don't shake me hand when I get out of 'ere then.'

I was finished in my cubicle before my neighbour. I was grateful for the cardboard tube.

As I returned to where my Dad was stood there were a few cheers coming from around the next corner. Muted chants of 'England's, England's, number one', could be heard over the mass of reds queuing for flights. 'Must be Kirkland' I said to Dad. Sure enough Liverpool's injury-blighted keeper came around the corner with his girlfriend, who looked about half his height. There was then a steady stream of Liverpool squad players making their way through gate number five where we were waiting. I was surprised to see some of them because I thought they would have already been out in Turkey with the squad, for experience if nothing else. I thought players like Stephen Warnock and Darren Potter were particularly unlucky not to already be out in Istanbul with the rest of the first team squad. Stephen Warnock is a player I like. I like his attitude and his commitment. Warnock broke into the first team early in the season and managed thirty games. He was an unused substitute for the Chelsea semi-final and the quarter-final against Juventus. Warnock was also an unused sub for the Bayer Leverkusen game at home but played the full ninety minutes in the away fixture. I felt it was really harsh for him to be excluded, particularly as he befell the same fate for the League Cup final defeat to Chelsea back in February. I'm not saying he should have played in Istanbul or even got on the bench, but not taking him in the squad seemed really harsh to me.

Other players to pass through were Neil Mellor, Zak Whitbread, Richie Partridge, Paul Harrison, Florent Sinama Pongolle, Anthony Le Tallec, and Mauricio Pellegrino. There were probably others I missed too. The biggest surprise of all was the appearance of Salif Diao, complete with black bandana. Diao had left Liverpool to join Birmingham on loan during the Premiership season and his presence caught a few by surprise, but not all.

'Thought you were a Birmingham fan?' one red shouted.

'You're doing a real fan out of a ticket!' shouted another.

Salif laughed nervously but he showed a decent turn of speed I'd not previously seen from him when getting through the departure gate.

I decided to call home using my mobile phone. The delayed flights meant I could at least say goodbye again to my wife Yvonne and my little girls. Yvonne was surprised to hear my voice as she assumed I'd be somewhere over western Europe by now. During our short conversation I could hear my three-year-old daughter Hannah demanding to speak to me. Yvonne had little choice to put her on the phone.

'Daddy I ate all my breakfast!' she shouted enthusiastically. I could picture her face beaming with pride. Speaking to Hannah made me feel good. It was obvious that she was unconcerned about Daddy going away for a couple of days. My 16-month-old daughter Jess was equally unconcerned. Jess came to the phone, breathed heavily for a moment, and then shouted, 'Ba-bye!'

At 9:10am an announcement was made to let us know our flight was boarding. A predictable cheer went up and the mass ranks of Scandic Airways flight number SCY9931 shuffled towards the gate. The mood instantly lifted and the first telling rendition Johnny Cash's 'Ring of Fire' rang out over the departure lounge. Rather apt I thought considering my numerous trips to the toilet! This tune was to become synonymous with the whole trip. In the queue for the plane I bumped into a mate from Runcorn, Nick Davies. Nick played football in the same six-a-side team as me and he is a die hard red. I knew he was going to Istanbul but it was something of a coincidence that we were on the same plane. Nick is a fairly laid-back sort of bloke and he looked really calm. I told myself that I really needed to take a leaf out of his book and chill out.

My Dad still wasn't showing any nerves so I decided to try and enjoy the journey as much as possible.

At 9:30am Dad and I boarded our plane in good spirits. It was two and a half hours later than planned but we were on our way. My stomach finally settled. It was as if somehow I still hadn't quite believed we were going. Perhaps boarding the plane had been the last psychological barrier for me to finally realise that this dream was a reality.

As we stood on the tarmac waiting to climb the steps to the plane I wondered whether it was obvious to others that we were father and son. I hoped so. I was very proud.

3. On the Wing

Our love was on the wing
We had dreams and songs to sing

Fields of Athenry – Pete St John

The plane was already two thirds full when Dad and I got on. The cabin crew were huddled in the doorway of the plane packed into a tiny corner by the toilet. They looked nervous and there was a distinct absence of a welcome. It was not the greeting I associated with boarding a plane for a holiday. They looked almost frightened, huddled together like they were trying to shelter from the rain in a bus shelter. None of the crew were giving advice to where fans might be seated on the plane. As a result the seat numbers on the boarding cards became meaningless. A good-natured free-for-all sorted out the seating plan for everyone, with reds finding a spot they liked and staking claims to them. I spotted three empty seats in the right hand aisle and we quickly got settled. Dad sat next to the window and I sat in the middle seat of the three. Everyone on the flight was travelling with hand luggage only so there was very little space to be found in the overhead lockers. The locker above my seat was already full. I stuffed my bag under the seat in front of me in between my legs. The plane was buzzing with the noise of reds sorting themselves out in preparation for the flight. After a few minutes a young black lad asked if the seat next to me was taken. I couldn't immediately pick his accent but he wasn't a scouser. I told him the seat was free and he somehow managed to stuff his bag into the already crowded locker above our seats. He spent a couple of minutes battering and stuffing his bag in there and then after three increasingly violent attempts he finally banged the locker shut.

The young lad literally dropped into his seat next to me. He puffed out his cheeks in exaggerated fashion. He was shaking his head and looked seriously stressed.

'You alright mate?' I asked.

'I'm just glad to be here,' he said, 'I'm not supposed to be on this flight.'

It turned out that he had missed his own flight after oversleeping the night before but Lonsdale Travel found him a seat on this flight.

'Overslept!' I thought. How the bloody hell could you oversleep the morning you are due to go to travel to the European Cup Final?

Despite being unimpressed by his timekeeping he seemed like a good bloke and I sympathised. If I had felt stressed out this morning he must have been almost hysterical.

'I couldn't have gone home, I'd have been suicidal.' he said. 'I'm supposed to be with me mate. He's on another flight. Thank God Lonsdale found us a couple of spare seats'. He stammered. He then started flicking through a football magazine as if he was speed reading it and then stuffed it into the pouch in front of him. He unfolded the tray attached to the seat in front and laid his head on it. He then just seemed to switch off completely almost like a video recorder switching onto standby mode.

Before long the flight was ready for take-off. A stewardess politely asked the bloke next to me if he would put his table in the upright position and he slowly, very slowly complied. He looked seriously knackered. The atmosphere was quiet apart from some muted chants of Ring of Fire as the plane left the tarmac.

About five minutes into the flight a couple of blokes made their way toward the toilet. They were strongly rebuked by a member of the cabin crew, a young girl.

'Please, please sir! Sit down! Sit down!' she called out, 'you must wait until the seatbelt sign is switched off!'

The two blokes gave a genuine look of 'who me?' and went back to their seats.

The cabin crew continued to look nervous and I thought the reaction was a bit dramatic. Almost immediately there was an announcement about not using the toilets 'inappropriately'.

There was a rumble of laughter. What did 'inappropriately' mean? I presumed that meant no smoking.

'Tell us when we're over France love, so I can go for a shite!' came a strong scouse accent, followed by a muted ripple of laughter and a few shaking heads.

A few short years ago it was a Frenchman Gerard Houllier leading us to European victory. How times change. It didn't stop me from laughing. Sometimes it can be basic stuff but I love the banter and the humour dished out by Liverpool fans. It was only just getting going as the atmosphere began to build in anticipation of leaving Liverpool on our long journey.

In my 27 years watching Liverpool at Anfield, the one thing that really hasn't changed is the humour and the banter. I have been to some great and some not-so-great games at Anfield over those years but the humour remains a constant. There is always an inspired Kop chant to make me laugh. Years ago singing 'Brian Clough is a homosexual' was a favourite chant of mine (he always waved, by the way) whereas these days 'Steve Bruce, he's got a big fat head' (he doesn't wave) is a contemporary comparison. As I mentioned it can be basic stuff but there's something about being in a football stadium and sharing that basic joke with forty thousand others that make it priceless.

Trips to cup finals normally bring out the best banter. I remember a coach trip to Wembley to watch Liverpool play Arsenal in the 1987 League Cup Final. That final stands out as the only final I have been to that my Dad couldn't get to. It was just my brother and me. On the journey down a couple of reds searched everybody's packed lunches. If they judged that your butties had Spam in them they chained you to your chair using a leg iron. If you refused to have your butties inspected they took it as an admission of guilt and you were chained up anyway. Their judgement of what constituted Spam was fairly arbitrary. Some of the butties were taken to the 'lab' at the back of the bus for forensic examination. Regardless of the test outcome they returned with large bite marks out of them.

There were lots of protesting and plenty of chained passengers. I was only 15, terrified, and I pissed myself laughing all the way to Wembley. Arsenal beat us 2-1 that day, the first game ever that Ian Rush scored for Liverpool and we didn't go on to win the game. On the way home the Spam inspectors walked up and down the bus offering cans of lager to anyone who wanted one.

For the first hour of the flight Dad read his paper. He kept pausing to tell me what various pundits were predicting. Ariggo Sacchi was predicting a Liverpool win, and Graham Taylor a Milan victory. Only Jan Molby was brave enough to suggest anything other than a low-scoring game. Most pundits leading up to the game were predicting a boring game and suggested our only way to win the final would be to shut up shop and hope to nick one.

I recalled very similar judgements before our 5-4 victory over Alaves in the 2000 Uefa Cup Final. I suggested that there could be a few goals predicting a 2-1 win for us. Dad nodded but he wouldn't commit himself. As you might imagine Dad and me talk about football a lot. I would even venture to say that 99.9% of the time we are together we find time for at least a few words about it. We don't always agree, but so far today we seemed to be agreeing on most things about the biggest game of our lives. Every now and then Dad added a point of view on behalf of my brother Stephen. 'Steve reckons we might do it in extra-time. He was thinking about sticking a bet on 1-1.' Dad said. It was almost as if Dad had to keep reminding us both that he should have been there. A good example of how touching my father can be without actually spelling out his feelings.

After trawling through a few newspapers my Dad decided to pass some time sleeping. The bloke next to me had been asleep for most of the flight already wearing an eccentric facemask. The only other time I'd seen a facemask like that was during the opening titles of Topcat.

I couldn't sleep because I had my contact lenses in. As I sat staring down the plane I tried to imagine what it would feel like to stand next to my Dad just before kick-off. I imagined a huge stadium full to bursting. I imagined we would be behind the goal and quite high up and I imagined singing at the top of my voice. I imagined that standing there side-by-side with my Dad waiting for the game to start would be worth seven hundred quid of any-one's money.

I whiled away a good 10 minutes listening to other pas-sengers' conversations. The bloke in front of me flicked through an FHM magazine. I casually peered through the seats and was grateful that he paused generously on every page; 15 minutes flew by.

The other passengers on the plane were a surprisingly diverse bunch. There was a fair share of women of all ages and also quite a number of families travelling. I couldn't help thinking that some of the children there were much too young to appreciate the enormity of the trip. I under-stood it would be an awesome thing for these kids to brag about in later life, to say 'I was there in Istanbul', but could a six year old really appreciate a trip like this? It seemed more of an adult expedition to me but I'm not entirely sure why. And how could a family of four afford a trip like this? There would certainly be no change out of three grand. Then again, if you have the money I couldn't think of a better way to spend it.

The journey was peaceful. The in-flight meal was a cheese roll described as 'breakfast' by the air Scandic cabin crew. About an hour before we were due to land a Liver-pool FC rep walked up and down the plane, checking a printed list and distributing match tickets. Everyone on the plane examined tickets with pride and protection. Everyone apart from the young lad next to me, that is. His ticket was presumably on another plane ahead of us. Sense told me that he would be united with his match ticket when we reached Istanbul, but I was glad not to be in his shoes. Examining our tickets we could see we were behind the goal at the south end of the stadium. I had visualised us being behind the goal and generally that's usually the best place to be and the most sought after spot, so we were both really pleased.

Years ago when we stood on the Kop we would have the same position left of centre behind the goal. If I wasn't with my Dad I'd venture as close to the middle as I could get. These days it is a rarity to be right behind the goal.

It was a good feeling to have the tickets safely in our possession. I had been nervous about booking the tickets in the first place. Strictly speaking, the ticket I had in my hand belonged to my mother-in-law Kathy. Just like my Dad, Kathy had been to every Liverpool home game throughout the season and by virtue of that she was entitled to go to the final. Adverse publicity about Istanbul, the reputation for violence at football matches there, and the distance from home all contributed to putting her off the trip. If the final had been in Paris, like it was a year later in 2006, Kathy would have gone to the final and I'd have missed out. I hadn't been to nearly enough games to go to the game in my own right, but when I was offered the chance to go using her entitlement I couldn't say no. I hope nobody reading this begrudges me that decision.

During my 27 years watching the club I've found money when I had none to get to Anfield week in week out. When I was 16 I used to earn £5.80 every Saturday for four hours working in a local library but somehow I still managed to fund my own season ticket. Almost every penny I had went toward watching Liverpool F.C. I could no longer do that with a very young family to support, so this season (of all seasons) I hadn't been to many games. At various stages during the booking process I had expected my application to be rejected, but now, sitting on the plane with the ticket in my hand, I had no such worries. I knew I had Kathy to thank for my ticket.

Our first view of Istanbul came from the sky.

It wasn't awe-inspiring. The landscape was pretty barren and the housing rudimentary, to put it politely. I can't say I was shocked, but the absolute nothingness of the land-scape was somehow a minor disappointment. There were very few comments from the other reds as bodies lay across each other for a glimpse of the landscape. My over-riding feeling was that we had just landed in the middle of the middle of nowhere.

Sabiha Goeken isn't the main airport for Istanbul. The main Istanbul airport was being used for the AC Milan fans and naturally we had to be kept apart. Sabiha Goeken *was* in the middle of nowhere. It seemed an odd place to have an airport, slap-bang in the middle of an area com-prising mostly dusty farmland. Agriculture is hardly a speciality of mine, but it was difficult to see how anything could be farmed there. Nevertheless there were plenty of houses dotted around brown fields of livestock, so some-one was making a living.

At 4:00pm Turkish time our plane landed to muted applause. The air of palpable anticipation increased my heart rate. My next priority was a smooth journey into the centre of Istanbul so we could get amongst it as quickly as possible.

4.   Coach 52

Those who remember the past are destined to live through it again

Banner – Liverpool Fan

A couple of hundred Liverpool fans fiddled around with passports and prepared to hand over photocopies of their photograph page to a stern-faced security guard in a tiny booth. The Lonsdale Travel information sheet sent with our ticket booking confirmation had told us the photocopy would save us from having to pay a £10 charge to enter the country. The security guard in the booth looked at us as if we were bonkers. We didn't need the photocopies. My Dad looked nervous as he was checked over by security. Thankfully Turkish security was more concerned about getting us through to the coaches quickly rather than searching Dad, so his butties escaped a strip search. The security checks through Sabiha Goeken aiport were quick and efficient. This is the last time you will read the word 'efficient' in this book in connection with any travel arrangements. I am sure that anyone who travelled on Lonsdale Travel coach 52 will remember the experience for a very long time. I am also sure that many other fans travelling on other coaches have similar memories to recount.

We were ushered into a large open area of the airport where we met a young Turkish bloke holding up a piece of A4 paper with the number 52 scribbled onto it. It must have taken ages for him to write the huge numbers onto the paper as they were written in biro. *You'll Never Walk Alone* was being played through the airport speakers in a constant loop, so we got to hear it about half a dozen times whilst we waited for everyone to get off the plane ready for the bus journey. My guess is the entire airport staff would have known it off by heart by the time the last coach left for Istanbul, having been force-fed our famous anthem all morning.

A few young lads were getting anxious about the amount of time we were waiting. I understood completely. Their main fear was that they wouldn't have time to join mates already in Istanbul before the game. Taksim Square in the centre of the Asian side of Istanbul was where Liverpool fans had been congregating for days before the game. Some of the lads in our bus queue were speaking to mates on mobile phones. It was obvious these mates were calling from Taksim Square and these lads were desperate to join them.

The delay to our flight had significantly shortened the time available to get there and the extra delay was winding them up further. As tempers raised the group of young reds decided to abandon the queue and head for the taxi rank, but as they moved away from the queue we were gestured toward the buses parked outside the front of the airport and they swiftly changed their minds.

On the bus there was more waiting around. After a twenty-minute wait for the driver, coach 52 set off for Istanbul. The coach crawled past a number of lengthy taxi queues. I spotted a number of old mates from Runcorn I hadn't seen for years. It's strange that living in a town of only ninety thousand people I hadn't seen some of them for 10 years or more but now there they were, standing at a taxi queue 1,700 miles from Runcorn.

After travelling about two hundred yards up the road the coach stopped. The co-driver had realised that the Liverpool FC steward assigned to coach 52 wasn't with us. Five tense minutes later another coach pulled in front of us. A Liverpool FC steward, complete with fluorescent jacket, lumbered off and got onto our coach.

Now I know hindsight is a wonderful thing and it's easy to judge months after the trip, but my first impressions of the Liverpool FC steward were not altogether favourable. He couldn't have been more Muppet-like with Jim Henson's right hand up his arse. I don't want to cast aspersions on all LFC stewards as I'm sure there are dozens of excellent people for every Kermit, but this bloke was clearly just along for the ride.

According to our itinerary the estimated journey time from the airport to our destination, The Grand Emin Hotel in central Istanbul, was fifty minutes. We immediately joined a motorway from the airport terminal and it was a pretty steady journey to begin with. The motorways were busy and the skies were grey. I had heard stories that the traffic in Turkey could be like the Wacky Races, but nothing could have been further from the truth. Okay, there was a bit of dodging and weaving but the speeding salesman and boy racers were conspicuous by their absence. Travelling on this particular Turkish motorway looked a lot safer than your average ten-mile journey on the M62 back in England.

Recognising us as Liverpool fans, we were waved on by passing cars and vans. Beaming, moustachioed van drivers gave us over-enthusiastic thumbs up as we steadied up the freeway. Coach 52 was quiet with patience and anticipation.

Before long we were amongst the residential areas alongside the motorway. Even at a distance it was easy to see the housing was overpopulated and underdeveloped. At least a quarter of the buildings we passed were unfinished, apparently abandoned. Crumbling houses sat divided by rotting businesses. Most of the housing we could see was high-rise and it looked grim.

After about an hour on the road and a couple of tollbooths later we crossed the unoriginally named *Bosphorus Bridge* over the river Bosphorus. The Bosphorus Bridge links the West to the East and Asian side of the city. It is a magnificent structure stretching high across the river. From the incredible height of the bridge we could see even more clearly the vast amount of housing crammed onto the banks of the river and up into Istanbul. Both sides of the riverbank were festooned with thousands and thousands of houses and high-rise flats. Dotted in between the housing were huge dominating Mosques that looked as if they were standing guard over the houses, protecting them like strategically-placed forts, looking out into the river for approaching enemies. Once over the bridge the landscape reverted to shabby tower blocks and crumbling businesses. I couldn't begin to estimate how many people lived there.

Having been given an estimated time of arrival of 5:20pm for The Grand Emin a few fellow passengers began to check their watches. Nervous glances soon became disgruntled voices. The LFC steward sat motionless. An hour and 15 minutes into our estimated fifty-minute journey coach 52 arrived in the centre of Istanbul.

The centre of Istanbul reminded me a little of Havana in Cuba. My wife and I had our honeymoon in Varadero, Cuba but spent a long and wonderful day in Havana as part of our trip. Just like Havana, the streets of Istanbul had some fine architectural aspects, but looked as though very little in the way of running repairs had been made for several decades.

Before visiting Istanbul I had heard the cliché about 'a Mosque on every corner' from a number of people. I guess sometimes clichés are there with good reason as this wasn't too wide of the mark. Generally the Mosques were in better states of repair than other buildings.

As we moved steadily through the centre there were western influences you would never see in a place like Havana. There were plenty of Ford cars, 99% of taxis were yellow, and before long we spotted a huge MacDonald's restaurant right in the middle of town. Is there anywhere in the world (other than Cuba) that doesn't have a Mac-Donald's? The presence of the world's largest junk food outlet was especially curious as another Istanbul cliché also had strong foundation. There were Kebab shops everywhere! Where I live in Runcorn there is a local joke that the Old Town has a Kebab shop on every corner. In the centre of Istanbul there were two Kebab shops for every Kebab shop. It made me wonder how the hell they could all stay in business – although forty thousand plus scousers would surely help for a couple of days at least.

Eventually coach 52 turned into a crowded side-street. The only feasible reason to turn into a side street so small must have been because our hotel was down there – or so I thought. Progress was agonisingly slow. The street the coach was attempting to negotiate was like Matthew Street in Liverpool during an August Bank Holiday music festival. It wasn't pedestrianised, not officially, so the coach had to negotiate every inch very slowly and very carefully. There were plenty of reds wandering the streets amongst the locals who waved to us as we edged through the chaos.

It took around 25 minutes to travel two hundred yards to get to the bottom of the street … and back out onto the main street we were on 25 minutes earlier! The fact we were lost was now glaringly obvious. Coach 52 parked up and the driver got out to ask directions. Our LFC steward sat looking out of the window at the traffic. The frustration aboard began to grow.

'What's going on mate?' shouted a strong scouse snarl from somewhere around the middle of the bus. After a few seconds the LFC steward peered around his seat back up the aisle of the bus with 'who me?' written across his forehead.

'What's happening lad?' the worried voice insisted.

'I don't know, I think we're lost,' replied the steward.

'You *think* we're lost! No shit Sherlock!' shouted the bloke just behind us.

'When will you know for sure like?' shouted another.

The steward now looked like his feelings were hurt.

'Get out and find out what's going on and get us some information,' the bloke behind me insisted.

At this moment a passing blind man on a galloping horse could see there was a situation here that could escalate. If I had been the steward I'd have got off the bus and found out as much 'information' as possible. If I had been the steward I would have at the very least pretended to find out something. Our steward chose to sulk.

There were now a number of people shouting down the bus and clearly some kind of leadership was needed. A young lad made his way to the front and spoke for a few minutes to the co-driver and the steward. He then asked everyone to be quiet and announced the bus driver had been following another bus to get to our hotel. Unfortunately, the bus he followed didn't know where the hotel was.

A few people laughed whilst most shook their heads in disbelief. Our estimated fifty-minute journey had already taken around two hours. Parked up at the side of the road at 6:15 pm local time left us three hours and thirty minutes until kick-off. My Dad isn't one to shout out suggestions but he turned to me and said he thought we might be just as well going straight to the stadium. Without really thinking too hard about it, I shouted out his suggestion.

'Just take us to the ground if you don't know where the hotel is. Just get us to the game.'

A generous amount of approval greeted my shout. The most important thing here was the game. We had all been travelling for something like 11 hours. I didn't really care about the hotel just now — I just wanted to get to the game.

Divine intervention was needed and it came suddenly. The bus driver got back into his seat and took a call on his mobile phone. Then after a fit of exaggerated laughter a Scooby Doo villain would be proud of, he started the engine. This irritated the life out of his young co-driver who began chattering and bouncing in his seat, but the driver seemed to be ignoring his younger animated counterpart and drove off.

By this time our LFC steward was trying so hard to hide in his seat that he was almost in the foetal position. At home playing hide and seek, my three-year-old hides behind our curtains shouting 'Daddy I'm behind the curtains'. Our steward was just as well hidden.

The driver looked like a man who knew where the Grand Emin Hotel was. It took about two minutes to drive up one slip road and down the other side. He parked the coach once more and pointed into a side street, grinning up the aisle of the coach. The Grand Emin Hotel had been sniggering at us around the corner all along.

The LFC steward stood up at the front of the bus and quietly mumbled we had 10 minutes to check into the hotel and get back to the coach. He was first to get off. I was happy to be at the front of the bus so I could hear his instruction. We passed his message down the coach like Chinese whispers.

At the hotel reception there were shouts of disbelief; 18 rooms were available for 32 people.

'Is anyone prepared to share?' shouted a scouse voice. 'There's not enough rooms?'

The reception area was now full of reds.

'Just check us all in eh love,' shouted a middle-aged man next to me. Somehow the girl at the front desk began checking us in. We were quite close to the front of the queue and check-in went something like this:

Receptionist: 'Name?'

Me: 'Bailey'

Receptionist: 'Room 414'

Security wasn't tight. No passports, no signature, no information about us, just first come first served gets a key. At Liverpool airport my Dad's butties had been checked more stringently. We didn't give a toss. The lifts were busy so we ran up the stairs and stumbled into our room. We had just about enough time to take a pee and change our shirts. Dad also laid out his turkey butties on the sideboard. They were battered, a bit warm, and suffering from the psychological after effects of a strip search earlier in the day, but they were very welcome indeed. A handful of jelly babies complimented them perfectly.

Dad then produced a couple of cans of red bull. What a blinkin' superstar! The Grand Emin was a three-star hotel. I don't know what stars are awarded for in Istanbul but it was hard to see how they might have gained their awards. The room was battered. The bathroom, in particular, was falling to pieces. The soap dispenser hung from the wall dripping its lime green contents onto the sink and I could smell the towels hanging from the towel rail. The toilet was more inviting than my last experiences in Liverpool airport, as it had an accompanying roll of toilet paper. I was grateful.

Over the road from the hotel there were three floors of workers hammering away at sewing machines. They were far too busy to notice a half-naked scouser peering across from the fourth floor of the hotel across the road. I changed my gold 1994 away shirt for a 2004 red one. Dad wore the yellow away strip Liverpool wore for the 2001 FA Cup final. The final that sometimes gets called *The Owen Cup Final.*

The quality of the hotel was the least of our concerns. We now had about two minutes to get back to coach 52. After a quick check for tickets and cash we grabbed our scarves and darted out. It was all really manic Crystal Maze kind of stuff. Dad was two steps ahead of me and made his way downstairs as I locked the hotel door behind us. The key fob was just about the largest object I have ever seen attached to a key. If we had tried to take that with us to the game it would have been confiscated as a weapon.

When I reached reception Dad wasn't there. After handing in the room key I turned around to find him at the bar. He had bought us two bottles of lager each. I was impressed that Dad felt a couple of beers were a priority given that we had about thirty seconds to get back to the bus. We drank our first bottles almost without speaking. It was cold and it didn't touch the sides. My first experience of Efes lager, the local brew, was that is was very drinkable.

We strolled out to the bus, taking marginally more time about our second bottles. As we got to the bus it became apparent that some of the other passengers on coach 52 had decided to use their 10-minute check in time more constructively. A couple of young lads were heaving two crates of beer onto the coach whilst another strolled on with a bin liner full of cans. How did they get them so quickly? Where did he get a black bin liner?

'How long does it take to get to the ground?' asked a boarding kopite.

'About half an hour,' mumbled the LFC steward.

At 6:30pm local time coach 52 was in high spirits. The beer was loaded onto the coach and the singing started up before the engine. A bloke next to us on the coach was eating something large and donut shaped. Dad and me tried to guess whether it was bread or meat based.

'What's that mate?' I shouted across.

'Greasy,' he replied. I gave thanks again for Dad's turkey butties. For me, personally, risking unidentified food would have been tantamount to arse roulette.

The Fields of Anfield Road boomed from the coach and the adrenalin pumped through every vein and every follicle in my body. Four seats in the middle of the bus were now occupied with crates of Efes. The two bottles I'd quickly knocked back before getting on the bus had been most welcome but I turned down the offer of another from a fellow red. I remember listening to a Bob Paisley interview when he said he didn't have a drink after the 1977 European Cup final success because he wanted to enjoy the victory completely sober. Bob said winning the trophy for the first time in our history was more than enough. I felt a bit like that. I fully intended to have a skin-full if we won the game, but for now I just wanted to enjoy every minute, drunk on the adrenalin.

Dad looked every bit as high as I felt. Not that I would ever criticise anyone who was drinking, far from it. It was just my personal choice to keep a clear head before this particular game. To be honest, I can only ever remember being drunk at one game in my life; the 1996 F.A. Cup final versus Manchester United at Wembley. My brother missed that one too, so it was just Dad and me. I met an old mate from Runcorn, a chap called Billy Wilcox. He was a good bloke Billy, really knowledgeable. It promised to be a glorious day as we sat drinking lagers on a grass bank outside the stadium. Everything was fine right up until kick-off! I haven't seen Billy since, funnily enough. I hope he made it to Istanbul. Anyway, the mix of too many lagers and defeat was a lasting experience for me. The journey home was the most miserable journey from any football match I have ever been to, a real post-pissed depression. When I got home I argued with my girlfriend and we split up. A really cracking 24 hours that was!

I haven't been drunk at a Liverpool game since.

As we left the centre of Istanbul, road traffic police guided us through each junction and each set of traffic lights. Loud cheers accompanied every gesture to pass through, and we appeared to be making good progress. After about twenty minutes the traffic became heavier and we began to pass other coaches, buses, and taxis packed with reds. Green public transport buses were full to bursting point with Liverpool fans.

We laughed and cheered as we passed bus after bus containing Liverpool fans squeezed up against the glass and each other, singing at the top of their voices. Some of them made mock wafting motions in front of their noses and it was easy to imagine the sweaty stench they had created. Condensation dribbled down the windows of every scouser-crammed bus but everyone on board was laughing and singing.

As each bus realised we were watching they would up the volume, singing ever louder. Before long, the traffic began to slow and it was obvious that most of it was headed in just one direction. The taxicabs were just as entertaining. Scores of battered, little yellow cabs attempted to weave through the buses with reds leaning out of the windows waving flags and singing. There were six or seven people in some of them, with blokes hanging out of the windows *Dukes of Hazard*-style, presumably because there was no room inside.

It was a really great sight, a huge rally of red. It looked like a vast, slow-moving carnival creeping through the packed streets, with locals lining the streets, cheering and waving us on.

On reaching the top of a hill we turned right onto a dual carriageway. After about one hundred yards someone spotted the Ataturk Stadium miles in the distance and a spontaneous rendition of *Ring of Fire* spread through the bus. The stadium was already lit up and was about three or four miles away, in a straight line across a huge area of wasteland. Despite the distance between the stadium and us, there really didn't appear to be anything much on the land in between, just scrubby greenery, rocks and litter, with the odd telegraph pole here and there. Everyone on our coach leaned over to peer across the wide expanse of no-man's-land to get their first glimpse of the stadium. The adrenalin level stepped up a notch. Almost as quickly we began to realise the length of the traffic jam we were in. Before long, you could literally see the queue of taxis and buses all the way to the stadium. Not directly to the stadium, but in a huge arc, bending off into the distance around the wasteland. The traffic jam was approximately four or five miles long and we could see almost every yard of it ahead of us.

But the realisation that we wouldn't be getting to the stadium anytime soon did nothing to dampen our spirits. The singing grew louder and the banter intensified.

The streets were lined with local people cheering and waving. There were children running in and out of the traffic and jumping up at the windows of buses asking for scarves and flags. On our side of the bus a couple of 10-year-old boys were break dancing on the central reservation of the carriageway to the cheers of passing buses. Other young lads had shinned their way up lampposts or sat on top of traffic lights. Loads of the kids had managed to blag themselves a scarf or a flag and waved them, showing off like only excited seven-year-old children can. Their little performances got them a cheer from every coach and cab and they looked like they were having the time of their lives. I bet some of them will remember the day the Liverpool fans came into town for a long time.

I couldn't help thinking about all of the warnings of trouble and violence I had from people at home. I knew there was a higher risk of trouble *after* the game, especially if we lost, but nevertheless I wished they could see this. If a row of steel bands had lined the kerbsides it would have been no more of a carnival. It was one long and spontaneous street-party.

Further along, we passed the Efes brewery in the middle of a built-up area. Crates of beer were being passed over the wall to waiting men, who then ran alongside the buses and taxis, trying to sell it on. The people lining the streets made the time pass quickly, though we still kept one eye on the clock. Some of the young boys lining the streets were wearing the football shirts of various English clubs, presumably especially for the occasion. The odd Liverpool shirt and homemade banner received huge cheers. One young lad went berserk as a red ran across and gave him his scarf. Another young lad wasn't so lucky. He was standing stone-faced next to a set of traffic lights in an old Manchester United shirt. The occupants of the coach in front were ferociously booing him and then when we took our turn at the lights we continued the relentless barracking. I couldn't help feel sorry for him. He obviously didn't understand the significance. He must have thought, 'the English are in town so I'll wear my English club shirt'. He only looked about eight years old. It was pretty cruel, but both Dad and me booed and laughed. I have no idea how long he had been there but I hoped he would soon get the message.

With the beer flowing freely it was inevitable that at some stage people were going to have to get off and pee. Our co-driver initially tried to prevent anyone getting off the bus but the LFC steward pointed out that people might begin peeing on the coach. The co-driver took no more than a moment to realise the steward was serious and began to let people off. It was hilarious watching lads jump off the bus a take a pee on the hard shoulder of the highway. When they had finished the bus had typically moved about fifty feet. That meant they then had to try and find the bus again. Relieved reds crawled like ants amongst the buses looking for familiar faces or the numbers at the front of coaches.

Our journey to the hotel had been such a complete shambles that it wasn't difficult to remember the number of our coach. This gave anyone on our coach an advantage in relocating their transport. It's at times like this that I'm thankful to be a bloke. Jump off, zip down, pee, shake, and back onto the bus. It's not so easy for girls. Any girls spotted scrambling across the wasteland searching for a secluded spot were cheered and accompanied by chants of *Ring of Fire*. Some could be seen scrambling great distances to get away from the lines of blokes at the roadside. As the girls came back from their expeditions they had a tougher time finding their transport. Even in this slow-moving jam, coaches could travel a reasonable distance by the time the young ladies returned. But the girls took the banter in great spirit and waved various gestures toward the cheering bloke-dominated coaches.

After about ninety minutes on the coach we left the overpopulated built-up areas and joined what looked like a two lane motorway. It was the newest road I have ever seen in my life. The tarmac was still pitch black and looked as if it had been laid earlier that day. Some of the Turkish coach drivers seemed confused by the motorway concept as a number of coaches reversed past us the wrong way down the opposite carriageway. And I'm not talking about a one hundred yard reverse after missing a slip road. Each coach could be seen reversing a couple of miles into the distance as the police sat and watched.

Also on the opposite side of the carriageway taxis began to park on the hard shoulder. This line of parked taxis stretched for about a mile all the way to the car parks outside the stadium. Our side of the carriageway was crawling with reds jumping off buses and out of taxis for a pee. The traffic was still bumper-to-bumper and inched slowly up the freshly surfaced freeway. It was a pain-free journey. The coach went through a varied repertoire of anthems as the atmosphere built and the adrenalin continued to pump by the gallon. My favourite song of the last few years has been *Fields of Anfield Road*. I have a habit of singing it around the house when I'm at home almost without realising I'm doing it. I started loving it even more since my three-year-old daughter Hannah picked up the words from me. I honestly didn't teach her to sing it she just picked it up herself. The first time I heard her sing it my jaw hit the ground. Hannah quite often bursts into a spontaneous word-perfect rendition. She knows it makes me smile so she does it all the more. Although Hannah has her own little Liverpool kit she is far too young to understand what the game is about. She knows we support Liverpool and that Manchester United and Everton are rubbish. At three years old that's all I could ask of her. I thought about her cheeky little grin as our coach sang yet another word-perfect rendition of my favourite Kop chant.

Dad was well and truly into the swing of things. Dad doesn't normally sing as much as I do at the games. He tends to join in during various points of a game when the crowd gets wound up but he doesn't sing constantly like I sometimes do. Sitting on the coach singing Liverpool anthems with my Dad made me far more relaxed about when we might arrive at the stadium. I was happy to sit there singing for a while longer. There were pauses in the group singing for some of the lads at the back of the coach to sing solo versions of Liverpool songs. One bloke sang a great version of 'The Fields of Anfield Road' start to finish that was really rather good. Another guy sang a couple of versions of the original Irish folk song 'The Fields of Athenry'. On the back of this blokes version I learned the words to the original song myself when I got home. I hadn't heard Liverpool fans sing solo amongst other groups of reds before but the atmosphere was so charged and emotional it seemed perfectly natural. The fact that the two guys singing solo were great hairy-arsed skinheads seemed appropriate too. It was a good day for the unexpected.

At 8:30pm local time the brand new road leading to the Ataturk stadium began to run out of tarmac and the awesome Olympic stadium came into view. At least it looked awesome from this distance. Many literally couldn't wait for their coaches and taxis to park and jumped out of their transport, deciding to walk the remaining eight hundred yards or so to the stadium. Hundreds of fans streamed across wasteland toward the stadium whilst others walked along the remainder of the freeway.

My first impressions of the stadium from my seat on the coach were that it was breathtaking. The huge East stand dominated the stadium with its gigantic freestanding crescent roof. The enormous car park at the south end of the stadium was a sea of reds. The combination of the two sights temporarily stopped us singing. The floodlights were in full effect as the last half hour of daylight began to fizzle away. We were here with the stadium in front of us and it was real. I grabbed my Dad by the shoulder and we clenched our fists.

A flawless rendition of *You'll Never Walk Alone* took us to our position in the car park looking down onto a sea of Liverpool fans. The tears welled up in my eyes but I was happy to control my emotion. It was now only one hour to the 9:45pm kick-off but there were still thousands of fans stood outside the ground at the south end of the stadium.

Our clueless co-driver attempted to tell us that the coach would leave at midnight, regardless of extra-time or a penalty shoot-out. There was no stressful reaction this time, just hoots of laughter.

'You'll be on your own lad,' came an instant reaction.

'Do you know your way home?' shouted another.

It was then politely explained to the driver that we would return after the game and that if we won, we would be staying to celebrate, whatever time it was…

5. The Fields of Istanbul

*The future belongs to those who believe in the beauty
of their dreams*

Banner – Liverpool Fan

Coach 52 parked up in an elevated car park directly facing
the Ataturk Stadium. As we got off the coach we looked
down onto the sea of reds. Dad and I took the direct route
toward the swarm by scrambling down a gravel hill and
onto the roadside. The sense of anticipation was incredible.
We crossed another section of freshly laid tarmac highway
and into the mass gathering of red missionaries. It was the
friendliest atmosphere I have ever experienced at a football match. Everyone was smiling and singing. It's hard for
me to estimate how many reds were still outside the
ground, but I'd say there was roughly 15,000 still out there
an hour before kick-off. It had taken Dad and me nearly
14 hours to get here but we weren't thinking about that
now. After a couple of quick photographs with the stadium in the background we decided to make our way
toward the main gates.

In all it took us about half an hour to get in. The first
line of security was a line of young boys in fluorescent
vests. I'd say these lads were 15 or 16 years old, maximum.
They were lining up to check we had tickets. I showed
mine and was waved through whilst Dad inexplicably
showed his coach ticket and was also waved through! The

match tickets were a deep red colour and about seven inches long whereas the coach ticket Dad showed was white and about half the size. To be fair to Dad, the coach tickets were printed on Liverpool Football Club ticket paper and identical to Anfield match tickets.

On the other side of the line of juvenile security, Dad was in a blind panic.

'Where's me ticket, where's me ticket?' he stammered.

My heart sank as I watched the strongest man in my life descend into momentary terror. I could see that he genuinely thought he'd lost it. But his terror was mercifully short-lived as he plucked the priceless crimson ticket from his back pocket. I laughed nervously as the colour flowed back into his cheeks and shook my head.

'For fuck's sake, Dad, do you want me to mind it for you?' I said, laughing nervously. I can't remember ever using that particular phrase in speaking to my Dad before, but on this occasion it was just about justified, and he knew it!

I don't think Dad let that ticket out of his fist until we reached the turnstile some thirty minutes later.

One of the things I love about being with my Dad at the game is that I can relax and be myself. At the game we act more like mates than at other times when the rest of the family is about. Dad understands what it is to be one of the lads, even if he doesn't revel in it himself. He understands that blokes shout and swear and sometimes push the levels of humour beyond reasonable levels of decency. I'd never dream of swearing in front of my Mum, well maybe sometimes to wind her up, but in front of my Dad at the game it was totally acceptable.

The next line of security was a line of police. This time we were body searched. The kind of up and down search you get at airports. We both passed through quickly but as there was no real barrier to speak of hundreds and hundreds of reds just walked past the police officers. It was almost like being searched by the police was voluntary. If you didn't want to be searched you just walked on through. I didn't see the police stop anyone. Some reds comically crept past behind huge scarves hiding cans of Efes. I saw one young girl on the other side of the police line pull four cans of Efes out of her enormous red and white foam top hat. A young bloke cheered and hugged her as she handed them to him. All this happened about 12 feet behind the police barrier.

As we approached the fencing at the south end of the stadium it became much more congested. It was almost dark now and the lighting outside the stadium was poor. The lights outside the ground were the type of orange sodium lights you might find on any housing estate in Britain and there weren't many of them. Thousands of fans shuffled up to the fences straining their necks to see if they could spot a gate or turnstile. There was a lot of confusion but everyone stayed calm. As the lighting in the car park was so poor no one looked sure of where the turnstiles were but we joined the massing fans moving in one general direction.

Progress was slow but reds all around us were reassuring each other that we would all get in soon enough. The crowd became more tightly packed and Dad and me were now firmly packed into the crowd. I began to think that if there came a roar from inside the ground there might be a surge forward, but it is to the credit of all those fans standing outside the Ataturk Stadium that the surge never came. Everyone waited patiently shoulder-to-shoulder until finally Dad and me appeared at a turnstile.

The turnstile consisted of a man stood next to a freely revolving gate. The man took your ticket, tore off the stub, handed the larger part of the ticket back and then waved you through the gate. In our case, the bloke ripped a small two-inch corner off the wrong end of our tickets and handed them back – as a result Dad and me still have our tickets almost intact. To be honest, I couldn't see what the bloke on the gate could have done about anyone who was really determined to get in without a ticket. It would also have been really easy for me to pass my intact ticket back through the fence to another fan. As it is, we made our way through the back of the stadium towards the seats.

We took one look at the queue for food and thought better of it. Anyway, the only food I could see on show was large sausages on bread rolls. More important to me was taking a pee. Considering the Ataturk was a brand new stadium the toilets were shocking. The urinals were about two inches deep on the floor and had long since overflowed. I had to wade delicately through the puddles to the edge of the long communal urinal. Although a lot smaller, the toilets reminded me of the toilets at the old Wembley stadium. We were always appalled at the state of the state of England's premier stadium and I wasn't surprised when they knocked it down for rebuilding. In the old Wembley Stadium you used to have to wade through puddles of piss before you even got into the toilets themselves. At least here it was only the inside of the toilets that were flooded.

As I stood peeing I could hear the team being announced in the background. There were no speakers in the toilets and the announcement was muffled. Before I had zipped up, reds began coming in declaring that Harry Kewell was starting the game. This turned out to be the only real shock in the starting line-up but it was a big shock. I don't mind stating up front that I'm a Harry Kewell fan. At the time of writing this book I'm still convinced he can do the business at Liverpool. Harry has been really unlucky with injuries and this has blighted his progress and led to some pretty unfair criticism in my opinion. Having said that, I think he was really fortunate to be in the side for the final. Rafa obviously rates him very highly. Personally, I'd have played Didi Hamman, but Rafa's choice was Harry and who were any of us to argue? Rafa had brought the club on a fairytale journey to the final and his judgements were the only ones that mattered.

Before I left the toilet I spotted a guy I used to play football with years ago, Jason Weigand. He was a bit of a star turn when we about 10 or 11 years old. I hadn't seen him for about 10 years. Perhaps if we had met after 10 years in a Runcorn street we would have passed each other without remark, but here we shook hands warmly and exchanged a few words. The atmosphere of generosity and wellbeing was palpable. As we walked out to take our first look out onto the pitch I bumped into another Runcorn lad, Steve O'Leary. The surroundings and the faces around me were beginning to feel familiar. I have been to hundreds of games at Anfield and various grounds around the country. I have been lucky enough to get to Wembley five times and not seen more than a couple of friends from Runcorn. Here in Istanbul, some 1,700 miles away from home, lads from Runcorn were everywhere.

Dad and I made our way to block 305, row 36, seats 287 and 288. Directly behind us a huge screen boomed out unfeasibly loud adverts. I can't remember what the adverts were for and I didn't care. It was thirty minutes before kick-off and we were in our seats. It had taken us more than 14 hours of almost constant travel but nothing mattered now. I stood side-by-side with my Dad just as I imagined on the plane. It was uncanny just how close our position was to how I had imagined it, but if anything, the view from our seats was even better than I had hoped for. Those first few moments standing by our seats were spent absorbing our surroundings, soaking up every inch of the stadium into the memory. Whenever I go to a stadium I've not been to before I always spend the first few minutes eyeing the place up. Usually it's a ground I have seen a thousand times before on TV and I'll be judging if it lives up to expectations. When I went to Highbury for the 1992 FA Cup semi-final against Portsmouth I was really disappointed. I had always fancied going to Highbury, as it looked every inch the classic old English football stadium on TV. In reality, it was uninspiring. Other grounds have surpassed expectations. Following my only visit to Villa Park, I left with the unexpected feeling that it was a great place to watch football. This was probably due to the fact that the usual resident Aston Villa fans weren't there that day. The Liverpool v Wycombe semi-final of 2001 served up a pretty unique atmosphere.

I had only seen a few photographs of the Ataturk Stadium via the official Uefa website, so I didn't have any preconceived ideas. I have read plenty of criticisms of the stadium since I got home from the final, but to me it was truly magnificent. I didn't care that this was in the middle of nowhere. I didn't care that it was primarily built as an athletics stadium. I wasn't interested about time zones, travelling distances, policing, hotels, organisation or stewarding. I really couldn't give a toss if it was a huge concrete white elephant of a stadium that even the Turks thought was crap. To me, at that moment, the Ataturk Stadium was the greatest stadium I had set foot in apart from Anfield. In my mind, it certainly beat the old Wembley stadium – and I'd seen us pick up a few important bits of silver there. I will always feel that the Ataturk was the perfect setting. I am so glad it wasn't in the San Siro, the Bernabau, Wembley, Paris, or anywhere else.

The Ataturk Stadium was the place I imagined during my wildest daydreaming. From the coach, an hour or so earlier, I had thought the stadium looked awesome and up-close I wasn't disappointed. To my right was the East Stand, with its huge crescent roof. To the left stood the West Stand, also huge, albeit a slightly smaller and less architecturally eye-catching than the dominating East Stand. Directly opposite us at the other end of the ground were the Milan fans in the North Stand. This stand looked like a mirror-image of our own section and was already fully populated with the *Rossoneri*. At first it looked like each of the Milan fans had a different coloured flag to make up their traditional black and red stripes. On closer inspection later I could see they were all wearing plastic bibs to achieve the same effect. I was happy the Liverpool fans weren't asked to adopt a similar dress code of red and white.

The Liverpool fans were a great sea of constant movement. It looked great from where I stood in the middle of it, but I bet it looked even more impressive from the pitch. Each fan in the Liverpool end seemed to have a distinctive red kit or hat. Thousands of different flags were flowing back and forth and it looked much more alive than the uniformity of the Rossoneri stripes. I was desperately happy to be one tiny ripple in this huge sea of Kopites.

More Runcorn faces appeared close by. Dave Wright and his brother Steve were about four rows in front of me. Dave and Steve were both handy amateur footballers when we were all a few years younger. They reckon Steve in particular could have played professionally, but didn't push himself hard enough. I knew Dave better but it had been about three years since I'd last seen him in a local gym. I then spotted a lad called John Perry about three seats away from Dave and Steve. John was in my class at school. I hadn't seen him for about 12 years. I was impressed that he even recognised me. He looked like he was on cloud ninety-nine, never mind cloud nine.

The players came out for their final pre-match warm up. I watched their every move as if looking for signs of nerves or a change in preparation. The players coasted through a familiar pre-match routine just as if it were Fulham at home in the Premiership. At 9:15pm on 25th May 2005 I stood by my seat in the Ataturk Stadium in Istanbul watching my beloved Liverpool warm up for the big-gest match of my lifetime.

I wanted Liverpool to win this football match more than I ever wanted us to win anything.

6. With Hope in Our Hearts

You may say I'm a dreamer
But I'm not the only one

John Lennon

The temptation to read through match reports and scan through my video and DVD collections making notes of the game before writing this chapter is very strong. There is no doubt that if I revisited a few web sites and dug out my copy of the *Daily Post* dated 26th May 2006 it would help me with specific details surrounding the most re-markable European Cup Final in history. I reckon I could compose a lengthy and detailed blow-by-blow account of the game if I set my heart to it. But precise detail of the match action is not really what this book is about. I want to recount to you what I remember.

This book is about my experiences with my Dad, be-fore, during and after standing in the Ataturk stadium in Istanbul, watching the game of our lives. I am going to write this chapter mostly from memory, albeit a memory reinforced by the numerous times I've watched the game on DVD since returning from Istanbul.

The Liverpool team chosen to live this particularly overwhelming dream lined up as follows:

Dudek

Finnan ~ Carragher ~ Hyypia ~ Traore

Kewell ~ Gerrard ~ Alonso ~ Riise

Garcia

Baros

Subs: Biscan, Carson, Hamman, Josemi, Smicer

I was happy enough with the tactics implied by the selection. Baros alone up front with Garcia playing behind him seemed to be how we would line-up. It had worked well against other great teams in the competition, most notably Juventus and Chelsea, so it seemed right to go with that against Milan. I didn't have much time for thinking tactics though. My mind raced around from tangent to tangent. I was thinking about all kinds of things not always entirely related to the game. How the players would be feeling, how their wives would be feeling, who was at the game, what former Liverpool players would be there, and how many other legends would be there.

I knew from the TV reports a day earlier that Maradonna was there and tipping a Milan victory. 'Milan would have too much for Liverpool' he stated. 'Hard work wouldn't be enough for Liverpool'. He also expressed his concern that Liverpool could make it a boring final. Despite his sentiments, I liked the idea of Maradonna being at the same game as I was. I thought about what my wife would be doing. I thought about my little girls, Mum, our Steve, all my mates at home, and in the pub. I imagined they would all be thinking about me and telling other people proudly that 'our Mike and his Dad are there'. I could sense that the whole of Liverpool would be watching us, and certainly every red worth his salt everywhere else in the world too. Every one of those reds would want to be where I was. Slap-bang in the middle of Kopite heaven. Jesus, I was proud!

Above all, what meant everything to me was being stood shoulder-to-shoulder with my Dad, my role model, the person I respected more than any other.

A short opening ceremony started about twenty minutes before kick-off. As a general rule, opening ceremonies at big sporting events don't interest me. I can only recall two brief things about previous opening ceremonies. I remember Diana Ross missing a spoof penalty during the 94 World Cup ceremony in America. I also remember that during the Euro 96 ceremony in England there was a Dragon accompanying St George that looked like it had just done the London marathon. But the Istanbul ceremony had my full, albeit slightly sceptical, attention. White skirted figures floated across the pitch holding what looked like huge champions league umbrellas. The skirted figures seemed to be on trolleys of some kind producing the effect of hovering six inches or so above the pitch. Male dancers also dressed in white cavorted around the turf to the sound of deafening drums and lines of children dressed in red ran across the pitch in formation.

The ceremony added to the fact that this wasn't any ordinary match. I haven't a clue what it was all about but it built upon the already sky high atmosphere as the anticipation of the kick-off grew around us. Most people around us were laughing and joking about the ceremony. I wasn't alone in wondering what the hell it was all about and I don't think anyone was taking it too seriously. By the time the dancers had floated over the touchline it was obvious the kick-off time would be 5 or 10 minutes late.

Again, this added to the tension of waiting for the biggest game of our lives to kick-off. As the cast of the opening ceremony twirled away from the pitch the stadium reverberated to the sound of Tony Britten's interpretation of George Frideric Handel's *Zadok The Priest* … or as it's more commonly known, the Champions League theme music. This is one Uefa gimmick that I like a lot. Five minutes before kick-off the magnificent chorus and classical choir music really had an effect. The hair stood up on the back of my neck and my arms were covered in goose bumps. My eyes welled up and I clenched my fists.

My Dad's expression mirrored mine. Every game, every goal, every minute stood on the Kop with my Dad and my brother appeared to lead up to this moment. It was highly appropriate that the highly esteemed Royal Philharmonic Orchestra and the Academy of St. Martin in the Fields Chorus should lead us to that moment. At that moment I really wished our Steve had been with us. He had walked every step of our journey with us and really deserved to feel this moment too. I told Dad as much and he replied with a rueful smile. There wasn't time to dwell on it thankfully.

Since the final, this music has had the same effect on me every time I hear it. If I hear that theme tune ten thousand times more during my lifetime it will only ever return me to that moment in Istanbul five minutes before kick-off.

The magnificent Champions League trophy was brought out and set upon a white column. The two teams then had to file past it. All eyes were pinned on the huge piece of silverware. There it was for all to see and in touching distance of the players. It was too much for one Milan player to resist as he gentle petted the trophy as he passed by; an act of arrogant folly, if ever there was one. I found out later, by watching the footage, that the player coveting the trophy was Gattuso. I'm not superstitious, but I was more than happy for the Milan players to give the trophy a cuddle as long as our lads left well alone. Tempting fate seemed a dangerous thing to do.

Maldini had called the toss correctly before kick-off and swapped the teams around. This meant that Liverpool began the first half attacking our end of the stadium. For most games there is a slight air of disappointment when we attack our own fans in the first half, but tonight it didn't matter a jot. Three sides of the grounds were stuffed with Liverpool fans so the Italians couldn't really escape us nor separate us from our players. The switching of the teams passed almost without comment.

The Milan keeper, Dida, spurned the opportunity to establish a fragile rapport with the Liverpool fans. He did this by ignoring the applause that greeted him into his goal. For as long as I have been going to Liverpool games there has been an unwritten rule. When a keeper runs toward the Kop he is applauded into his goal. If he waves or applauds back in recognition he gets an easier ride. If he ignores the Liverpool fans he gets hammered for ninety minutes. Only the stupid or the ignorant don't acknowledge the Kop. The only keeper I can ever remember not being applauded into his goal was Peter Schmeichel. Despite his obvious world-class talent as a footballer he always did his best to incite the Kop. Every other keeper I can remember received the applause, Shilton, Southall, Barthez, and all. They were all applauded into their goal-mouths and most of them graciously acknowledged that applause. I am sure that Dida was blissfully ignorant of this tradition and could easily be excused. It wasn't a pressing concern for him or us.

How Liverpool started the game now had my focus.

In the moments before kick-off I raised my eyes to the jet-black Istanbul sky and closed them tight shut. For a few moments I thought of my wife sitting in the living room of her parent's house staring at the TV clenching her fists in desperate hope. I knew that Yvonne would be thinking about me and wanting this victory for me more than herself, or anyone else. I thought about my little girls, no doubt safely tucked up in bed, totally unaware of the magnitude and importance a game of football could possibly have. I thought about my mother-in-law, Kathy, who made it possible for me to get there. I knew Kathy would be thinking 'That could have been me' but I knew she would be living every moment at home with me. I thought about my family, I thought about my life, and I revelled in the fact that I was standing in the Ataturk stadium next to my father.

It was one of those all too rare moments when every aspect of my life seemed right. If the Liverpool players were 'living the dream' as a Liverpool fan I was doing the same. I'm a kopite, a family man; I'm one of the boys. In every aspect of my life I was very much living the dream.

Everything in my life seemed right in that moment. I was on a spiralling natural high as forty thousand fellow reds roared in anticipation of the first whistle. I could smell the adrenalin as the Spanish referee signalled to his linesman. As the first whistle blew I filled my lungs to capacity with the intoxicating air of excitement.

Having lost the toss and Maldini deciding to switch the teams around, Liverpool kicked-off. I remember distinctly that the first ball of the game was fed out to Traore at left-back and he knocked it long down the left flank. At this point my mind was racing. Dad and me stared, glued to the pitch. In what seemed like the very next instant Kaka had the ball and attacked Traore down the right wing.

A feature of European competition is often a stream of dubious free-kicks and Traore gave away the first of the night in a dangerous crossing position almost level with our penalty box. It was a daft tackle and it was the obvious option for Kaka to go to ground. Perhaps a stronger referee might have made a stand early against any hint of gamesmanship. Perhaps Traore should have stood off him and guided him into the corner. Perhaps it was a foul.

Only thirty seconds into the game we had our first serious threat to deal with. I was terrified. I remember thinking that surely they couldn't score in the first minute. Surely my dream couldn't begin to end before it had even begun at all. Pirlo took the free-kick. He swept the ball in flat in front of the defending line almost level with the penalty spot and there to meet it on the volley was the unlikely figure of Paolo Maldini. As the ball hit the net there was total disbelief amongst us.

'It's in!' said the bloke next to me, as if I needed confirmation. Perhaps he was convincing himself. It didn't feel right. Twelve thousand Milan fans went wild and their bench ran down the touchline. We were one nil down almost before the game had started.

A couple of days after the game I found a Ladbrokes betting coupon for the final in my desk at work. Maldini was 80-1 to score the first goal. I expected him to have been longer odds than that. He hadn't scored for God knows how long and it was only his 2nd European Cup goal in a million appearances. It was like that goal was fate.

At the time I seriously feared that it was fate.

Traore's nervous start continued as the ball seemed to seek him out in the opening minutes. Barely moments after the restart he gave away possession and then gave away a foul in trying desperately to recover. He looked like he could hardly keep his feet – like Emile Heskey on ice.

If anything the atmosphere amongst the Liverpool fans intensified. We had a full ninety minutes to sort this out. We stood up as one and roared our support for the boys. The immediate response was good. Baros won a corner running at Stam on the right. Gerrard knocked it to the edge of the box to Riise and a trademark thunderbolt was blocked as it screamed toward Dida's goal. Spirits lifted amongst us. Before possession broke down, a cross into the box was met strongly by Hyypia. He planted a strong header straight at Dida but it was a good response all the same, a statement of intent.

But that was as good as it got for some time. Milan started knocking the ball about, around us, and through us.

Shevchenko and Crespo crisscrossed along the frontline. Milan didn't pile on the pressure but when they attacked they looked like they would score. Worst of all, we looked fragile from set-pieces. Much of our success in the competition had been built upon our strength in defending set-plays, but now we looked uncertain. Garcia cleared the ball off the line from a Crespo header as we struggled to calm our nerves.

If some of the Liverpool lads looked nervous, Milan's Kaka was the epitome of calm and confidence. He didn't see a lot of the ball at first but as we passed the twenty-minute mark he started to become more involved and more assured with every touch. Everything he did spelt danger for us. In the final of the world's premier club competition he looked like he had all day to pick a pass. Kaka nutmegged Alonso in the centre of the pitch, a zone controlled by Milan and for all his valiant efforts Gerrard could do nothing about it.

After twenty minutes of the final there were two significant changes. First Harry Kewell pulled up with an injury. It would later transpire that he needed an operation to repair a torn groin muscle. This injury typified Kewell's season; Benitez had placed his faith in him time and again only for Harry to pull up injured and unable to repay that faith. The Liverpool fans were sceptical. A few shouted disapproval and I even heard a few boos. I felt sorry for Kewell. The media had pilloried him by questioning his commitment, but the truth is that he had terrible luck with injuries in 2004/5. Instead of sympathy, Harry had the likes of Andy Gray bleating on about how he 'owed us big-time'. Yeah, like Gray wanted to see those instalments deposited!

On in his place came Vladimir Smicer. Vladi had many similarities with Kewell. Smicer was technically superb, unlucky with injury, and had unquestionable ability. The twist in Vladi's tale was that this was undoubtedly his last game for Liverpool. The second significant change in the game was that Milan noticeably stepped up a gear.

Midway through the half Crespo was flagged for offside when in on Dudek. Jerzy made the save but my heart was pounding. A couple of minutes later a Garcia flick went astray and Seedorf burst forward. Inevitably the ball found Kaka, who played in Shevchenko. The Ukrainian superstar slotted past Dudek and wheeled away to the corner flag to celebrate.

Thankfully, a more important flag waved above the linesman's head to signify offside.

I thought it was a goal. I thought it was all over. Milan looked as comfortable as any team can when only 1-0 ahead. Liverpool struggled to create half-chances. Baros hooked one over from the edge of the box when Alonso was better placed but our first real chance was yet to sur- face. Meanwhile Djimi Traore's nerves were still jangling like a Mike Oldfield album as he tangled with Shev- chenko in our penalty area. Traore momentarily deserted the line of four in defence and wandered into a deep posi- tion where the white hot Shevchenko happily terrorised. Dudek scooped the ball away from the tangling players and gave us some temporary relief.

The first half was now following a simple pattern. Liv- erpool pushed forward, attacks were broken down, and

Milan countered. We all longed for halftime. If we could just get to halftime then maybe we could change things around. 1-0 at halftime would be OK; we could recover from 1-0 against anyone, even the great AC Milan. No game is ever over at 1-0. But the pattern of the game continued and as halftime approached Milan stepped on the gas and the counter attacks got quicker and quicker.

It was horrible and frustrating to watch. Crespo broke through on Dudek once more and Dudek made a great save. Again the flag was up but I had the feeling that Milan would get one right soon.

Then, out of the blue, Liverpool threatened the Milan penalty area with real purpose for the first time. Garcia stepped inside Nesta just inside the box and just as the door opened for Garcia to step through, Nesta blocked the ball with his arm and swept the ball from the Spaniards feet. Penalty - no question. We had a clear view of it and all the Liverpool fans and players went up as one.

But the Spanish referee didn't give it! He didn't even wave play-on, he just let the game continue. Dad was going berserk. All his frustrations built up during the previous thirty-odd minutes let loose.

To equalise at a point when we were in danger of conceding a second would have been a real boost. To go in at halftime level having played second-fiddle to Milan for 45 minutes would give us all real hope.

Instead, disaster struck quickly and clinically and the three best players on the pitch during the first half combined to strike a cruel blow. As Liverpool reeled from the decision not to give a penalty, Milan zigzagged through us with Kaka finding Shevchenko on the right. Shevchenko cut it back for Crespo who stroked it home. It should have been a penalty to Liverpool and most likely 1-1. Instead it was 2-0 to Milan and we were miles away from them. No one could deny they deserved the second goal, 1-0 didn't do them justice.

It crossed my mind that on balance of play 2-0 at half time wouldn't be all that bad for us. At 2-0 there was still hope. I was hopelessly clutching at straws. That fragile hope was put under threat by another Traore mistake. A terrible attempted cross left us short at the back once more and Milan swept forward again, this time winning a corner. Traore was out of his depth and Liverpool were in no position now to carry passengers. The corner was wasted and I breathed relief. I couldn't contemplate 3-0. I didn't want to contemplate 3-0.

Then, a minute before half-time, I had no choice.

Gerrard gave the ball away to Pirlo who, of course, gave it to Kaka. Kaka then crowned his superlative first half with a simply perfect through ball; a ball that would have unlocked any defence in the world; a ball that could have opened my front door at home.

Waiting on the other side of the keyhole was Chelsea's on-loan striker Hernan Crespo, who sumptuously chipped Dudek before he could plant his feet.

It all happened so quickly it was like a flash flood.

7. Doom & Gloom

When you walk through a storm,
Hold your head up high
And don't be afraid of the dark...

Rodgers & Hammerstein

At half-time I wasn't feeling nervous anymore. Dad didn't look nervous anymore. Nobody felt nerves. We felt sick. The game was over.

No one was making eye contact, much less ready to *talk* about the first half. To my right, a Liverpool fan was raging on the gangway of steps between the seats. Shouting at no one in particular, his disappointment boiled over into a frenzied outburst. After a few moments he headed up the steps, out of sight, out of the stadium and into the gloom.

He needn't have bothered leaving the stadium to find gloom. There could have been no darker place in Istanbul than on the south terrace at half time. There was no escape for most of us. I've heard numerous tales of fans streaming out at half time, but truly and honestly, the only person I witnessed leaving was that one red who lost his cool on the stadium steps. Most of us stood silent. A young girl behind me sat down and cried. She was the only person I saw actually cry tears at half time, but thousands certainly felt exactly the same.

I didn't feel comfortable making eye contact with anyone. I turned to Dad for some inspiration. He didn't have any. Looking at Dad was like looking in the mirror. He was shaking his head and muttering to himself and looked really tired. Fourteen hours of travelling started to take its toll for the first time. Most of the Liverpool fans were standing but I sat down and held my scarf either side of my face and over my ears. If I had been alone, the emotion I felt would have been more than enough to make me break down. I didn't want to cry in front of my Dad. Strangely enough, I recalled an incident when, as a young boy, my school team lost a big cup final replay. What made it worse was the school gave out the wrong directions to the game and my Dad missed the match. When I returned home after the game I burst into tears and Dad hugged me until I stopped. I felt like that now but much worse. I was in total despair.

Many of the fans around me were busy on their mobile phones. Some were taking calls but most were reading and replying to text messages. A bloke a couple of rows in front started to lose his temper. He was on the receiving end of a gloating text message from someone. I guessed it would have been an Everton or Manchester United fan. The thought of people sitting back at home revelling in my despair made my blood boil. I wished I had sorted my phone out so I could speak to or at least text my wife at home. I needed comfort from somewhere, but it was never going to come.

After a long 10 minutes of stewing in my seat, I stood up and nudged my Dad.

'All we can do know is show a bit of pride.' I suggested.

Dad agreed. Even though it was very much a cliché and a statement of the bleeding obvious, Dad was happy to engage my opening line. At that point, my old school mate John Perry made his way up to see me. He clambered over a few rows of seats to join me briefly. He gave me a warm handshake and a hug and I could hardly blame him for over-emotion in my own current fragile state. He probably needed a hug as much as I did.

'All we need is four penalties and we're laughing,' John said.

In the same way as my own father accepted my crap attempts to revive our spirits, I accepted John's feeble attempt. That one sentence is all John had to offer but it was nice of him to make the effort to clamber over several rows to shake my hand.

As the second half approached I could feel the gloom lifting slightly. Everyone around us was chatting inanely and attempting somehow to lift each other. The recovery of the massed ranks in red was growing. The first muted chants of 'Liver-pool, Liver-pool' started to creep around the terrace and flags were hoisted once again. Looking back with the benefit of a particularly bright and glorious hindsight, this was the moment that the miracle of Istanbul began. From total despair came an adrenalin rush that swept across the South Stand of the Ataturk stadium. An enormous banner that can be seen drifting across the Kop at every Liverpool home game now came slipping across the open terrace as the chants of *You'll Never Walk Alone* got louder and more vociferous. The world could watch us in our hour of despair stand up with our chests pushed forward and sing the reds back onto the pitch.

By the time Steven Gerrard led the Liverpool team back onto the pitch they were greeted by forty thousand reds celebrating being part of England's most successful football club. This was a mood-swing like no other. From the depths of despair we stood as one. If any member of the Liverpool team hadn't yet grasped what it means to be part of this magical club then surely this would erase any doubt.

8. Mission Impossible

Liverpool's mission impossible started with a change of formation. An injury to Steve Finnan gave Traore an undeserved reprieve and Didi Hamman took Finnan's place on the pitch. Liverpool were now playing with three at the back, Carragher, Hyypia, and Traore. Didi would sit in midfield protecting the back three and feeding Gerrard and Alonso in the centre of the park. Riise and Smicer would stay wide with Garcia pushed further forward to join Baros.

What we all needed as fans was for the Liverpool players to take on our raucous suggestion. We needed signs of fight and determination. The first signs of both came from the most obvious source. Steven Gerrard charged through the first fifty-fifty ball of the second half like it meant something much more. His attitude was infectious and the beleaguered Traore made another strong challenge following Gerrard's lead.

Despite the fighting spirit I was still only too aware that Milan were still directing traffic. A terrible Cafu cross was inexplicably spilled by Dudek and a fourth for Milan looked far more likely than a Liverpool riposte. Even so, the attitude of the players is what we were all feeling for. With the game lost, we were hungry to salvage some pride. Even if Milan went 4-0 or even 5-0 up, I still wanted to see a Liverpool team prepared to battle for 45 minutes. I wanted to salvage second half pride from the first half carnage of my European Cup dream.

Despite Milan's thinly veiled threats, there were signs that we could achieve this aim, at least as we roared the players on. Smicer looked lively as Hamman added to the successful fifty-fifty count in the first five minutes of the half. Alonso then hit a speculative screamer a foot wide of Dida's goal. The keeper looked comfortable but it fitted my bill of attacking intent and physically determined football. On the rare occasions I have seen Liverpool well beaten I have always joked that the least I wanted before the end of the game was to see a Liverpool player knock someone into next week. I like to see players try to take some of the pleasure out of winning from the opposing players. My fellow Kopites stood on their seats and bellowed out *The Fields of Anfield Road*. I felt so impassioned I wished I could get closer to the game. I gripped a fistful of my Dad's shirt at the shoulder as Jamie Carragher won yet another crunching tackle, this time with the Dutch hardman Japp Stam. This was great, four or five crunching tackles in the opening five minutes of the half. Dad looked better, happier now and miles away from our half time misery.

The Liverpool lads looked more determined, if not assured. Perhaps the feeling of having nothing to lose had helped the side lose its inhibitions. The consolation prize we were hoping for was increased passion and commitment and in the opening minutes of the second half it looked as if we would at least get that. In the midst of this early promise, Djimi Traore was close to crushing our early resolve. A simple square ball from Carragher slipped under the Frenchman's boot to – who else but Kaka? I swear the Brazilian knew it was going to happen or else he willed it to. Sami Hyypia bailed out his defensive partner with a body check on Kaka. Hyypia earned a yellow card for his last ditch challenge but it was an acceptable result as Kaka threatened to steer the game back onto its first half course.

After waiting an age for the free kick, Shevchenko speared a shot toward the bottom left hand corner. Dudek made a great save and we sighed with relief. Tension was beginning to mount within me again. Desperate optimism had the massed red ranks groping for some kind of sign that we could get out of this game with our pride intact, but after the Traore slip and Dudek's save I began to panic again.

In the 54th minute of the 2005 European Champions League final a spark was ignited. In footballing terms Steven Gerrard's goal to make it Liverpool 1 AC Milan 3 was as simple as they come. Cafu blocked John Arne Riise's initial cross from the left, but Cafu could do nothing about his second attempt. It was a textbook cross, met by Steven Gerrard, who planted a perfect looping header into the top corner of Dida's goal. The giant Brazilian keeper didn't even attempt a token dive, there was no point. At the time it seemed to happen in slow motion.

My first instinct was to look for a linesman's flag and then check if the referee had given the goal. The Spanish referee spun away toward the centre circle.

There was no flag.

I remember turning to my Dad to see his face contorted with emotion. Rather than looking elated, he looked like he might just shake the life out of someone given half a chance. He was shaking both fists in time like a mime artist banging on a door. A girl in the row behind me, who had been in tears at half time, now choked with relief. I reached out a hand and she quickly squeezed it and beamed a broad smile.

It had only taken 10 minutes of the second half to restore our pride. We were no longer taking a beating and a lively imagination might even begin to think in terms of a miracle. My Dad was happy enough to entertain such thoughts. Barely had play restarted when my Dad pulled me toward him and shouted into my ear.

'We can do this Mike! If we get another they will shit themselves!'

You couldn't disagree. If we scored another to make it 2-3 it would pile the pressure onto Milan. The Olympiakos game that ultimately helped Liverpool qualify for the first knockout stage had a similar scenario. At 1-0 down at half time at Anfield, having lost the first game 1-0 in Greece, Liverpool needed to score three in the second half. Florent Sinama-Pongolle scored in the first minute of the second half. Liverpool then knew that if they could manage to score a second goal, Olympiakos would be under incredible pressure for the remainder of the game. It was just a question of when that second goal could be scored. It didn't matter if the second goal came with thirty minutes, twenty minutes, or two minutes of the game remaining. What was guaranteed was that the remainder of the game would be unbearable for the Greek side as long as the second goal was scored.

As it happened, Neil Mellor managed to score the second with 10 minutes to go and this turned out to be enough time for Liverpool to turn up the heat and get the third, a screamer from Gerrard. Who else?

I turned around to look at the giant screen behind us. AC Milan 3 Liverpool 1. It looked so much better than before and Liverpool were now in the Olympiakos scenario once again. But this time it wasn't a Greek side with a disastrous away record in tow. This was an Italian side, six times winners of the trophy, and reputedly the best club side in Europe if not the world, defensively as well as offensively. With this in mind I'm sure there were plenty of Manchester United fans all around the south of England still sitting comfortably in their easy chairs. Two minutes after the Gerrard lifeline, however, the game changed completely. If the Gerrard goal had been a redirection of footballing traffic, Vladimir Smicer was about to set a juggernaut freewheeling down a one-way street.

Didi Hamman fed Smicer twenty yards out and the whole game opened up before him. A slashing right foot drive spun toward Baros, who did a passable impression of Patrick Swayze to let the ball somehow get through him. More importantly, it got through Dida too, who could only push the ball into the net.

This time I didn't check for a flag or even think about the referee. I grabbed my Dad in a bear hug and we somehow leapt up onto the back of our seats without losing our footing. It was total bedlam. Arms, scarves, and flags, tangled and punched holes into the night sky. Screams of ecstasy and celebration filled my head as I looked across the terrace, punching 10 times my weight in happiness.

'We're gonna win this son!' my Dad raged.

I believed him.

I looked back at the screen behind us. AC Milan 3 Liverpool 2. I was dreaming and beginning to understand what was going on around me. We were going to win, this was going to be our night and everything that I thought was lost just four minutes earlier was now reappearing in front of me. The Liverpool fans sang so loudly that I couldn't hear myself singing, although I was shouting as loud as I could. I bounced on my seat to *The Fields of Anfield Road* as Liverpool immediately won a corner.

Milan were now looking so nervous they were making Traore look like Beckenbauer. The corner came to nothing but it was only a matter of time. Using the Olympiakos principle, we now had at least 33 minutes to capitalise on Milan's fear and desperation.

Liverpool were now surfing forward on a tide that Milan were never going to stop. Twenty thousand Rossonieri sat silently watching the floodwaters rising to consume their once invincible charges. Carragher fed a ball through to Baros, whose deft back-heel was taken by Gerrard in his stride. The Liverpool skipper surged into the box and looked set to knock it past Dida only for Gattuso to bring him down.

Penalty!

No arguments, no debate, a stonewall penalty.

Somehow Gattuso kept his place on the pitch, despite denying Gerrard the opportunity to pull the trigger. We were mystified to how Gattuso could get away with just a yellow card, but there wasn't a prolonged debate on the terraces. The protests and punishment surrounding Gattuso's punishment were lost somewhere in the frantic celebrations.

As with any penalty decision there is celebration tempered by the fact that a goal hasn't yet been scored. Wild celebrations and disbelief were replaced quickly by astonished glances and anxious looks into the night sky. Reds of every religious denomination, and perhaps even the atheists, pressed their shaking palms together and prayed.

The miracle of Istanbul, created in six frantic minutes was a penalty kick away from reality.

Xavi Alonso, a young footballing aristocrat with an artist's touch, was the man with the considerable weight of responsibility. The Milan players did their utmost to delay the kick and give Alonso time to dwell upon the enormity of the task in front of him. You couldn't blame the Milan players for that. Their panic had turned to desperation and now desperation was turning into resignation.

Alonso stood still, with a billion Scouse prayers wishing him on. From the South terrace it would be over in a flash.

I grabbed a fistful of Dad's shirt at the shoulder and braced myself.

Alonso stepped up ... saved ... rebound ... goal!

A great save from Dida only served up the chance for Alonso to crash in the rebound. It happened so quickly there was no time to feel the pain of Dida's initial save.

A bolt of lightning surged through me. Wild uninhibited joy and celebration picked me up and flushed through every vein in my body. For 10 seconds or more Dad and me embraced, jumping in time and screaming with joy. Every game, every trophy, every goal we had ever witnessed at Liverpool games passed through us. Our footballing lives passed before our eyes as the dreams of Anfield Road became reality.

As I opened my eyes the scoreboard behind us had already changed – *AC Milan 3 Liverpool 3*. Six minutes of blitzkrieg had restored pride and parity. The Roseneiri sat motionless victims of Liverpool's shock and awe tactics. The celebration continued unabated. The girl behind us in tears at half time was nowhere to be seen. Convulsing bodies in red stumbled across seats and clambered to their feet. A bloke behind me grabbed the back of my head by the hair and roared into my face. I grabbed the Liverpool badge on his shirt with my fist. Around three sides of the ground there was mass hysteria in stark contrast to the motionless disbelief on their side.

At some point the game had restarted. Liverpool were now confident and assured, stroking the ball around with an air of 'mission accomplished'. In reality, we had only achieved parity. There had to be more to come. In my mind there could be no doubt that we would go on to win in normal time. Milan had been clinical in the first half but in the second half Liverpool were merciless. No team could brave this storm.

But even the strongest winds blow themselves out and Liverpool's storm abated and Milan dusted themselves down. Before long, the game reverted to a weaker version of the first half, with Milan assuming dominance and threatening the Liverpool back line. What was clearly different from the first half was that Liverpool now had belief and determination.

Jamie Carragher grew a foot taller in height, casting a Yeats-like shadow across the Liverpool back line. Milan attacked but Liverpool stood strong. Traore looked like a born again defender, clearing off the line from Shevchenko. Carragher blocked a Kaka effort on the edge of the six-yard box and followed that with a last ditch tackle on Shevchenko in the dying minutes.

Strangely enough, I don't remember an awful lot about the second half following Alonso's equaliser. What I do remember is the injury time board going up and thinking that Liverpool looked absolutely knackered.

There is something about the injury time board that induces panic in me. The knowledge that a goal scored during that time would normally always prove fatal is a terrifying prospect. The two minutes of injury time at the end of the ninety minutes were agony. Milan didn't really threaten but nevertheless I was hurting.

The whistle at the end of ninety minutes was a blessed relief. I couldn't really rationalise how I felt compared to what I experienced at half time. Total despair was now growing confidence. The instant that normal time ended I turned to my Dad. He was laughing nervously, whilst wiping his forehead with the palm of his hand. We mirrored each other's feeling for the game. Having come back from the dead it was unthinkable that we could lose. Our emotions were stretched to the limit. At half time there was no question of a comeback, we were beaten. Now at full time we didn't dare consider we could lose. At half time we were desperate to save face but now we were on the brink of much, much more.

9. Holding On

In my memory, extra time is a blur of emotion punctuated by moments of panic. I remember as extra time began it began to look more and more obvious that the Liverpool players looked spent of energy. Increasingly I felt that Liverpool could only win the trophy by one of two ways, a moment of magic or penalties.

During the first five minutes of extra time I realised that it was 'backs to the wall' for us now. Milan grew in confidence as Liverpool defended deeper and deeper. I remember Tomasson missing a decent chance on the stretch and Liverpool playing lots of long hopeful stuff up to Cisse, who had replaced Milan Baros in the closing minutes of normal time. Cisse was having real trouble holding the ball up and possession was surrendered to Milan over and over. Several Liverpool players looked to be suffering with cramp. I remember Vladimir Smicer needing lengthy treatment at some stage in the first period and I vaguely remember a number of other reds struggling in the second.

In the second period of extra time Jamie Carragher showed exactly why he is adored by kopites. Carra stretched to cut out a cross from the Milan left and succeeded in conceding a corner. In making the block he hit the turf in agony, riddled with cramp in what appeared to be his groin. Carragher is not a man to show any pain if he can help it, but he looked in serous discomfort as he received treatment to get him back on his feet. Barely two minutes later, Carra limped back into the action and was immediately called upon to make yet another diving intervention to cut out another cross from the Milan left. You could see Carragher was in agony, but he got back to his feet nevertheless and took up his position for the corner.

One of my only other recollections from extra time is a Milan free-kick, taken by Pirlo from a crossing position. I had hold of my Dad's arm like a tourniquet as Pirlo knocked in a cross that we scrambled clear.

Then came a moment I could never forget, a save that defies physics as much as it does my own personal belief. Yet another cross from Serginho was met powerfully by Shevchenko. For a moment Shevchenko had the European Cup at his mercy; it was a chance he would take 99 times out of a hundred, his bread and butter. He wouldn't need to practice putting away a chance like this; to a player of Shevchenko's class this would be a natural instinct. But somehow, and I still don't know how, Dudek managed to get a forearm in the way and deflect the ball over the bar. It was a moment of freak physics.

How the ball hit Dudek's arm and deflected over the bar at that angle and that speed is still incomprehensible to me, but the moment it happened it became Liverpool's night. I don't have much time for Sky commentator Andy Gray, but he summed the moment up perfectly when he said, 'You may as well start engraving Liverpool's name on the trophy'.

Of course it didn't feel that cut and dried from my point of view at the time, but with hindsight Gray was spot on. The game restarted and Milan took their corner, but really they could have blown the whistle there and then.

Amazingly, Liverpool had the last chance of the game, in extra time injury time. A rare break up field resulted in Didi Hamman inducing a poor tackle on the right edge of the Milan box. For a moment we all held our breath and thought maybe we could win it without the need for penalties, but really it was never going to happen. A weak and tired free-kick routine between Gerrard and Riise was the last action of extra time.

Penalties were now a cert and we were more than happy to accept them. The pain of half time was so acute that I could still taste it under my tongue. Every Liverpool fan in Istanbul would have snatched your arm off at the elbow given the offer of penalties when we were 3-0 down. I bet there wasn't a single Milan fan that would've dreamt it would go to penalties.

10. Penalties

Our faith is the weapon most feared by our enemies

Banner – Liverpool Fan

Sometimes when you watch a big game on telly and it goes to penalties it seems to take an age to get round to the first spot-kick. The players are invariably knackered and need a massage and some fluid. The managers have to recruit at least five strong characters to put their hand up for a kick and rally their beleaguered troops. But the time elapsed between the end of the game and the first spot-kick seemed to fly by in Istanbul. I don't know why. Perhaps I've just watched the game too many times on DVD, where the intervening minutes have been edited out. All I know is, I have very little recollection about waiting for the kicks to be taken.

The one thing I do remember is watching Jamie Carragher waving his arms frantically in front of Jerzy Dudek. At the time it looked like Carra had lost it. It was shown on the giant screen behind us and everyone was watching and talking about it. It was Dad who pointed it out to me. It seemed inconceivable that they would be arguing at a time like that, but that's what it looked like from the Liverpool end. Dad and me were in high spirits.

It would be a long time before any of this sank in properly and at the forefront of my mind was still the horror of half time. It was a great feeling to have watched Liverpool come back from the dead. After all the magnificent triumphs I'd witnessed first hand – the Wembley cup finals and the league winning sides – here I was amidst the greatest of them all, and it just so happened to be the European Cup final.

On the wave of that emotion my Dad was as confident as I've seen him at a big game.

'We're gonna do it Mike, we're gonna do this …' he kept on saying. I believed him because I wanted to believe him.

The penalties were taken at the end where the Milan fans were. A rumour flash-flooded across the Liverpool fans that this meant Liverpool would be taking the first penalty. This would be a good thing, the general consensus being that the team taking the first penalty has a small but sometimes significant advantage. Taking the first kick would give us the chance to forge ahead and heap more pressure on the Milan takers. And if we missed a kick there was still pressure on Milan to take advantage.

But the general consensus was wrong. Milan would be kicking toward their own fans and also take the first kick.

Milan's first taker was Serginho. I won't pretend that I knew much about the prowess of the Milan penalty takers, apart from presuming Shevchenko would be taking one and he would be an expert. Serginho's penalty taking skills were a mystery to me, but only 15 minutes earlier I had watched him curl in numerous superb left wing crosses only for him to be single-handedly foiled by a wall of Carragher.

There was no Carragher to stop Serginho now. This time Jerzy Dudek was the man standing in his way. As

Serginho approached the penalty area Dudek was waiting for him with the ball. I once watched a David Seaman interview when he said he used to hand the ball to the kicker wherever possible deliberately, to gain a psychological edge over the penalty taker. He would hold on to the ball so the taker would have to come to him. Sometimes he would even drop it so the taker would have to pick it up from in front of Seaman's feet. The odd word to unsettle the players mind would also be used.

Dudek seemed to be using all of these tactics, but he wasn't finished there. When he retreated to his goal-line he started waving his arms and bouncing around all over the place. Even in this desperate pressurised atmosphere most of us were laughing.

Somehow the best efforts of Dudek to distract Serginho worked. He skied his kick high, and wide. Dad and me went berserk but only for a few short seconds. It was like celebrating a goal and then seeing a flag for offside. The elation came as we watched the distinctive Champions League ball swerve high and wide. This was curtailed by the reality that there was still a long way to go.

LIVERPOOL					0
AC MILAN	X				0

Didi Hamman would take Liverpool's first penalty in the penalty shoot-out. Dad and me had hoped Didi would make the starting eleven. It seemed like light years since we talked about that very issue in a Manchester Airport café only that morning. Didi had helped turn the game in the second half, now we were counting on him to turn the screw.

Now I used to take penalties when I played football and there is always a certain amount of pressure. Pressure from within, from team mates, from opponents and those watching who are willing you to score or miss. I always just ran up and side footed as hard as I could into a corner chosen about five seconds before I took the kick. I once took a penalty in a friendly game and missed. If I had scored it would have been my hat trick and I was gutted. About a minute after my miss we got another one and I stepped up to take that one as well. The extra pressure of potentially missing two in a minute had me panicking. I stepped up, abandoning my usual methods, and just hit it as hard as I could. Fortunately, it went in, right down the middle.

Now if I felt pressure taking a meaningless penalty in a friendly in front of one man and his dog, then the pressure on Didi Hamman must have been almost overwhelming. As he placed the ball on the spot I clenched my fists and held them in front of my mouth, my elbows tucked into my stomach.

The pressure didn't tell on Hamman. He took one of the classiest penalties I have ever seen; a smooth, stuttering run-up followed by a curved right footer into the roof of the goal. It was the type of penalty I might have attempted in a kick-in to take the Mickey out of our keeper – and more than likely miss. This was as important as it gets. Eighty million people watched Hamman take that penalty.

LIVERPOOL	✓					1
AC MILAN	✗					0

Next up to the plate was Pirlo. I'd almost forgotten about him. In the first half of normal time he was everywhere complementing the industrious Gattuso and feeding the ball hungry Kaka. The first half of normal time seemed a long time ago. Dudek employed the same tactics that, perhaps, did for Serginho. He offered the ball to Pirlo, retreated to his line and then started weaving up and down like he was reviving some ridiculous sixties twist. As Pirlo took his last step toward the ball Dudek set himself. A week effort was parried strongly by Dudek who then leapt to his feet to punch the air with both fists. This time Dad and me celebrated a little longer without as much inhibition, without the thought that Milan could recover. My eyes filled to bursting as I gritted my teeth and started to really believe the dream.

LIVERPOOL	✓					1
AC MILAN	✗	✗				0

Liverpool's next kicker strode forward confidently. Djibril Cisse, looked like a man in a hurry. He marched to the penalty area stuck down the ball and took three steps back. With the minimum of fuss he then side-footed the ball firmly to Dida's left as the keeper guessed wrongly and dived the other way. Cue another quick burst of emotion quickly stifled by a reality check.

LIVERPOOL	✓	✓				2
AC MILAN	✗	✗				0

If Milan were to haul themselves back into contention Jon Dahl Tomasson simply *had* to score Milan's third kick. A successful kick would put pressure on the Liverpool player stood back on the halfway line, waiting his moment in the spotlight. Tommasen strode forward purposely towards Dudek, who went through the same routine as before, ensuring that Tommasen came to him for the ball. Tommasen placed the ball on its spot and took a few strides backwards. He then sprinted into his penalty kick and scuffed a sweeping right footer low into the net. It wasn't a great penalty but it beat Dudek and his zany semaphore and that's what mattered most.

LIVERPOOL	✓	✓				2
AC MILAN	✗	✗	✓			1

Next up, John Arne Riise. Riise was possibly the most powerful striker of a ball at the club, bar perhaps Steven Gerrard. Confidence grew amongst us.

'Leather the bastard down the middle!' screached a woman behind me. It raised a laugh from everyone in the general vicinity, we had started to relax, just a little. With the power Riise possesses it was a nailed on certainty that he would blast it, probably down the middle. But he didn't. Riise struck the ball to Dida's right and the giant Brazilian keeper kept it out at full stretch. A purist might say any missed penalty is a poor penalty but it was hard to criticise Riise's miss. Notwithstanding the immense pressure, it wasn't actually a bad penalty and technically much better than Tomasson's kick a few moments earlier. He hit it hard and low and right in the corner, but somehow Dida got there. It was an inspirational save. I bet Riise wished he had battered it down the middle. At that moment we all wished he had. It wasn't exactly 'panic stations' but it was a sobering moment.

LIVERPOOL	✓	✓	✗			2
AC MILAN	✗	✗	✓			1

If there was one player who had terrorised Liverpool in the first half of the final it was Kaka. Crespo had scored twice in that first half, and his second goal was a clinical piece of marksmanship, but Kaka made all the bullets. His through ball for Crespo's second will live long in the memory. It was like one of those freak forty-foot golf putts you see at the Open every year that you just know is going straight into the hole as soon as the ball is struck. Only this particular monster putt stopped at the feet of Crespo for him to slice into Dudek's goal. I often think if that goal hadn't been scored then Milan would have come out for the second half with a different attitude. Milan were arguably a victim of Kaka's own brilliance as the third goal had led them to believe they had won the game. Not that any blame could be laid at the feet of the Brazilian. After half-time he didn't have quite the same impact on the game. As taker of Milan's fourth penalty he had a chance to heap more pressure onto the next Liverpool kicker. Kaka's penalty was struck with purpose into the net. Dudek's bouncing suddenly looked a little futile as the ball arrowed home. Suddenly Milan were on terms, albeit having taken one kick more than us. The Rossonieri found their voices as I felt my feet weld to the floor.

LIVERPOOL	✓	✓	✗			2
AC MILAN	✗	✗	✓	✓		2

Next up for Liverpool strode Vladimir Smicer, for what would be Vladi's last contact with a football in a Liverpool shirt. Kaka's penalty meant that Milan had pushed the door open ever so slightly. A miss from Smicer would blow the door off its hinges. This was the ultimate win or bust. Score and Smicer would become a Liverpool legend. Miss and he may well fade into ignominious folklore. I don't think there was ever a doubt in Smicer's mind to where his fate lay. A trademark bouncing gait preceded a precise side-foot finish. As Smicer stretched his shirt out in front of him Dad and I pumped our fists and celebrated. I don't remember much after Smicer's kick until someone pointed out that Shevchenko was next up for AC Milan.

| LIVERPOOL | ✓ | ✓ | ✗ | ✓ | | 3 |
| AC MILAN | ✗ | ✗ | ✓ | ✓ | | 2 |

To a player like Shevchenko a penalty is like a black off its spot to Ronnie O'Sullivan. But when it's a black for the World Snooker Title or a penalty to stay in the European Cup the rules change. Perhaps O'Sullivan would miss more important blacks if we stuck a crazy Polish bloke in the jaws of the pocket. Dad nudged me purposefully and made a nodding gesture toward the pitch, 'Shevchenko' he said. By simply stating his name I knew what Dad was implying. Milan were certain to draw level again and force Liverpool to score their fifth kick to become European Champions. I was comfortable with that. I hope you will pardon me for referring back to half time yet again but a single penalty kick to become European Champions sounded like a great deal when you consider that we had lost the final approximately two hours earlier.

Shevchenko wasn't going to miss. Forty thousand kopites in the Ataturk, millions of kopites around the world, millions of football fans around the world must have been in agreement with me that Shevchenko would score. A great player on the big occasion, that's what happens, they do the business.

Dudek reserved no special treatment for the great Ukrainian striker. He made Shevcheko come to him for the ball. He dropped it in front of him so he had to bend down to pick it up. Dudek later revealed that he spoke to Shevchenko as he dropped the ball onto the turf.

'Same place as always, Andrei?' he said.

If there was a flickering flame of indecision in the Ukrainian's mind, Dudek was pouring on petrol. Dudek's psychology, eighty million pairs of eyes, the very fate of the European Champions trophy sat upon Shevchenko's shoulders.

Liverpool's Polish keeper easily palmed out a weak, half-baked chip down the middle of the goal and the European Cup was ours.

The Final Score:

| LIVERPOOL | ✓ | ✓ | ✗ | ✓ | | 3 |
| AC MILAN | ✗ | ✗ | ✓ | ✓ | ✗ | 2 |

Dad and me bear-hugged each other and bounced up and down on our tiny red seats. I'll never know how we managed to stay on those seats whilst jumping up and down like they were mini-trampolines. We held each other so tightly that I couldn't see Dad's face. I could feel his chest reverberating as we both screamed 'Yesssss! Yesssss! Yesssss! Yessssssssssssss!' into the night sky. When we came up for air I could see three quarters of the stadium were following suit. It was total pandemonium. I have been involved in some wild celebrations on the old terraced kop. My feet didn't touch the ground for most of a Liverpool v Genoa Uefa Cup tie. I was once thrown into the moat on the North Bank at Highbury when Liverpool equalised against Portsmouth in the 1992 FA Cup semi-final. I lost my voice completely when celebrating a League Cup quarterfinal win against Everton in the lower bullens at Goodison Park, the night Jim Beglin broke his leg. But nothing, nothing at all had ever come close to these celebrations. Pure elation, the stuff dreams are made of, the ingredients of folklore, the greatest moment a football fan could have. Thousands of miles from home, beating the best team in Europe on the biggest stage for the most important club prize in the world.

I feel uneasy that there might be people who read this, people who deserved to be there that couldn't go, who might feel that I am somehow gloating that 'I was there'. I don't intend to do that. I just want to record a little of what it was like. My problem is that describing it is almost impossible. I have been to big European games at Anfield, semi-finals, Wembley finals, derby victories, I been to all kinds of games … but the game at the Ataturk beats them all. If I could buy the 2005 European Cup Final in drug form from a dealer in a side street I'd be slumped in some doorway with a smile on my face. As I sit here now typing these words, a part of me still doesn't believe we did it. That's what makes this victory so enduring. All I need to do is think about our half-time position. If I take all of those facts in, then somehow the knowledge that we went on to become Champions still had a fresh taste of disbelief about it. I hope that doesn't fade and I don't think it will.

After the initial burst of ecstasy the next thing I remember is *You'll Never Walk Alone* belting out over the public address system. After the first few words of the song it wasn't really required. Forty thousand reds took up the anthem and sung every syllable with meaning. Dad and me had our arms around each other with scarves held high above our heads. On the pitch the players were running around celebrating and doing interviews. Before long some of them were in front of us on the running track punching the air and applauding us. My eyes swelled with the chorus of our famous anthem. I fought the tears at first but I didn't really want to. I freely let the tears run down my cheeks. There were plenty of reds in tears all around us, significantly more than during half time. I looked at my Dad and he bear hugged me once more. For a moment I thought he would crack too. My Dad's eyes filled up but he held onto his equilibrium, as resolute as ever. He needn't have bothered, his face was stretched with happiness.

Over the next twenty minutes Dad and me hugged anyone that moved in red … unless they hugged us first. It was a big red love-in. Every shape and size, every age, gender of Liverpool fan was ready to congratulate the other. If penalties are a lottery then six numbers had just come up for every one of us. This went on until the presentation platform was assembled and the players were beckoned back to the halfway line to conduct the ceremony. Cheers rang around the stadium as an official carried the beautiful shining trophy toward a tall white podium. I wish I could say I stood and applauded the Milan players as they collected their medals but I don't have a single recollection of them collecting their slim consolations.

I remember the Liverpool players collecting their medals. I remember Cisse doing a kind of improvised limbo around the trophy. I think every one of the players gave the giant trophy a kiss before taking a position on a rostrum behind the awesome silverware. The presentation platform was crawling with Liverpool players and staff by the time Steven Gerrard was beckoned forward. Next to the platform on the right hand side, the Liverpool squad players we had seen passing through Liverpool airport gathered to join in the big moment.

As Steven Gerrard lifted our European Champions trophy, red and white ticker tape sprayed the squad and the Champions League theme consumed the stadium. A magnificent firework display began all around the stadium high into the cool Turkish sky. It was a glorious sight to witness. I had never before seen anything like it, no victory ever tasted so sweet. There is something particularly powerful about classical music that induces the adrenalin. I must have produced enough adrenalin to kill a racehorse in the previous thirty minutes alone but there was no relenting. The players cavorted and paraded with the trophy. In no time at all, the trophy was in front of us, and the players celebrated with us. They stood in front of us and sang with us. At that moment the gap between player and fan seemed very small. It felt like we had achieved the night's success together.

Thirty minutes or so of singing, hugging, and laughing came to a close as the players finally made movements toward the tunnel. I would have been happy for that part of the evening to go on forever but I wasn't greedy. Dad and me agreed we should make a move but it was hard to leave the stadium. I tried to soak up every last bit of my surroundings before we left. I wanted to remember the stadium in intricate detail. A place I brought my dreams to and a place I left singing about their fulfilment.

11. On Top of the World

What we achieve in life echoes in eternity

Banner – Liverpool Fan

Dad and I staggered up the steps of the stadium drunk on happiness. When we reached the top of the steps where the exits were I noticed a familiar face. It took me a few seconds to place the face of Rob Palmer, the football commentator and presenter with Sky Sports. He was decked out in a Liverpool home shirt and had a youngster in a wheelchair in front of him. As I extended my right hand to him he opened his arms and we gave each other a manly backslapping hug. 'We're European Champions! I can't believe it!' he shouted.

The scene was becoming more surreal by the minute! I tried to point him out to my Dad but he didn't hear me. He was standing in a kind of semi-hypnotised state, staring out at the pitch. I went over to Dad and stood next to him. We then stood at the top of the steps for a few moments and surveyed the scene. The stadium was now emptying and the players slowly heading toward the tunnel area. Fans streamed out of the back exit gates running and singing into the huge car parks behind the stadium. *You'll Never Walk Alone* still bellowed from the giant speakers all around the ground and those with any voice left gave it their all. It was a difficult scene to walk away from. I almost wanted to walk out backwards so I could take in every last available memory. But I already had plenty. Memories in the making lay within every moment. Eventually Dad convinced me we should go. We got about twenty yards out of the stadium before I ran back for one final look. I looked skyward and thought again about my wife at home. I hoped she could feel just one iota of what I was feeling at that moment.

I turned away from the Ataturk pitch for the last time and ran back to my Dad. He stood with open arms. My quiet and reserved Dad whose shows of open affection can sometimes come years apart held his arms wide open. I greeted him like Carra greeting Dudek's penalty save from Shevchenko. Arms around each other's shoulders we then began to stagger across the gigantic car parks in the general direction of our coach.

The huge car parks at the back of the stadium were poorly lit with orange sodium lamps scattered indiscriminately. It took a while for our eyes to adjust to the gloom after hours spent staring out onto the floodlit pitch. Dad and me staggered through the car park, our arms around each other's shoulders. For a while we just celebrated and wandered in the general direction of the coach park. *You'll Never Walk Alone* continued to choir out of the Ataturk and we gave it our best shot. In front of us, behind us, all around us, Liverpool fans raced around throwing themselves in pure unbridled joy. Fans with huge flags zigzagged across the gravel screaming ecstatically. People hugged and kissed and sang together. Progress across the car parks was slow as we were stopped and greeted by stranger after stranger. Dad kept stopping to take photographs and every time he did a fellow red offered to take one of the both of us. We had a number of photos taken of the two of us outside the stadium after the game. Unfortunately the reds taking the photos didn't exactly hold still and most of the resulting photographs turned out as a slightly blurred, hazy mixture of sodium light, and waving scarves. In truth a reasonably good representation of what I remember. It was totally understandable.

Dad and me scrambled up the gravel slope into the car park where coach 52 was waiting. The coach was at the edge of the car park directly facing the stadium. The coach wasn't even half full when we got there so we stood in front watching legions of Liverpudlians drain out of the stadium celebrating in the orange haze of the gravel car park below. The noise of fans greeting each other as they returned to their coaches could be heard all around us. When our bus started to fill we decided to get on as well. As I returned to my seat there were a dozen or so beaming reds staring at me.

'I quite enjoyed myself there,' I said, to a generous amount of laughter. I couldn't have got close to saying how I felt so understatement seemed my best bet. The chatter on the coach was deafening and Dad and me tried to make sense of it all. We kept looking at each other and shaking our heads, repeating the same things over and over again.

'I don't believe this ... we were dead and buried ... Gerrard will never leave now ...' and so on.

Although I was physically and mentally battered by the celebrating in the stadium I still had plenty of voice left. As the coach filled the singing got louder. As our coach made its way slowly out of the car park other coaches, full of reds bouncing in their seats and celebrating, mirrored us. The journey back would take a different route. The long since departed Rossoneri had made it possible for us to leave by the North end of the stadium and a potentially quicker route back to the centre of Istanbul. Very quickly the coach made it out onto a motorway and we gathered pace. After twenty minutes or so the noise on the coach reduced down to an excited chatter and the songs became more sporadic. Although we were travelling down a motorway there were no overhead lights and I stared out of my window into the darkness. I wondered what my family and friends would be doing. I wondered if my brother would still be standing? Would my wife still be celebrating with her Mum and Dad? I bet they were all thinking about us.

We sang all the way into the centre of Istanbul. As we got into the centre I recognised parts of the route and had a feeling we were only five minutes or so from our hotel. But then the route became less familiar and I wasn't so sure. The journey out to the stadium had been so slow it was difficult to estimate how long the journey back should take. Another five minutes would pass and I'd recognise some of the buildings again ... and then I wouldn't.
'

At the risk of sounding stupid,' said Dad, 'are we going around in circles here? I'm sure we passed here 10 minutes ago.' It wasn't a stupid question. We were lost again. Same coach, same driver, same co-driver, and the same result, we were lost. The anxiety and anger that accompanied getting lost earlier in the day was nowhere to be seen on our journey back. As the whole coach began to realise we were going round in circles the atmosphere of celebration prevailed. Somebody at the back of the coach played the Benny Hill theme tune on a mobile phone. Then the whole coach sang 'We've been this way five times' to the confusion of the co-driver. He looked like he expected a riot, what he got was a European Champions party bus. The Liverpool steward sang with us as we chanted 'We only travel Lonsdale'.

A couple of laps of Istanbul later we finally stopped at the bottom of a street I definitely recognised. As we got off the coach I turned to my Dad. He looked shattered and I knew how he felt; 14 hours travelling and three hours of concentrated emotion takes it out of you. We headed up the street, into the hotel, and headed straight for the bar. Half a dozen reds joined us. It really should have been me dipping my hand into my pocket but Dad was insistent that the beers were on him. He bought everyone a beer and we collapsed onto the leather sofas next to the bar. The first one didn't touch the sides. Over the next few hours the exact state of play with regard to whose round it was became very blurred. The beer flowed freely and we recounted the match erratically moving from one point to the next. There was too much to say, too much to explain, and too much to share. I managed to get my hand in my pocket after an hour or so and bought a double round to make sure I was pulling my weight.

Dad and me were really hungry now. There is only so far a homemade turkey sandwich can take you. The hotel had stopped serving food hours ago but Dad managed to broker a deal with the barman to make us some cheese rolls. It was just as well I had bought us a double round as the barman disappeared for ages before returning with the largest cheese sandwiches I will ever see. We demolished them in minutes. Cheese and beer, the meal of European Champions!

I can't recall too much about the exact detail of what we talked about during those hours sat drinking at the bar. It was pretty much an open forum for everyone to chip in and talk about any element of the game they wished to. There was an outpouring of opinion and disbelief as the most incomprehensible of matches was randomly dissected. It was the ultimate in footy pub conversations. I know I talk too much when I've had a beer so I'm pretty sure I talked for Britain that night. I also recall on more than one occasion I laughed so hard I nearly choked but I can't remember what it was about. I can remember the barman, who doubled as a late night chef, asking me repeatedly for my scarf. There was no way I would part from it and I laughed with him as I tied it ever more securely into a not around my neck. In the same way that I couldn't imagine any of the Liverpool players would want to give away their shirts from the final I wouldn't part with that scarf. Before the game it was a lightly rated accessory, now it had become a thoroughbred memento.

Dad and me met some great blokes in that bar. I hope I bump into some of them sometime at Anfield. I will recognise them and I will stop them to say hello. Naturally we eventually ran out of steam. At about 5:00 am Dad said he wanted to call it a night and I was happy to do the same. Some protracted goodnights then followed to blokes we would undoubtedly see only a few hours later. I remember walking up the stairs to our room in almost complete silence, drained of emotion and my head humming with Efes. I stripped down to my shirt and shorts and climbed into bed. Like a seven year old schoolboy with his first ever Liverpool top I didn't want to take my shirt off. So I slept in it! This was boys' own stuff but many of my wishes as an adult were also coming true.

12. The Day After in Istanbul

I was only in the game for the love of football – and I wanted to bring back happiness to the people of Liverpool.

Bill Shankly

I don't know what it is about my Dad that makes him get up at the crack of dawn every day, but he has done for as long as I can remember. Maybe it was all those early shifts at Ford Halewood or the thousands of early morning miles he has trained as a marathon runner. Whatever the reason, he can't help himself. I have been on nights out with my Dad when he has sunk six or seven pints of Guinness and then has got up first thing next morning and gone for a run. I'll grant you that, to some, six or seven pints isn't a heavy session, but try getting up at 8.00 am next day and going for a 15-mile run! That takes real stamina.

Over the years, I've had plenty of mates who have boasted about playing footy the day after a skin-full but none of them ever covered 15 miles on a football pitch sober, never mind with a hangover! Dad never bragged. He just got up and ran. Even if he isn't running, Dad gets up early every morning.

The morning after the greatest football night of my life I woke to the sound of running water … and a fair bit of cursing too. I lay in a semi-conscious slumber for a few minutes before I reached for my watch. It was 8:10 am and I'd had about three hours sleep. I didn't have much of a hangover, but I felt battered and bruised. The cursing from the bathroom continued for a few minutes until the running water stopped and Dad appeared at the bathroom door.

'I can't get that thing to warm up; it's bloody freezing!'

I smiled broadly at his discomfort and eventually he smiled back. Before I could say anything Dad continued, 'That did happen last night didn't it?' a massive smile that Jack Nicholson would have been proud of then beamed across his face. All the previous evening's joy flooded my body instantly. I was happy to be up early today, hangover or not. We had a full day to enjoy in Istanbul and I couldn't wait to get out onto the streets and enjoy the very warm light of day.

On any given day of the year, Dad and I are capable of talking football for as long as we think we can get away with it. Today we would talk fantasy football for as long as we liked. In fact, at that moment, I couldn't envisage talking about anything else for a very long time. I still didn't quite have my head around what had happened the night before. You take hopes and dreams into any game, particularly a final, but you could never imagine a result the like of which we had just witnessed. There was nothing to compare it to. We were both at the Liverpool v United 3-3 game at Anfield, and both of the Liverpool v Newcastle 4-3 games, but this was something totally different. The European Cup Final of 2005 was in a different league, a different stratosphere, a different world entirely. What was there to compare it to? We began the day shaking our heads in disbelief.

I grabbed a pair of shorts and went to brave the shower. As showers go it wasn't the most complicated to operate. The showerhead hung precariously off the wall and the colour of the soap in the dispenser looked a bit suspect, but the water was powerful and hot. I don't know what Dad had been trying to do, soft sod, but it was fine for me. After my shower I spent a few minutes gloating about how refreshed and clean I felt. Dad, who was fully dressed by that time, stripped off again and jumped back in the shower.

We decided to venture downstairs for breakfast. Whenever I've been away with the lads I'm rarely up in time for breakfast, so this was a novelty for me. Describing the content of the breakfast as a novelty would be kind in the extreme. There were slabs of bread you could use to replace your front door step and a cold meat counter displaying meats in various shades of grey. Dad found a basket of hard-boiled eggs and we both took a couple. The outside appearance of the eggs flattered to deceive, as inside they were a slightly deeper shade of battleship grey than the cold meats. Dad tried to convince me that this is how eggs should really look and that at home farmers inject all kinds of chemicals into them to make them bright white and yellow-yolked. He had me half convinced but I left them alone anyway. I settled for a coffee that tasted fine.

By my own admission, my brew-making skills aren't great. My wife insists that I make a crap cup of coffee to make sure I don't get the job on a regular basis. The fact that I'm used to my own brand of crap brew probably made the coffee served up at the *Grand Emin* much more palatable. Dad was less fussy and polished off his Turkish-style organic hard-boiled eggs without a fuss.

Breakfast wasn't a lengthy affair. We spent most of the time wondering what state my brother would be in, lying face down somewhere in Aya Napa, probably grinning from ear to ear. Dad mentioned Steve's absence repeatedly; I'll always remember that. It was touching to see that Dad thought about him all through the trip, wishing he could have been there with us. He might not have done it consciously or deliberately, but it was clear that Dad really did miss Steve.

After breakfast we ventured up to the bar area of the hotel. There was a bloke sitting on a huge leather sofa, staring at a television set. He was part of our coach party and his seat was fairly close to ours at the game. We had some brief conversation with him before the match and even briefer words after. He sat in front of us on the coach and had me in stitches on more than one occasion. The last I saw of him at the stadium he was heading toward the front rows to get as close to the team and the cup as he could. It's fair to say that I was in the mood to sit and talk pleasantries with just about anyone, but I had taken to this guy already the day before. He was the type of Liverpool fan the club has been built upon. He was stocky, a few stones overweight, completely bald, and had the type of face that would frighten your dog. In fact, he had more than a passing resemblance of Buster Bloodvessel. He had a scouse accent so broad that it was virtually a whole new dialect and he made me sound like a member of the gentry in comparison. The type of scouser I love and the type of scouser other people, who live in our wonderfully diverse culture, love to pre-judge and stereotype. From conversations I had with him the previous day, I could tell he was knowledgeable, intelligent and polite. He was travelling on his own and had a very strong sociable character. I could well imagine that three syllables from him to anyone living south of Watford would strike fear into their hearts. He was excellent bigot fodder.

There was a news programme on the TV in German, but he stared at it nevertheless. When he saw us approaching he leaned over to shake our hands in turn.

'Am opin' de footy's gonna be on in a minute just to prove last night really did appen,' he snarled.

I knew what he meant. Although I didn't exactly need evidence of the victory, the desire to see the goals on the small screen was strong. I could still taste the despair we felt at half time. In my mind we had lost the game. It didn't feel like we were 'up against it' or that it needed 'the biggest comeback of all time'. We needed a genuine miracle. Not just a footballing miracle, a biblical one. We were dead and buried.

When I got home after the game, I was initially irritated by comments made by Andy Gray and Alan Green during their commentary, but with hindsight I understand why they pronounced us dead and buried. Andy Gray's victorious shout of 'game well and truly over' was understandable. In my mind it was too. At half time we had lost the game and it was hard to forget that feeling of despair. Next day waiting for my first glimpse of the final from a German news station our victory was still a lot to take in.

Of course Andy Gray's commentary of the game for Sky Sports involved much more than a statement of his opinion that we had lost the game. Gray's wallowing in our agony is something I have come to resent since the final. More of that later.

After ten minutes of waiting and more head-shaking between us, the news programme reached its sporting slot. The evidence, as if we really needed it, was there before us. The Maldini volley that had fate written all over it, the Crespo tap in that came seconds after a stonewall penalty claim at the other end of the pitch, and Crespo's incredible finish to make it 3-0 at half time. The report then focussed on some of the Liverpool faces leaving the pitch, Garcia shaking his head and the Milan players striding off purposefully. Then the six miracle-filled minutes were played out on screen before us. By now a number of the hotel staff had joined us in front of the TV screen. The hotel staff were grinning almost as uncontrollably as Dad, our red companion, and me. Gerrard's stunning header, Smicer's skidding drive and Alonso's penalty rebound were there right before our eyes, replayed in less than 15 seconds. So it *did* happen!

Next up was the save by Dudek from Shevchenko at the end of extra time. I wasn't quite sure what I had just seen! It would take many replays of that save for me to understand just quite how the ball managed to go over the bar. There seemed to be some fundamental laws of physics shattered during my first viewing. Subsequent viewings haven't come close to explaining to me quite how Dudek managed that save. The report then cut to the first two penalties missed from Serginho and Pirlo. The Riise miss was cut from the footage too but no doubt got a mention from the German sports reporter. The final piece of evidence was then given to us. A one-handed save by Dudek from the deadliest striker in the world, Andrei Shevchenko. A one-handed save that put the European Cup permanently into red hands all across the world.

It was ours, we did win it and we were keeping it!

It was still early. At 9:30 am we took our first proper stroll out onto the streets of Istanbul. One of the first things we came across was an old battered newspaper shack selling a whole host of Turkish newspapers. Two sporting publications caught our eye immediately, *Fotomac* and *Fanatik*. Both were thin broadsheet newspapers devoted almost entirely to football. On 26th May 2005 *football* translated loosely as 'Liverpool, European Champions' and therefore the pages of these broadsheets were covered in huge colour images of our triumph in the Ataturk. A quick calculation and recalculation told me that these papers were available at about roughly eight pence each so we immediately picked up a couple of each publication. 'We should get a pile of these to take home,' Dad enthused, 'our Steve would love these'. We agreed that on our return to the hotel later we would buy a good number to take home for a whole range of deserved recipients.

We hadn't a clue where we were going, so we ambled off along the street next to the main highway. There were plenty of shops alongside the main road but mainly kebab shops. I don't mean kebab shops in the English high street sense of the word – i.e. a chippy with a doner kebab spit-roast in the corner. These huge kebab shops stood side by side, offering every size and shape of cooked animal you could imagine. The doner kebab spit roasts were in evidence, albeit three or four times the size of any I'd seen at home, but more noticeable were the enormous skewers with what can only be described as 'sheep' roasting on them.

Further up the road we decided to turn down a side-street that we hoped would take us into the centre, but all we found were restaurants and bars open early to accommodate any red stragglers. Most were empty, as at this early hour there were very few reds about. After a short discussion we decided to head back to the hotel and come out again later, having pinpointed a few bars we quite liked the look of. We were only out of the hotel for about 45 minutes on this first occasion.

In hindsight, I reckon the only reason we came out so early and after so little sleep was because we were just too eager to get up and talk about the game. The game was alive in my head every waking moment. We decided that a couple of hours more sleep might set us up nicely for a trip round a few bars, when no doubt a few more reds would be out on the streets.

Back at the hotel, sleeping was impossible, at least for me. Dad slept like a baby and snored like a warthog. It wasn't his snoring that kept me awake though. I lay on my bed, on my stomach, facing the window. I watched the workers in the building opposite the hotel, going at it hammer and tongs, and my mind raced. Whilst trying desperately to relax, my head spun through images of the miracles of the previous night. Penalties, half time, Alonso's rebound equaliser, Maldini's first minute goal, all raced through my mind as I tried to make sense of it all. I couldn't and it felt great. I lay for two full hours thinking about the game whilst contemplating the surreal view of an Istanbul workhouse. There was no way to make sense of it. It was a genuine miracle.

By the time Dad woke up I had been attempting to find some news footage of the game on the TV we had in our room. I had been trying for twenty minutes to no avail. Having seen the goals briefly I was gagging to see them again … and again, and again. One of the pleasures of going home would be the waiting video's to plough through. I hadn't asked her to, but I knew my wife Yvonne would record the game for me. Knowing Yvonne, she would somehow manage to have ITV's coverage and Sky's coverage waiting for me when I got home.

Dad sat with me on the edge of my bed as a Turkish news programme threatened to give us a glimpse of the game, but after 10 minutes of waiting we decided to go out. We had to check out of the hotel at 12:00 pm, so packed up and took our bags down to the foyer. The checking-out procedure mirrored the checking in procedure for security and attention to detail. I handed our key to someone in a uniform who dropped it into a box. I then asked if there was a room we could leave our bags in and was invited to put them in a cupboard alongside reception. The cupboard was already full of sports bags and rucksacks, no doubt belonging to our fellow red travellers. We dumped the bags and strolled back out onto the streets of Istanbul.

The streets of Istanbul looked very different at 12:10 pm than they did at 9:00 am. The pavements were now packed with people and the roads were busy with traffic.

Most noticeable of all was the number of Liverpool fans amongst the locals. Reds were everywhere, and mostly heading in one direction, toward the bars and restaurants we had located earlier. Before we headed in that direction as well, we decided to phone home. One of my minor regrets about the trip is that I didn't sort out my knackered old mobile phone to make and receive calls whilst we were away. It was pure laziness on my part and it meant that when we called our families next day just after lunch it was our first contact with them since we left Liverpool. I called Yvonne first. As soon as she picked up the phone and I heard her voice I could tell she was on cloud nine. It was a short conversation but one of mutual disbelief over the game. She said she had thought about us non-stop since the first whistle of the game. She said she cried at half time and then she cried after the penalties. It was a familiar story. My baby girls were fine and couldn't wait to see me. At that moment, after speaking to Yvonne, I just wanted to go home.

Dad then phoned my Mum. Mum was really happy for us but was less enthusiastic. As Dad spoke to her the expression on his face changed from jubilation to one of deep concern. He wasn't on the phone long. Mum had told him that my brother Stephen had spent last night in a Cyprus hospital with food poisoning. We had imagined him in a bar with his girlfriend, sinking lagers and celebrating with like-minded reds when he had, in fact, been on his own in a hospital bed, in agony, with not even an English voice to keep him company.

For God's sake! Dad looked crestfallen. We walked, almost without talking, to the newspaper stall we had visited earlier. We picked up another eight or nine copies of *Fotomac*.

'We had better pick up some more of these in case they sell out', Dad said. We walked up the street toward the bars we spotted earlier that morning and I wondered what to say. It didn't seem the best time to start up again about the game but it was hard not to. In the end Dad broke the silence.

'Just imagine if he had been in hospital and we'd have lost!' he said. He had a good point. Perhaps for a Liverpool fan like our kid even watching it in hospital must have been an awesome experience. We were clutching at straws though. He must have felt like shit.

As we wandered into a busy area of cafés, restaurants and bars there were reds everywhere. As we passed, locals were jumping out at us and shaking our hands. 'Gerrard!' 'Dudek!' they shouted at us, beaming and waving their arms about. At first I stood back, as I expected it was a ploy to get me into their shops or bars, but I couldn't have been more wrong. They just wanted to shake hands and celebrate with European Champions. It was a great and unexpected welcome and none of the shop owners that jumped out at us offered to sell us a thing. Every red that walked the streets that day must have felt like a celebrity. Dad and me didn't even have our Liverpool shirts on, but I guess we stood out like English distress flares.

As we got further into the centre we decided to sit down outside a café. We were served instantly and ordered a couple of beers. There was no question of what I was going to order, a kebab, but I took a look at the menu for a while to see what was available. There was already a group of about a dozen reds sitting outside the café and we joined a table next to them. Across the pedestrianised road was another line of cafés, also populated by reds. The group of reds we sat next to had been there since they arrived back from the game in the early hours. They were still lively and bantering with each other. Every one of them was draped in souvenir flags, or a scarf from the game. Surprisingly we hadn't seen many souvenir sellers at the stadium, but then again we did only get there 45 minutes before kick-off. Before I had the chance to ask one of them where they had bought their gear, a Turkish bloke appeared from nowhere, draped in scarves, pendants and flags. We asked how much they were and they were very, very cheap. Dad and me bought a whole load of stuff for people back home.

The Turkish bloke looked very pleased with himself. From the attire of the surrounding people I think he was having a good day.

Dad and me both ordered a chicken kebab of some description and the obligatory side salad and chips. As we sat waiting for our food a couple of young Turkish boys approached with a plastic crate and a small wooden toolbox stuffed with rags and polish. One of them looked about 13 years old. He was overweight and wearing a tracksuit that was a size or two too small. The other looked about eight years old, was painfully thin, and had a mop of brown hair. He was dressed like a bonfire-night Guy. They both looked in need of a bit of spit and polish themselves. The older boy prodded his younger counterpart in the back and he stumbled one step forward. The young lad then offered to shine my Dad's shoes, an offer Dad declined. He then offered to polish my white New Balance trainers but I also declined, slightly puzzled at how he might have attempted the task with a box full of black and brown polish. As the thinner of the two lads retreated to his mate he was wildly gesticulated at by the older lad to approach the larger group of reds. The older boy then stood away from the group across the street.

'Oh go on then lad!' shouted one of the Liverpool fans on the table next to us 'you can do mine.'

This bloke looked every inch the head of the party, sat with everyone else circled around him and a short crop of distinguished black, but mostly grey hair. He was sat about six feet away from Dad and me. The young lad didn't understand at first, but the older boy barked an order at him from the other side of the street. The older boy then disappeared up the street and out of sight. The young lad came forward and hurriedly attended to his scouse client and his black Chelsea boots. Hernan Crepso's footwear apart, these may well have been the only Chelsea boots to get to the European Cup final in 2005! After a few minutes furious buffing the lad young lad stood up and waited. The group of scousers applauded and he was firstly presented with a Liverpool scarf and then a Turkish Lira note of some description. 'That's about a tenner, I think, mate. I'm feeling pretty generous today.' said the silver haired scouser enthusiastically. The young Turkish boy stood and stared as if he wanted to say something but didn't know how. He looked really miserable in his newly acquired Liverpool scarf.

'What's up fella? Did your Dad not let you stay up for the second half?' I asked. 'We won mate, we won it,' I insisted to him, pointing to a European Cup on one of my newly acquired souvenirs. My offering got a generous laugh, which made me feel about a million quid. One or two of the group started singing a lazy rendition of 'In Istanbul we won it five times' which made me feel even better.

A smile cracked on the young lads face as he enjoyed his moment of attention and then he turned without saying anything and walked off slowly down the street. He walked so slowly he managed to retain our attention and we watched him all the way to the bottom of the street. He stopped where the pedestrianised street ended and met the busy traffic and stood motionless. Then just at the point where we had begun to look away the older boy returned. The younger lad handed over his earnings and then turned to walk away. Instantly about five or six scousers, each in Liverpool home shirts and decked out in Champions League regalia, charged up the street shouting. The older boy froze as a mini red regiment lumbered toward him. I am certain he would have legged it if he had realised it was him they were targeting. A very minor commotion followed, as the Liverpool fans demanded the money back, which he handed over instantly in something of a terrified daze. The bloke who had his shoes polished took hold of the note and gave it back to the younger. He then pointed at the boys in turn, youngest lad first.

'You, go and spend that money. You sod off' he said. In any language it was a crystal clear message. The Liverpool fans returned to their seats next to us looking self-satisfied.

'I wouldn't like to be in that little lads shoes when fatty catches him in ten minutes,' Dad whispered.

As Dad and me ate our surprisingly palatable kebabs Dad mentioned he had seen an old mate of mine a few weeks earlier, a lad called Robbie Gibbons. I hadn't seen Robbie for something like five or six years.

'Oh yeah,' I says, 'did he recognise you?'

'Yeah,' says Dad. 'He stopped to talk for a minute. He's got young kids now.' Now there are times in all our lives when the world seems like a really small place, and there are other times when a coincidence can almost do your head in, but when two minutes later Robbie Gibbons walked past us I nearly choked on my skewer. As a Liverpool fan that goes to the games, I suppose there was a reasonable chance Robbie might get to Istanbul, but bloody hell! The first thing I told Robbie was that we were just talking about him. He didn't need to say 'Why the hell would you be talking about me?' because it was written all over his face. I wish I hadn't said it, because I think it made Dad and me seem a bit strange. Robbie stood next our table and chatted for a few minutes. He had the same problem all reds that went to the game had. It was impossible to describe how he felt. The day after the miracles of Istanbul it was hard to make sense of it all. We were all in some kind of ecstatic shock.

After lunch we had a few beers and the time began spinning by. Dad said his head was starting to spin as well so we decided to take a walk around the shops for an hour to walk off some of the Efes. Almost without noticing, we had managed to put away six beers each in little over ninety minutes. There's something about talking footy that makes you drink two or three times your normal pace, a fact that has had me in trouble on many occasions. It's worse if you watch a big game in the pub. England's game against Argentina during the 2002 World Cup in Japan is a fine example. The game kicked off 12:00 pm UK time and I went to watch the game with about 10 of my mates (and my Dad) at a Runcorn pub. Five of us split into a round and I decided to get the first one in. My thinking was that if I got the first round in just before kick off I wouldn't have to battle my way to the bar during the game and miss any of the action. Selfish I know, but sometimes it pays to be one step ahead.

I managed to get my order in just before the 12:00 pm kick off, five pints of Stella. We drank so quickly during the first half that it was my round again just as the half ended. Somehow we managed to stick away five pints of Stella each in under an hour. I like a beer and my beer of choice is still Stella Artois, but five pints in an hour is madness. We all slowed a bit for the second half but we had still managed eight by the time the final whistle came. I was feeling pretty good about the game as I had a couple of quid on a Beckham 1-0 scorecast at 40-1. We were all supposed to be out for the night. A pub-crawl followed by a late night bar. Only my brother in-law Simon made it to the pre-arranged meeting place at 8:00 pm. The rest of us, me very much included, only succeeded in crawling home. My wife was really surprised to see me when I came home early evening. What's worse, I completely wasted an all-day, all-night pass out!

Dad and me weren't on the same kind of mission I was on during the England-Argentina game but it was tempting to sink a few. Instead we decided to have an hour off the Efes and take in a few shops. It was a good decision. I enjoyed milling around the various shops and stalls of Istanbul. The shops varied from ramshackle to pristine. Interestingly enough, the sports shops were as expensive as any back home and were decked out in similar fashion. Perhaps I was being naïve and even patronising to expect anything else, but I must admit I expected things like football shirts to be a bit cheaper than at home to reflect the wealth of the country. Fenerbace and Galatasaray shirts were selling at the equivalent of around £40 to £50, so any ideas I had about flirting with Turkish football culture dissipated quickly.

As we walked round the shops there were reds everywhere. None of the shop assistants were hassling us. Red shirts wandered around as if they were regulars and no one pulled us aside or tried to browbeat us into buying a thing. I bought a cracking pair of sunglasses for the equivalent of about a fiver from a guy on a street corner. The guy selling the sunglasses had about fifty pairs pinned to a huge board. There were no prices on them so I was asking the prices as I tried each pair on I liked. He was a jocular kind of chap and happy for me to try on as many pairs as I liked. His attitude changed though when I picked one particular pair up. He frowned and gestured for me to give them back saying 'For ladies! For ladies!' They looked the same as all the rest to me but he wasn't about to let me buy a pair of sunglasses that were 'for ladies!'

After choosing a pair of 'mens' sunglasses, we both bought the obligatory chocolate and Turkish Delight for the children and family back home. If you are in Turkey you have to buy Turkish Delight. I don't know why. As Harry Hill would say, 'I don't make the rules up.'

After an hour of mostly window-shopping we retraced our steps and headed back to the busy area of bars and cafés where we had earlier had our kebab lunch. It wasn't difficult to find a place that looked hospitable, not least because every bar we passed had around twenty or thirty reds sat outside. Dad spotted an empty table and we sat down. Within seconds we were served and about a minute later we had two large Efes to enjoy in the accompanying afternoon sunshine. It was really warm now and we managed to park ourselves in a cracking little suntrap. We browsed through some of the sports papers we bought earlier for next to nothing. The issue of *Fotomac* we were scanning had an enormous photo on the front of the moment Steven Gerrard lifted the European Champions trophy. It's was a fantastic front spread with the headline 'destanpool'. Even if you haven't seen the front cover of this particular publication its a scene you will no doubt be familiar with. Stevie G holding the trophy aloft, ticker tape jetting out from behind the players platform, and an ecstatic Liverpool squad behind him. When I look at that picture the hairs stand up on my arms. The giant broadsheet sized photo immediately got the attention of a group of kopites sitting at a nearby table. A guy wearing a white t-shirt with a black and white print of Shankly on the front asked me where we had bought the paper. I had hardly begun to explain when a nearby waiter came over. He had noticed us passing the paper across for the other reds to look at and came over.

'Fotomac? Fotomac?' he asked gesturing at the paper. The reds around us nodded quizzically. The waiter then pointed to each of the Liverpool fans in turn, counting the copies they wanted. He then disappeared. Five minutes later he returned with an armful of Fotomacs. Our fellow kopites were ecstatic and began offering notes in exchange. Even though I explained they cost the equivalent of about eight pence they were not to be deterred. The waiter smiled as five or six Liverpool fans insisted he take at least twenty times the face value of the newspapers. Soon everyone around us seemed to be holding up these giant images of Stevie G and the most magnificent piece of silverware available in modern sport. I felt amazing. Sat in the sun, with my Dad, drinking beer, basking in the glory of a European Cup win. The lads around us all wore the same expressions of disbelief. By soaking up these great images plastered across nearly every page of this Turkish sports paper, reality was really hitting home. It would be a long, long time before I would come down from this high.

The bloke in the Shankly shirt thanked us as if we had published the newspaper ourselves. He was most welcome. He then beckoned Dad and me over to his mobile phone. In his phone he had a long list of texts he had received the night before. He had 15 or 20 texts he received at half time alone. As I mentioned earlier, one of my only minor regrets about the Istanbul trip was not sorting out my mobile phone before we left Liverpool. It meant that I missed out on what would surely have been a flood of messages from home. When I did get home I had messages from mates who assumed I would have sorted my phone out to work abroad. The bloke in the Shankly shirt wanted to show us one text in particular. It was from an Evertonian mate of his back home and was sent at half time. It must have taken most of half time to type, it was that long! It was a rambling paragraph of a text message, the gist of it being that we had been out-classed, out-fought, out-played and found out. The message then finished with something about red-shite and a further line of expletives. The guy in the Shankly shirt then showed us his reply sent after the game. A one-word reply, 'Prick'. There must have been thousands of similar messages flowing back and to from Merseyside throughout that night. For my part I know that even if I had sorted my phone out I wouldn't have received any abuse. I have loads of Evertonian mates, but whereas they would have enjoyed Liverpool taking a beating, they would never have rubbed our noses in it. One Blue I know may have even wanted us to win, but it would be unfair of me to give you an identity! Knowing just exactly how much rival fans would be hurting after our win in Istanbul felt great. For me personally it was the certainty of how much our victory would hurt *Manchester United* fans that was most satisfying. The prospect of Mancs all over the world watching us perform the greatest comeback in European Cup Final history was a sweet concept to me. I bet there were plenty of beers cracked open during half time in Salford and plenty of phone calls between Mancs enjoying a gloat-fest on the back of our impending famous defeat.

After a glorious afternoon drinking Efes and quietly celebrating amongst the red masses, we inevitably had to make tracks to the hotel. Our faithful and much-loved

Coach 52 was due to take us back to the airport at 4:30 pm. When we arrived at the hotel to claim our bags the foyer was already scattered with tired, half-cut Liverpool fans sitting on and around their overnight luggage. I felt sad to be leaving. I took a good look at the hotel surroundings and tried to take in as much mental imagery as possible as I left the hotel and walked down toward the coach. The Hotel Grand Emin in central Istanbul was one of the worst hotels I have ever stayed in yet I have nothing but fond memories of the place. Dad and me made our way to the coach. If the journey here was anything to go by, we had a long journey ahead.

13. The Bell from the Hotel

An impromptu song rang out from the back seats of Coach 52:

> *We've got the bell − ding-ding*
> *From the hotel − ding-ding*
> *We've got the bell from the hotel − ding-ding*
> *I wanna be in that number*
> *With the bell from the hotel − ding-ding-ding-ding*

The voices on the coach were still going strong and now had accompaniment. After a reasonably quiet and relaxing afternoon, spirits were high again at the prospect of heading home victorious. Coach 52 filled quickly but one seat at the front remained conspicuously empty. The coach was full apart from the LFC steward. Ah yes, our official steward, probably couldn't find his arse with both hands so finding the coach may have been tricky. We waited ten, twenty, thirty minutes, full bus, but still no steward. Throughout our waiting time the suggestion that we go to the airport without him gathered momentum. A couple of fans came down the coach to ask why we were waiting when the bus was full. The Liverpool FC steward had earlier insisted the coach would leave promptly at 4:30. Even though he wasn't here, 5:00 seemed like a reasonable time to set off. Finally the driver turned on the engine and there were ironic cheers from the back seats. But instead of the driver pulling out onto the busy carriageway he turned right up the tiny side street which led to the

Grand Emin Hotel! We now found ourselves in the same narrow side street that took us 25 minutes to negotiate on the day of the final. The driver then parked the coach outside the hotel and a nervous co-driver leapt from the bus with four or five Liverpool fans bouncing down the bus in hot pursuit. The driver followed, somewhat more sedately, lit a cigarette and stood back to watch the pavement debate. The reds jumped from the bus and began pleading with the co-driver for a few minutes. I could see from their anguished faces they weren't making much progress. Then one of them came back.

'We need permission from Lonsdale travel to leave because there's no rep with us,' he shouted to everyone. Tempers soon began to rise as missing our 7:00 check-in started to look like a real possibility. Before long there were eight or nine scousers on the pavement next to the bus, demanding the driver take us to the airport. Dad and me sat and watched whilst doing the maths of how much time we had. We needed to set off by 5:30 if we were to make it comfortably. Any later and we would be cutting it desperately fine.

At 5:30 a very attractive, smartly-dressed woman parked a convertible Citroen in front of the coach. As she got out of her car she brushed back her immaculate shoulder-length brown hair with her hands and pinned it back with a pair of sunglasses. She was smiling broadly and greeted the agitated group like she knew them all individually. She began to calmly address the Liverpool fans whilst flirting outrageously, flicking her hair and leaning on their shoulders. The Liverpool fans gobbled it up and seemed happy with what she had to say. She then spoke to the driver and co-driver, who were less impressed, but she continued to beam smiles at them nevertheless. The smartly-dressed woman with the perma-smile turned out to be a representative for the coach company and within a minute the driver was back on the bus and the co-driver reluctantly followed. The woman then gestured for the coach to follow her in her car. In truth, there was nowhere else to go. The side-street was so tiny the coach just about fit and her car was parked in front. About one hundred yards up the road the Citroen stopped at a tiny crossroads, barely big enough to get the coach through. In front of the Citroen there was a small white van blocking the road. The smartly dressed woman got out of her car to look for the driver. She found him in the entrance to a nearby shop but he was in no hurry to move his van, despite her exaggerated gestures and more grinning. What she did next met loud cheers from the whole coach. The bloke in the shop doorway had left the keys to the white van in the ignition. Our grinning heroine promptly jumped into the driver's seat and drove the van thirty yards up the road, with the van driver much more willing to hurry after her this time. She then parked the van, jumped out and ran back to her own car. The Liverpool fans on the coach cheered her all the way back to her car as she skilfully sidestepped the Turkish white-van man. I think she enjoyed her moment of glory.

It took another twenty minutes to snake out of the tiny Istanbul side-streets and onto a busy road. It was now 6.00 pm and we were pushing it to make our 7:00 check-in, but at least we were on our way. There was certainly more concern about the lack of time than for the lack of steward.

Thankfully the journey back was fairly smooth. The motorways were busy, but they flowed freely. Dad was quiet and he looked knackered. We were both now concentrating on getting home. I was really looking forward it. Our trip to Istanbul had certainly felt longer than an overnight stay.

We approached the airport at 7:00 pm with our check-in due to close at 7:10 pm. Our flight was scheduled to leave at 7:30 pm so we were prepared to move quickly. At least we only had hand luggage, so check-in would be quick. The journey to the airport should have taken fifty minutes, but in the end it took just over an hour because of the pantomime back at the hotel. As we approached we could see the airport terminal on our left, but instead the coach turned right and parked alongside an enormous marquee. A young bloke then flagged the coach to stop and jumped on board the coach. The coach fell silent in anticipation and suspicion of what he would tell us. Bizarrely, the young man had an American accent and proceeded to tell us that our flight had been delayed for three hours. Amid the groans he then told us there was food and drink available in the marquee.

Liverpool Football Club had just won the European Cup for the first time in 21 years. The manner of the victory involved the greatest comeback in European Cup final history. It was these two shining facts that got me through the next few hours. I mentioned in the previous paragraph that we had been directed to a huge marquee. But *huge* probably doesn't cover it. This tent made Billy

Smart's look like a wigwam. It was set upon a huge car park, the entirety of which was enveloped by the giant canvas. Billy would have been less impressed by the circus inside. When we arrived there were probably something like two thousand people inside, providing their own amusement. Anarchy, fuelled by boredom and a substantial amount of Efes, raged in every corner. We tried to avoid the chaos and attempt to find out more about our flight. We didn't have to look far. A giant departures board with flight times, destinations and expected delay times was flashing furiously in the centre of the marquee. Dad and me quickly found our flight number and discovered to our horror that we could expect a *nine-hour* delay. We hadn't been particularly pleased about a three-hour delay so nine-hours came as a bit of a blow. There was no cold comfort in the fact that a number of flights to Ireland had *24-hour* delays flashing against them!

We decided to get some food. All around the perimeter of the marquee were souvenir stalls, bars and food count-ers. The bars were doing a roaring trade but the souvenirs had long gone and the food was a little past its best. We weren't really that hungry, but it was a question of killing time. The food was a mistake. The best on offer was chicken drumsticks and rice. I took a leap of faith in be-lieving the chicken was intentionally a pale shade of yellow and decided that's how they eat it in Turkey. How my arse survived two of those I'll never know. The rice was served in gluey dollops, like some kind of shredded Pritt-stick. It was foul and we both ate it. After our gastric roulette we decided to take a seat on some plastic chairs in a position where we could see the flights board. As we walked across the marquee to find some seats the full picture of chaos in this giant makeshift departure lounge became clearer. We sat a reasonably safe distance away from where an impromptu football match was in full flow. The game resembled one of those ridiculous ancient rugby matches played by upper-class twits at places like Eton, where two hundred blokes try to take the ball across a village in a giant scrum. It was not a match for the faint-hearted. Every now and then the ball would emerge before disappearing in a melee of trainers and tangling legs. White plastic chairs bounced across the concrete car park as the games swept violently from one side of the marquee to the other. A group of lads nearby took the concept to another level by dispensing with the ball altogether. An improvised three a-side game used a plastic chair instead of a ball. Every so often the games would merge as the ball bounced amongst the chair kickers and pinballed out again.

Dad looked impervious to the whole situation. He is a really quiet bloke who dislikes confrontation but sometimes he can look so solid and resolute. He wasn't going to move to accommodate a game of chair football even if the six participants looked like they may have boosted Efes' share price in a single afternoon.

For the next thrity minutes we sat in what was effectively no-mans land in between raging football wars. We sat browsing through newspapers left lying around whilst glancing up at the flights board in hope of positive change. After about thirty minutes the board changed. Our flight information disappeared altogether! At first I thought I was losing it, that I'd looked at that great flashing neon board of numbers and letters once too often and developed some kind of numerate dyslexia. But pretty soon the reality set in that our flight had fallen off the end of the board. Even the 24-hour delayed flights to Dublin were still angrily flashing away but flight SCY7742 to Liverpool had gone.

I immediately asked Dad to double check for me. He looked puzzled before quickly turning his quizzical expression into an angry one. Dad slapped his newspaper onto his hand luggage and got up out of his plastic chair. He wandered toward the flights board until he was almost too close to read it and then returned shaking his head. By this point a number of faces I recognised from Coach 52 had also noticed our flight's disappearance and were assuming the same perplexed look as we were. What do we do now? Just sit and wait for it to reappear?

What we needed now (in the absence of an LFC rep) was someone whose anger could translate into action. I wanted to do something, but what? It looked like the Turkish authorities had deliberately housed us in Billy Smarts nightmare, away from the main airport building, so we couldn't protest about the delays. We were encouraged to drink as much as possible so we would be more interested in kicking lumps out of each other than worrying about when we might get home.

Eventually an unlikely source provided some hope. The mother of a young family I recognised from Coach 52 came across shouting, 'Anyone for Scandic 7742?' I stopped her and told her we were on that flight. She said she was desperately trying to round up everyone she could find as the flight was departing in thirty minutes! This lady *had* lost her temper and made her way across to the main airport building to let off some steam. Whilst venting her anger at an information desk the steward behind the counter quite calmly told her that the flight wasn't delayed nine hours, or even three hours. The flight would be leaving in thirty minutes time.

Dad and me decided to have a quick look around to see if we could see any familiar faces from our coach or from the flight the previous day. Luckily I spotted Nick Davis, a mate from Runcorn, sitting with his mates, quietly reading through newspapers. I let them know about the flight and they quickly ditched their papers and picked up their bags. We noticed another couple of blokes from our coach and gave them a shout, but couldn't hang around any longer. Leaving behind that tent felt like were legging it from an open prison.

The airport terminal building was crowded and noisy but at least it didn't feel like Trafalgar Square during the poll-tax riots. A helpful scouse voice shouted across the crowd 'there is no check-in lads, you just go straight to departures'. Unlikely as this might seem, we were caught up in the crowd that almost instantly moved toward the security gates. The security gates were right in front of us, so we headed straight for it with a swarm of other hurrying kopites. Security staff at the metal detectors beckoned us through impatiently, with no one being asked to stop for further examination. Even Dad escaped having his bag rifled or his pockets turned out.

At the other side of the gate, passport control required everyone to show a passport, boarding card, and ticket … unless you didn't have a boarding card and ticket, when your passport would be enough! On the other side of passport control we were ushered toward huge glass windows through which we could see an *Air Scandic* plane sitting on the tarmac.

All in all it took about four minutes to get from the first line of security to the boarding gate. Five minutes earlier we had been standing amidst a Big-top riot, contemplating a nine-hour delay. Now, somehow, we were standing with a couple of hundred others staring at Air Scandic 7742 sitting patiently on the tarmac. The super-mum who had tipped us off about the impending departure was stood about twenty yards in front of me, so I fought my way through the crowd to thank her in person. Without her, we may well have missed the flight altogether. My mate Nick from Runcorn would possibly have missed it too. It was a complete shambles.

Dad and I had hardly time to speak from the time we left the tent until arriving at the departure gate. We now had time to take it all in as we waited for twenty minutes packed in like a rush hour tube-train, staring out at the plane.

Dad looked worried. 'I don't remember half of these on our flight out Mike', he said scanning the heads around us.

'It's a flight to Speke and we're getting on it Dad', I said, 'that's all that matters'.

But it was our flight and we were in the right place. Plenty of others weren't, including a couple of Scottish lads next to us in really high spirits.

'You flying to Liverpool?' one of them asked me. The question confused me at first, until he explained that he was due to fly to Glasgow but him and his mate fancied a few days in Liverpool so they thought they'd chance their arm. They giggled like two schoolboys who had just booby-trapped a schoolbag, fidgeting in the knowledge that their wheeze was only a short walk to the plane away.

'Our plane was full on the way out so some unlucky sod must be missing out,' I said to Dad. Still, there must have been a reasonable number of reds still wandering obliviously around the set of 'When Big Tents Go Bad'. Security was so carefree there could have been any number of unauthorised passengers standing with us, waiting for the OK to board. All you needed was a British passport and you were in. I began to worry if there might be more people waiting to get on the plane than seats.

The twenty minutes wait for the departure gate was actually quite good fun. The 250 or so waiting reds went through a repertoire of anthems to pass the time. All the songs we had sung with such passion at the Ataturk were given noisy but far more relaxed renditions. After a while the airport staff stood by the departure gate doors tried to join in, waving their two-way radios like scarves. They seemed to find particular amusement in the Jamie Carragher anthem 'We all dream of a team of Carraghers'. Perhaps they recognised the tune of Yellow Submarine, I'm not sure, but all of the staff at the front gate were trying to join in with that one.

I noticed Dad sang every word of every song that we sang whilst waiting to get on the plane. It was great to see. I didn't want to stand there staring at him but I could see he looked really happy, elated almost, but also really relaxed. That was to change in a few short minutes as our pendulum of a journey took one last calamitous swing.

As soon as the departure gates opened I could see we were in a bad position to get through the gates. We were slap-bang in the middle of two gates and it became obvious we would be one of the last through. This wasn't a problem though. Naturally I wanted to sit with my Dad for the journey home but avoiding a huge delay was the first concern and having avoided that I was just happy to be boarding.

Although the plane was no more than thirty metres away from the terminal building the airport staff insisted that everyone must get on a bus and be ferried to the plane steps. As ludicrous as it seemed everyone just laughed about it and got on the bus. The turning circle of the bus was almost bigger than the journey to the plane and I could hear scouse cheers as the driver swung the bus around to the steps. I watched as each busload got onto the bus, was driven thirty metres in one huge arc. The bus would then stop to let everyone off and when empty would swing around another thirty metres back to the terminal to pick up the next lot of forty or so passengers to take them on the same journey.

Finally it was our turn. Dad and I got on the bus with about 15 others, the final passengers for the flight home. But instead of making the usual micro-journey the bus driver turned off his engine and got off the bus. Nothing happened for about five minutes until frustration started to build amongst us. You could almost reach out and touch the nose of the plane but we had to stand and wait on the bus. The driver then came back, sat in his cab for another few minutes, before getting off again and walking back to the terminal building. Pressure began to grow and two lads at the back of the bus tried to get off to ask questions. The door of the bus opened easily enough but the stewards at the gate just ignored their questions, not even turning around to acknowledge them. The two blokes took one look at the distance to the plane and decided to take the thirty-second walk to the plane steps. And they made it OK in fact got halfway up the steps until they were chased by two security staff. The security staff walked them all the way back to the bus from the plane and shepherded them back in with us. I started to seriously think that the plane might be full.

We waited another five minutes, meaning we had been waiting on the stationary bus for over 15 minutes with the plane just feet away from us. The bus driver returned once more to his cab, switched on the engine, switched it off again and then turned around smiling at us from behind the Perspex that separated him from the rest of the bus. Dad and me flipped almost simultaneously! We must have looked quite funny banging on the Perspex like a couple of demented chimps, demanding he take us to the bastard plane! Safely seated in his cab he didn't blink an eye. Our tempers were infectious as the lads who made a break for it five minutes earlier joined us and demanded to know why the hell we had been left standing on a bus for twenty minutes whilst the rest of the passengers were waiting to go. Just when we thought we had seen bus ride cock-ups done to perfection, here was a new level, the cock-up of a thirty-metre bus ride, a journey so short that Geoff Capes could have pulled us there.

Our twenty-minute wind-up came to an end as finally we were transported to the plane steps. Dad looked like he might split an artery by the time we got up the steps and into the cabin. Predictably the whole plane was seated and strapped in waiting for us. A significant majority had 'you dozy bastards' written across their faces. There was no point in trying to explain to anyone. Apologetically, I shuffled down the plane, looking for an unlikely couple of empty seats together. As there had been no check-in to speak of and plenty of passengers without boarding cards, it was a first-come-first-served seating plan. Incredibly, there were two empty seats about half way up the plane that I gratefully claimed. As I sat down I did a double take as I spotted the dozy-arse LFC steward that had missed our coach. Heaven knows how he managed to get himself onto the plane; he certainly didn't guide any of us there.

We were happy to get safely into our seats and to be heading home. Unlike our outward journey we were greeted onto the plane by warm smiles and genuine respect by the cabin crew. There were a number of stewards busying around as Dad and I settled into our seats. I noticed three of the cabin crew in particular. There were two attractive stewardesses, one blonde and one brunette. There was also a very tall male steward with wavy dark hair, who was particularly friendly toward the Liverpool fans. He also looked strangely familiar. As our fellow red passengers stuffed the overhead lockers to bursting point, he chatted and joked with anyone who caught his attention. Everyone on the plane was in high spirits. There was a huge sense of relief at escaping from the shambles of the airport and this fuelled the sense of elation we were all feeling from the night before. It felt great to be European champions again.

With everyone seated the tall dark steward stood at the front of the plane. Everyone faced forwards, anticipating the captain's usual announcements about flying time, cruising speeds, and weather reports back home. There would also be the safety demonstration to look forward to. It was then that someone realised who the tall steward reminded us of. 'Pe-lleg-rino!' came a chant from the back of the plane. A wave of laughter in agreement rumbled throughout the plane. Mauricio Pellegrino was a centre half we had at Liverpool on a short-term contract for the second half of the 2004/05 season. Putting it kindly, he was past his best when he arrived at the club and he put in some abject performances during his brief spell at Anfield. I don't think a lot was expected of him and as a result he didn't suffer any rough treatment from the kop. The tall steward looked bemused and continued to smile at the head of the cabin. The two stewardesses took up their positions ready to perform the safety demonstration. Facing the back of the plane, the brunette stood at the front and the blonde halfway down the cabin.

The tall steward took hold of a microphone and addressed an excitable plane of kopites.

'Good evening ladies and gentlemen and welcome on board this Air Scandic flight to Liverpool.' A huge cheer greeted his first sentence causing him to pause and laugh. It was now immediately obvious that the entire cabin of passengers were hanging on his every word and focussing on the young stewardesses. The blonde stewardess, startled by the cheering passengers, turned to look behind her. The stewardesses now realised that their performance could well be scrutinised like never before. I am sure both girls will have performed plenty of safety demonstrations for passengers barely able to look up from their duty free magazines. This was something entirely different as every Liverpool fan stared mischievously toward them. Pellegrino composed himself 'In a moment you will receive a safety demonstration,' he then paused, smiled broadly continuing, 'and are you boys lucky tonight!' The plane roared in approval and almost immediately burst into a rocking rendition of *Ring of Fire*. You could now hardly hear yourself speak as 250 kopites chanted to a favourite Istanbul anthem. I got the feeling that our Pellegrino look-alike was fully aware of what response his unexpected introduction might bring and he revelled in it. He then began to read out the safety instructions for the stewardesses to demonstrate. As each instruction was read out the Liverpool fans started a low humming noise that then developed into a huge cheer as each action was performed. It was almost impossible for the stewardesses. Rarely could a safety demonstration have been so appreciated.

'There are exits at the front and rear of the plane.'

Huge roar!

'Your life jacket can be found under the seat in front.'

Huge roar!

The demonstration was interrupted completely several times for more renditions of *Ring of Fire*. The loudest cheer was reserved for the moment the stewardesses demonstrated blowing into the top up pipe on the life jackets. Both stewardesses fell about laughing and the blonde girl closest to us buried her head in her hands.

The singing continued throughout the demonstration until both girls finished with a bow. They both received long, raucous ovations from every red on the plane, with the obligatory wolf-whistling and a final rendition of *Ring of Fire*.

Mauricio Pellegrino didn't do anything on the pitch worthy of real note, although he did have a decent game in a 2-1 win over Everton at Anfield. His lookalike did more to ensure I wouldn't forget him.

As the plane took off and we all settled down into our seats I wondered when this particular story would end. The wonderful truth is that it never will. The greatest European cup final will be remembered forever and I was there with my Dad.

The journey home was a quiet one. Most people slept whilst others quietly contemplated. Twenty minutes before landing a young kopite handed round *Hillsborough Justice* stickers. I stuck mine to the back of my passport. As he handed the last ones out he shouted toward the back of the plane, 'remember the 96 that should have been here with us'. There was a quiet hum of agreement and respect for the intentions of the statement. My Mum once told me after her Dad (my Grandad) died that if we always talked about him he would always exist for us to love him. By calling out in memory of the 96 Hillsborough victims I am sure they were with us in spirit.

14. Home

Liverpool was made for me
and I was made for Liverpool

Bill Shankly

The reds streaming through Liverpool airport on our return from Istanbul were now contemplating rather than
celebrating. The happiness that came with witnessing the
miracle of Istanbul first-hand was still etched on our faces,
but most fans headed out of the airport quietly reflecting.
The flag-sellers were still doing a brisk trade outside the
airport, despite the fact it was now well past midnight.
Dad and me were shattered. As we left John Lennon Airport Dad spotted our hired cab for home almost
immediately. We were both really happy to avoid any waiting around. The journey home was quiet. The driver was
the same guy who had taken us to the airport forty-odd
hours earlier. He struck up gentle conversation about the
game, but he didn't seem overly interested. He was probably looking forward to his bed as much as we were.

In particular I remember two things about the journey
home from the airport. Firstly, I wondered about the party
that would have let loose just six or seven miles or so from
the airport in Liverpool city centre. The homecoming had
been just a few hours earlier, with millions of reds bringing Liverpool to a standstill to celebrate the lads giving the
European Cup a new, more permanent, home. And of

course that particular trophy that we now had for keeps is the self same trophy Manchester United won in 1999. Could things actually get any sweeter? OK, I'm sure United have a replica somewhere in their museum, but if United fans want to see the actual trophy they won they will have to come to Anfield to see it. The homecoming party in the city centre was no doubt going on into the night as we drove home would have been an event in itself. I wondered how many of my mates might have made the trip and if they were still hung over from the final itself. I had been so wrapped up in going to the game I had no idea where my mates were planning to watch the game.

The other thing I remember is talking to my Dad about Michael Owen. It was Dad who instigated the conversation. Dad felt that it was a real shame that Michael Owen had not been part of the victory. I have heard lots of arguments since the final, but at the time my Dad was firmly of the opinion that the he deserved to have enjoyed the night as a Liverpool player. Owen had chosen to leave Liverpool in the summer of 2004 to join Real Madrid. Later he would join Newcastle when many felt that he could have dug his heels in with Madrid and demanded a move to Liverpool. After the Newcastle move, Dad was one of the reds who lost sympathy for him. For many kopites, with his move to Newcastle Michael Owen surrendered a large part of his legendary status.

Had Owen's move to Spain been successful, perhaps he would have had more sympathy from Liverpool fans. But Owen left Liverpool to 'win trophies' and ended empty-handed. Liverpool, meanwhile, went on to win the greatest prize in world club football, despite (rather than because of) Owen's departure. I think, in general, most Liverpool fans still loved Owen at the time of the final. Certainly, we all hoped he would return to Liverpool when he came home to the Premiership in August 2005. The fact that he moved to Newcastle ruined any chance of belated sympathy.

Immediately after the final my Dad wasn't looking at specific whys and wherefores. In my Dad's opinion Owen had given Liverpool so much in terms of success, he deserved to be there. If you look at certain facts, it's hard to disagree. Owen won the 2001 FA Cup almost single-handed against Arsenal at the Millenium Stadium. That final isn't known as the 'Owen Final' without good reason. He had also played a huge part in winning the Uefa Cup the same season and his goals lifted an inconsistent Liverpool team into 4th place in the Premiership to earn the Champion's League qualifier that started the road to Istanbul. Finally, Owen showed loyalty in not holding out for a Bosman to line his own pockets like Steve McManaman had *reputedly* done a few years earlier. Owen promised he would never leave on a free and he stuck to his word. Ironically, if Owen had followed the McManaman route he would have stayed at Liverpool another season and been part of the Champions League adventure. C'est la vie.

I agreed with my Dad and added that I felt similar sentiments for Robbie Fowler. From a purely sentimental point of view, I had wished Fowler had been at the club in the same way that Dad thought Owen deserved to be there. It later transpired that Robbie Fowler was in Istanbul for the final as a Liverpool fan. There is no doubt that Fowler has Liverpool Football Club running through his veins. The love and respect Robbie has for the club and its fans are mutual. At the time of the Final I thought that Fowler deserved to have been there as a player and had sympathy for his cause. His shock re-signing for Liverpool by Benitez in January 2006 seemed to make up for that loss somehow. Maybe Robbie Fowler's time will come again. Who knows, perhaps it will for Michael Owen?

Coming home felt like I'd been away for weeks. So much had happened in between walking out through the front door and returning some forty-odd hours later. I dropped my bag in the hall and went up to see my girls, all safely tucked up in bed. There was no danger of waking up either of my little girls. The pair of them have always been incredible sleepers. At that age I could have walked in dressed as a one-man-band and they would have slept on.

My wife Yvonne woke momentarily to welcome me home. I gave her an easy time of it by telling her to go back to sleep. There would be plenty of time for me to fill her in on everything. And it would take time. Safe in the knowledge I was home Yvonne turned over and went back to sleep. Despite the temptation of climbing in to a warm bed for some much needed sleep there was only one thing on my mind. I needed to see some of the footage. I crept back downstairs and into the living room. Three neatly stacked tapes sat waiting for me on top of the television cabinet. I was desperately tired and eager to get to bed, but the lure of a glance at those goals was too much to walk away from. Yvonne had taped the Sky coverage at her parents' house, the ITV coverage at home and also taped some footage of the homecoming that took place whilst we were flying home. I chose the tape labelled *Sky*, pushed it into the video recorder, and sat down on the carpet in front of the telly.

I have a main theory to why I love to watch Liverpool games on tape so much. Years ago, before the Sky Sports football revolution and the televising of anything remotely resembling a professional football match, me, my Dad and my brother used to rush home from the match in the hope of getting home in time to see the game on telly. Sometimes that would be 15 minutes of highlights on *Sportsnight* or the *Midweek Match*. Other times we would charge into the living room at 10.28 pm in the hope of perhaps catching our goals on the end of the news. We used to videotape everything. We had a videotape sat next to the video recorder at all times ready to throw in whenever there was a hint that a Liverpool game was going to be shown. My Dad has archives of tapes filled with random footage like our 3rd round FA Cup ties at York City on *Match of The Day* and midweek goals against QPR taped from the news. They are all really badly linked together and taped over episodes of *Coronation Street* and *Tenko*. Every now and then, squashed in between news items of 80s Liverpool games, Curly Watts or Japanese soldiers make brief appearances. It all adds to the charm of those videos. So different to games these days, where every game is edited to perfection. I'm convinced that those days as a young lad, chasing back from games to catch us on the telly, is a big reason why I have the urge to watch Liverpool victories at the very earliest opportunity, even when I've just seen the real thing in the flesh. There's nothing quite as satisfying as watching a famous victory over again on tape.

We even did it when we travelled home from Wembley. I can remember us clock watching after Liverpool beat Everton 3-1 at Wembley in 1986 to win the double. As we came up the M6 we sat trying to work out if we could get home to see the match. We made it home just in time that night. When we got home my mum had a load of lagers in the fridge for my Dad and a load of butties and crisps waiting on a table in front of the telly. What a woman! I think this was one of the first times Dad let me have an alcoholic drink of my own. I was only 14 at the time. I remember Dad let me have a glass of lager. I felt like a real man and although I thought it tasted like shit I wasn't about to tell anyone. Dad was in a great mood that night!

There were no mobile phones then of course so there was a real possibility we would have got home way after midnight and my mum's efforts would have been wasted. I remember us all sitting watching that game and roaring laughing when we spotted our Steve on the *Match of The Day* coverage in his Liverpool flat cap. But that's another story.

I was dead on the bones of my arse sat on the living room floor but I had to watch some of the game. I decided to wind through the tape and stop at the goals. That included the Milan goals. There's nothing painful about watching a team score against Liverpool when you know we go on to win. I rewound each goal a few times to have another look before moving on to the next one. I sat ridiculously close to the television, basking in the green glow of the Ataturk pitch, at a distance I wouldn't allow my daughters to watch *The Tweenies*. It sounds daft saying it now, but my heart raced as I watched those goals for the first time in the comfort of my own home.

The hairs on the back of my neck curled as I watched Maldini score Milan's first goal. I didn't pay much attention to the commentary at first, but when I watched the third Milan goal I recoiled in disgust at the tones of Andy Gray. I quickly recognised that here was a man simply wallowing in Liverpool's demise. His now famously inaccurate line '… game well and truly over! And I hate saying that.' had me shaking my head in disbelief. When I watched the whole of Sky's coverage the day after I was less than impressed. Surely Sky Sports could have found someone with a little less hatred for Liverpool Football Club than Andy Gray. Boris Johnson or Gary Neville perhaps? Clive Tyldsley and Andy Townsend conducted the ITV coverage and it couldn't have provided a bigger contrast. Clive Tyldsley is a Manchester United fan, by the way, but his commentary was everything you would expect from a British television station covering an English team in a European Final. There was no attempt to disguise they wanted Liverpool to win. On Sky Sports Andy Gray didn't even have the decency to be impartial. Ultimately his commentary on the first 53 minutes of the game has served only to confirm what Liverpool fans already know. His commentary also serves as a stick with which I am happy to beat him over the head. I hope he never lives down his 'game well and truly over …' gloat. The fact that he followed his first statement with 'And I hate saying that!' simply confirmed his enjoyment. No other commentator would have had to say that. I think Gray realised, that as he rubbed his hands together, he had got carried away and tried to immediately repair the damage.

As mentioned in a previous chapter, I honestly didn't get a kick out of the knowledge that plenty of Evertonians would be hurting following the final. My close mates who are Evertonians are fairly reasonable and talking to them when I got home I could see they were hurting. It didn't need me to ram the point home. Andy Gray was the one Evertonian I was sure would be hurting perhaps more than most and I was very happy to imagine his despair. Gray is a former Everton player who somehow manages to carry the title of legend amongst their fans. 22 goals in 68 games somehow gave Gray an over-inflated reputation as a player at Goodison. In truth if he had been any good he would have spent more time playing for big clubs rather than spend his career with Wolves and Aston Villa. As it was, Everton coming in for him was a surprise and I don't think they fought off too many rival suitors for his signature. Gray had signed for Wolves for a then record transfer fee of £1.5 million. After four fairly ordinary seasons his stock had diminished considerably and Everton sprung a surprise by signing him for £250,000.

Andy Gray had a purple patch in arguably Everton's greatest ever side. But Andy Gray's two years in the limelight at Everton are not entirely the reason for his over inflated reputation. Sky Sports have effectively billed Gray as a modern day football guru. Each week Gray is given license by Sky Sports to preach to the nation. Richard Keys wilfully indulges Gray by asking him to please explain how the simplest of tactical substitutions could possibly work. Gray even has the audacity to explain how the best managers in the country got their tactics wrong. Even managers like Sir Alex Ferguson and Arsene Wenger are subjects of the Gray lectures. Gray himself has no managerial experience and therefore no success or failures at the role. In the early 90s he had the opportunity to manage his beloved Everton but turned down the chance in order to continue educating the masses on Sky television.

Co-commentators constantly digress during live matches to massage the Gray ego. Many of the younger generation of Premiership addicts watching coverage on Sky Sports could be forgiven for thinking that Andy Gray's abilities somehow deserve comparison with Kenny Dalglish, Gary Lineker or, dare I say it, Eric Cantona. The truth is, he was good enough to play at the highest level and he deserves respect for that, but his qualities are more comparable to players like Michael Robinson, Paul Rideout and Gary Birtles. Younger viewers may be startled to hear that, apart from a lot of promise and an Indian summer, the career of Andy Gray was nothing special.

You could also successfully argue that it is Sky Sports that have created the Andy Gray persona, something that Gray is not entirely responsible for. I don't know if he has any choice when it comes to which game he commentates on. I assume he is told what games he will be covering. I have a little sympathy for him if this is the case. Andy Gray has a strong dislike for Liverpool football club and as an Evertonian in the limelight I understand this entirely. He has to be seen to dislike Liverpool or else risk his somewhat tenuous legendry status. It's a tactic Gary

Neville is still working on. Neville knows that if he shows United fans how much he hates Liverpool consistently enough, he might just earn himself a legendary reputation.

In the weeks following the final I watched footage of the game over and over. In the initial weeks I was on a diet of at least one screening a day. That may seem excessive and indeed obsessive but I was so caught up in the whole experience I couldn't keep away from it. That obsession would be revived in earnest a full seven months later when Father Christmas brought me a number of DVD's about the final. On the Sunday after the final, my Mum had the idea that we should watch the game as a family at her house. I think this was mainly aimed at getting my brother Steve involved in a joint experience. Remember Steve had not only missed going to the game because he was going on holiday, he fell ill whilst abroad and watched the game, alone in a hospital bed, in a foreign country. He got home from his 'holiday' on the Saturday after the final and Mum organised a gathering for the Sunday. Of course it would never compensate Steve for his holiday and there was no suggestion it would make up for missing the final, but it was a nice gesture by Mum.

I expected that my sister would come around to watch, but was surprised when her husband, Simon, came along too. Simon is a season ticket holder at Goodison Park and must have already had his fill of five-times European Champions in the full knowledge that Evertonians may never be allowed to forget about it. I should also point out that Simon is also one of my closest mates, so I'm always likely to sing his praises. Nevertheless, here was an Evertonian who was strong enough to not only welcome us home but also man enough to come around to a house full of reds reliving the final to do it. It was a warm sunny day and Simon sat out in the garden whilst the game was on. He had watched the game live on the Wednesday and I'm sure once was enough for him. But the fact he was there and asked us about the trip has always impressed me. I'm not sure I would have been as generous to go into a house of Evertonians or Mancunians had the roles been reversed.

My brother Steve was fairly reserved that day. I know he was still feeling the effects of the illness that caused his Cypriot hospital stay. I know he won't mind me saying that he looked like crap that day. Steve is a fairly lively character especially when it comes to Liverpool FC, but it would be a good while before I saw him really eulogise about the final.

Later in 2005 Steve and me were part of a group of mates who went to Torremolinos for a stag weekend. Steve was pretty vocal about the final that weekend and I remember thinking 'he must be feeling better now!'

For my part I have learned to enjoy remembering the Champions League Final success of 2005 quietly and with dignity. At first it was impossible for me to keep my mouth shut about what Dad and me went through before during and after the final but even in the early days after the final I don't think I gloated too much. That's not really my style. I don't want any of my Evertonian mates to hate me for rubbing their noses in it. If ever there was a game where winning was always more than enough for me it was this one. I didn't need to make others hurt on the back of it. Sorry if that sounds smug.

On the rare occasion I get time to myself at home I watch the DVD of the final, or sometimes I go through my newspapers and memorabilia. The elation of winning that final, in the way that we did it, is still fresh. I like to rummage through all the stuff I have connected to the final as it feels like I can still physically touch elements of that great night. When I hear the Champions League theme music the hairs stand up on the back of my neck. I love that music. I have the full version on my pc at home and at work and I play it every now and then. It transports me back to those intense moments just before kick-off. Other times I think about Steven Gerrard lifting the trophy high above his head, holding my Dad tightly, screaming pure joy at the top of my voice, and let the tears flow freely. Moments like that don't come around too often. I don't think that particular moment ever will again.

15. In My Life

There are places I remember
All my life…

John Lennon

My Dad is a reserved man and keeps his feelings to himself. Me, my brother and my sister, are completely aware of how much Dad loves us but I can't remember him telling us in words. He wouldn't feel comfortable with doing that so I wouldn't want him to. He is the same with my two young daughters and my sister's daughter too. You need only watch Grandad Tommy interact with them for a minute to see how much mutual adoration there is. Even when faced with raw emotion my Dad isn't comfortable using the spoken word to impart his feelings for us. When my first daughter was born I drove to my Mum and Dad's house early in the morning straight from the hospital. It was about 6.00 am when I arrived at my Mum's and I'd been up all night. I remember hugging my Dad and telling him how much I loved him. He didn't reciprocate my words for him. Even in that emotionally charged situation he wasn't comfortable with replying. I remember my Mum was like a boxing referee prising us apart. 'You're just tired and emotional son, you're just tired and emotional, come and sit down', she interjected. Naturally enough, yes I was! Mum knew better than anyone that Dad needed rescuing. He needed to be at arms length.

The fact is he didn't need to say a word. One look at my Dad's face that morning told me how elated he was to be a Grandad for the first time. Later that day when he eventually got to hold his baby Granddaughter later that day he looked like he might swallow his own ears he grinned so much.

The richest legacy I brought home from Istanbul was that for only the second time in my life I saw my Dad drop his guard completely. The only other time I saw him do that was in the minutes after his Dad, my Grandad, died in Fazackerley hospital. In those moments I saw a devastated, helpless and broken man where I'd only ever seen power and strength before. When Grandad died I moved closer to my Dad than ever before. I had only ever known my Dad to be indestructible. Grandad dying was Dad's Kryptonite.

I don't want to forget or understate the part that the game of football has played in my life. Between the ages of 7 and 14 I was very small for my age. In my first year of Comprehensive school the smallest size of blazer had to have the arms hemmed to the elbow to make it fit. I was tiny. The only reason I wasn't bullied was I was a decent footballer. My school team once went 18 months without losing a game. I played up front with the hardest lad in our year. If I was a decent player he was sensational. Between us we scored bags of goals but this lad was head and shoulders above me and everyone else in our team in terms of physique and technique. Other lads my size were obvious fodder. You could tell that he had been busy when someone would walk past you in the corridor with a felt tip moustache and earrings. We were never good friends or anything like that, but because we played footy together I got off scot-free. It wasn't just the smaller lads in our year that he singled out, he would take on all-comers. But he never pissed in your shoes or threw you out of the changing rooms in your y-fronts if you belonged to the football team. Playing football certainly paved an easier path for me in school.

Football has been kind to me and I am fortunate to have been born a Kopite. But salvation from a school hard-man is truly insignificant compared to the gifts of Istanbul.

In the first chapter of this book I stated:

'I hoped to come home with an experience of a lifetime under my belt. I hoped to come home having watched Liverpool regain the European Cup after 21 years. Most of all I wanted to bring home memories of my Dad and me together that I could cherish for the rest of my life.'

Istanbul didn't leave much room for disappointment.

My journey to Istanbul to watch Liverpool win their 5th European Champions Cup has left me with a number of priceless legacies. In Istanbul my Dad and me laid the final pieces of our relationship. My Dad is a young Dad. Mum and Dad must have been in some kind of hurry to have three of us by the time they were 24! Luckily for us it means that it's not unreasonable for us to hope to have both our parents with us for another 25 years and hopefully much longer. But in terms of my relationship developing with my Dad, I don't think things will change a great deal. There is nothing else I could ever ask of him and no one can take away Istanbul from us. Istanbul was a defining trip in my relationship with my Dad.

I guess in this book I'm partly following in my father's footsteps. By writing a book to at least partly to tell someone how I feel about them, rather than telling them face-to-face, I'm taking my father's trait to another level! I think Dad would corkscrew himself into the ground if I tried to stand in front of him and tell him some of the things I mention in this book. But I don't think I'd be brave enough to try anyway and it means my Mum doesn't have to form a human wedge between us to save her hubby's blushes. I want Dad to know that he doesn't have to say a word to me about how he feels about me or any of us for that matter. It's all been said.

At many times during the writing of this book I didn't think I would get it finished. I'm not a professional writer and this is the first book I have written. It has been a co-lossal effort for me to get to this line of my story. If there is one last miracle to squeeze out of the dreams and songs of Istanbul it's that this book has been written at all. Whoever you are I hope you have enjoyed reading my book and I hope you will forgive me for reserving the last couple of lines of this book for my Istanbul travelling companion.

Dad, if there is one ambition I have in life it is for my daughters to grow up feeling the same way about me as I do about you. Thank you for Istanbul. You are a great man and a great father. I love you very much.

~ *End*~

Marching as to War
Shrewsbury School 1939–45

Marching as to War

Shrewsbury School 1939–45

MICHAEL CHARLESWORTH

GREENBANK PRESS

Published by Greenbank Press
Greenbank, East Horrington, Wells, Somerset BA5 3DR

© Michael Charlesworth 2005

British Library Cataloguing in Publication Data
A catalogue record for this book is available from the British Library

ISBN 0 9523699 3 1

Designed and typeset by Bob Elliott
Printed by Hobbs the Printers Ltd, Totton, Hampshire

1939–1945

TO THE MEMORY OF THOSE
WHO LEFT THE FIELDS OF KINGSLAND
FOR OTHER AND WIDER FIELDS
AND DID NOT RETURN

Mementote fratres, memento Domine

The author wishes to acknowledge with gratitude
the support and sponsorship of the Old Salopian Club
in the publication of this book.

Preface

THE idea of writing this book came from Lieut Col Richard
Sinnett (Oldham's 1941–45) who suggested to me that
Shrewsbury School in the Second World War might be an
interesting subject, hitherto covered only superficially. Being
in a state of octogenarian idleness, I was happy to pursue this
suggestion, though I had no experience of wartime Shrewsbury,
having been overseas for five years in the army.

The School archives produced some material and there were
the *Salopian* magazines and Governing Body minutes; but these
sources provided only an outline. So I sent a circular to 500 Old
Salopians who were here in the war years. The response was
remarkable; I received about 150 letters from these wartime
Salopians, some writing at considerable length. Obviously I had
touched a nostalgic chord in that generation, now in their
seventies. So if this book has any merit it is because so much
material has been thus provided. My gratitude to them is
unbounded.

There will be inaccuracy in this book. Memories are often
unreliable and often it is difficult to date various experiences or
to set them in the right context. Those who have read what I have
previously written will find some repetition but I am afraid this
is inevitable.

Quite separately from my researches, Richard Sinnett has
been conducting his own researches into the Roll of Honour –
the list of those killed in the Second World War. His very
thorough work has produced much that was unknown about
these men and has both corrected and expanded the existing
record. It seems right that this research should be recorded and
published, and this revised Roll forms an appendix to this book.

Despite the fact that he has turned from being a full-time

publisher to being a schoolmaster, Richard Hudson has re-activated the Greenbank Press and found time to edit and oversee the publication of this volume. As always, I am most grateful for his advice and hard work. Linda Wason has made sense of my rough original draft and efficiently typed the manuscript; my thanks also go to her.

MICHAEL CHARLESWORTH

November 2004

Contents

1

Cheltonian Invasion

A T this distance it is not easy to remember and recreate the atmosphere which prevailed in September 1939 after Neville Chamberlain's doom laden broadcast that fine Sunday morning on the 3rd of September. The general expectation in the country, founded on Stanley Baldwin's statement a few years earlier that 'the bomber will always get through', was that the skies would immediately fill with German bombers. In April the Government had provided local authorities with one million burial forms; coffins had been stock piled and the Air Ministry forecast was that there would be 600,000 dead and 1,200,000 injured in the first two months of the war. There was a very considerable fear of gas attack and, from the first day of the war, all civilians were urged to carry their gas masks at all times.

It was against this background that arrangements were made for various Government Departments to be evacuated from London to areas thought to be safer. Cheltenham was one such area and the Headmaster of Cheltenham College received a *diktat* ordering him to move his school in its entirety to make way for a Government Department. The Headmaster, John Bell, at once contacted the Headmaster of Shrewsbury, H. H. Hardy, to ask if Cheltenham could come to Shrewsbury. Hardy, who had himself been Headmaster of Cheltenham, at once agreed.

Thus was the peace of the Salopian summer holiday shattered. Term was to begin on 28th September which left a fortnight to work out how two schools could share the same buildings and site. 338 boys and 38 staff were to move. Householders on Kingsland and beyond were canvassed as to whether they could accommodate a boy or boys, or a member of staff. Remarkably, this was achieved. It must be remembered that in those days there were cooks and housemaids so the billeting process was not quite the burden that it might have been. Also there was much billeting activity in the country in general with the evacuation of school children from what were thought to be threatened areas and also, in some families, a voluntary move of children and the old to relatives in country districts.

The heaviest administrative burdens were borne by the Bursars of the two schools, Denys Woods of Shrewsbury and A. R. Pelly of Cheltenham. It was decided that the rooms above the Boathouse should house the Cheltenham Bursary. There being no made-up road leading down to the Boathouse, the whole of the bursarial impedimenta was taken to the river and transported across in the ferry, managed with cheerful enthusiasm by Fred the Ferryman. The room at the top of the shop became the Visitors' Masters' Common Room; the so-called 'Art Room' in the Alington Hall became their Orderly Room. The whole of the Alington Hall was taken over by the Cheltonians for their daily assemblies and the gathering together as best they could of their Houses. The whole of the College's baggage arrived in fourteen railway vans, collected from the station and unloaded on Central.

What then of the hosts – the Shrewsbury School of 1939 – facing nearly six years of war? The seven years during which Henry Harrison Hardy had already been Headmaster could not be called entirely peaceful – in fact so far as the Housemasters were concerned the period had been a seven years war on the subject of salaries and emoluments, for these were the days when Housemasters owned and ran their Houses (except for the School House and Dayboys), gathering the fees from parents and running their own establishments as businesses, passing on a percentage of their income to the School. What proportion should this be? Herein lay the battleground from which Hardy had emerged as the winner but leaving much blood on the ground. His autocratic stance had stood in stark contrast to the easy going style of his predecessor, Canon Sawyer, and it had taken both boys and masters time to adjust to the new approach which was essentially bureaucratic and centralised. The initials H. H. H. had been transmogrified – by the boys – into Herr Hitler Hardy.

Early in his time Hardy had remarked that running Shrewsbury was like running a battalion without second-in-command, quartermaster or adjutant. The appointment of a full time Bursar gave him a quartermaster but no second-in-command (because, in Hardy's estimation, there was no senior master suitable), and no adjutant. So the rule of the Headmaster was all embracing. A study of the Notices Book, which the school porter Hartshorne carried round the form rooms every period, showed head-magisterial control of every detail of routine, each notice being written in his own scholar's handwriting, down to such minor matters such as the re-timing of a lesson by five minutes to accommodate a lecture.

He is remembered by Francis King 'in his tight fitting dark suit, the trouser legs extremely narrow, all jacket buttons fastened, and a gold pince-nez dangling on a chain from a button of his waistcoat which he wore in even the hottest weather, Hardy managed to project two images simultaneously; that of the Army officer which he had been in the First War (he always liked to be known as Major Hardy), and that of the clergyman he might have been. Holding himself stiffly erect as though by a conscious effort of will, so that even as an adult I felt a constant discomfort in looking up at him, he spoke in the clipped manner of someone who not merely demanded but expected to be obeyed'.

Discipline was strict and boys – until they were very senior – were wary of encounters with their Headmaster. They noted, with suppressed amusement, the way that he mounted his bicycle with one foot on a back step and so forwards on to the saddle. It was said that he had been wounded in an unfortunate place in the war which made this procedure essential – a rumour which was wholly false. For a man so devoted to detail, the boys found it odd that he always arrived for First Lesson, which began at 7.45 am, ten minutes late. Thus to arrive at 7.54 was safe – an extra nine minutes in bed. On Sundays, the Revd J. O. Whitfield, taking the early communion service in Chapel, delighted to start the service as the clock struck eight knowing that Hardy would be half way across the Common at that moment. Beside his desk Hardy always kept the Bradshaw railway guide. If a boy went away for any purpose he had to have his Exeat Form initialled by the sage and the train times carefully checked.

Hardy's capacity for organisation was put into full flow with the coming of Cheltenham. It is remarkable that the two schools were able to exist side by side and share the facilities virtually without any friction at all, and the major share in this achievement must be credited to Hardy.

He was a generous host and a model guest but he could be brusque – and more than brusque – on occasion. He frequently crossed swords with parents and with Prep School Headmasters. Writing to him about her son's progress, the mother of John Lea was surprised to receive, with the answer, her original letter with the misspellings corrected in red ink.

The Housemasters were a formidable team. With one exception, they had all run their Houses for more than seven years – in most cases much more. 'Cuddy' Mitford had joined the staff in 1908 and had reigned in Severn Hill for fourteen years, a man not to be treated lightly, whose tongue easily turned from sardonic to sarcastic. J. R. Hope-Simpson had already spent many years in School House, as Tutor then Housemaster, looking after eighty-four boys, a rock of dependability; no one better personified the Roman virtues. J. O. Whitfield ('the Joe') was in Churchill's, a man whose temper might erupt in the House or form room and who therefore had to be humoured with care. (A familiar punishment was 'Write out the Bible backwards, each letter in alternating red and black ink'. The punishment was always cancelled at the end of the period. Street and Tombling once started the task and calculated that it would take a hundred years, not allowing for sleep or food). Jimmy Street, a brilliant teacher of the classics and a man of wide general culture had succeeded his father-in-law in Rigg's. His knowledge of Salopia and Salopians was unrivalled. His close friend was J. H. Tombling ('the Bling') who concealed a sharp wit beneath an unsmiling countenance. His House was currently outstandingly successful in the sports fields. A. E. Kitchin ('the Bull'), the outstanding schoolboy rowing coach in the country, had already been in Ridgemount for fourteen years and was sadly showing the first signs of Parkinson's disease which was to cripple him. In Oldham's the urbane Sopwith ('the Swith') presided over a House more civilised and orderly than some others like Sale's where the popular Dick Sale interfered little and was a benign presence, always preceded by a tuneless hum; games were his main interest. His slow speech was, according to popular rumour, attributable to shell shock in the war – which was quite untrue. In contrast to these stalwarts of what was becoming the *ancien regime* was Alan Phillips in Moser's, taking office in the very year that the war began, younger and both athletic and energetic with a young family – the first ever in that House. Finally in Dayboys, Hans Pendlebury had taken over from James West for the duration. His real name was not Hans but his resemblance to a prosperous Bavarian Count had led to this nickname – he was also known as 'Pendlehoff'.

This then was the front line team which faced the Cheltonian invasion and was to face the expected German invasion. But the burden in the Houses, heavy as it was to be, was heavier for the Housemasters' wives. Before the days of labour saving domestic gadgets, the Houses were entirely dependent on man and woman power. As time went on, domestic servants were desperately difficult to find and ever-tighter rationing made the feeding of the boys a constant worry. The unsung heroines of these years were Ray Sale and Joan Tombling (sisters); Kate Street and Megan Whitfield (sisters); Effie Sopwith, Ruth Kitchin and Ethel Phillips. Cuddy Mitford's sister kept house for him; in the School House were two capable sisters who filled the housekeeping role. Later Hilary Bevan and Mary Taylor were to play their parts in Ridgemount and Churchill's respectively.

The war meant that for other members of the staff there were new and unaccustomed roles. Heavy responsibility was to fall on such as David Bevan, Stacy Colman, Jim Pitts-Tucker and others. The Government had ordained that teaching was a Reserved Occupation so that schoolmasters were exempt from conscription but were, of course, able to volunteer to join the Forces if their school and the Government would allow it. In London a special Board was set up to decide who should and who should not join up. Hardy defined their decisions as 'inscrutable'. Both David Bevan and Stacy Colman tried to volunteer but their presence was regarded as too important at Shrewsbury to secure their release. Stacy even tried to join the Australian forces on the strength of his one year's residence as Headmaster of Melbourne Grammar School but was told that the Australian army only recruited in Australia. Hardy had to report to this Selection Board from time to time with details of people he could spare – an invidious situation for him - but the Board generally ignored what he had to say.

The Michaelmas Term of 1939 started with 484 boys. There had been fifteen late withdrawals in the holidays, some for financial reasons (with threatening wartime taxes), others, according to Hardy, due to 'unjustifiable panic'. Three of the staff were at once called to the Colours – Major J. M. West, veteran of the First War; Major V. C. Knollys whom Hardy had signed up in 1938 to act as Adjutant of the Corps and Master in charge of Physical Training and who was on the Reserve; and – to everyone's surprise (including his own) – Hugh Brooke. It transpired that when he had joined the OTC he had inadvertently signed a form which stated that he was immediately available in case of emergency. James West had various postings and in the end commanded an NCO training camp, duly receiving his red tabs and becoming Colonel West, as later Salopians always knew him. Vernon Knollys was a company commander in his Rifle Brigade battalion which fought to a standstill at Calais, leading to his being a Prisoner of War for five years. Hugh Brooke was in the KSLI until a fall off a Welsh mountain in 1944 brought to an end his military career. (As he fell he is said to have exclaimed 'HIG' – or 'Here I go').

In the summer holidays of 1939 the boys in the OTC had had

a taste of army life at camp in Wales at Pentre Pant. This was run by the School, the army being too busy to organise cadet camps. It involved a march spread over two days, bivouacking overnight. ATS girls undertook the cooking and there was a remarkable readiness to volunteer for potato peeling. In a different sphere the school had had a taste of Nazism when, a year previously, Herr Werner Kränzlin had been a temporary addition to the staff in exchange for Hugh Brooke. His enthusiasm for Hitler was one hundred per cent. He was bronzed, fit and athletic and soon had his form singing the Horst Wessel Song. (Salopian humour he did not quite grasp. Jim Gladwell asked if they could have a window open – 'Ich bin warm,' he said, well knowing that this was a polite way in which a woman would say that she was pregnant). It was rumoured later in the war that Kränzlin had been killed on the Russian front.

In the early days of the term much time was taken up with ARP (Air Raid Precautions). Before the boys returned trenches had already been dug as shelters on either side of Central and in other parts of the Site. They soon filled with water and were later given roofs which protruded about two feet above the ground, reminding one boy of early British barrows. Each House had a shelter designated – there was a cluster for Ingram's and Churchill's whose traces were found when the Gymnasium was built in the 1970s. In School House the basement was thought to provide sufficient protection.

There were elaborate plans as to what to do 'when the sound of the siren is heard in the land' – a Hardyism. Directions were detailed:

IF THERE IS AN ALERT –

i. During School. Those on ground-floor immediately draw all blinds and stay there.

Those upstairs go down to ground-floor (routes and destinations posted up in each room) and shut doors as soon as all are down.

Later when ordered all go to House trenches or basements but Severn Hill to Central trenches, Ridgemount to School House.

ii. During Chapel. Stay till ordered then go to the nearer shelters leaving Chapel by indicated exits. Those in Gallery go to Chapel crypt.

iii. For First Aid and Fire Parties separate instructions will be issued.

iv. If caught in the open when missiles fall, lie flat face down.

Fire watching was undertaken by groups of masters and boys, the roof of the School Buildings being the prime point of observation. Classes in First Aid were held and teams could be quickly deployed. A large number of sandbags were piled at different places on the Site. These were not so much sandbags as earth bags, filled, with considerable sweat, by the boys.

The Black Out provided problems. Hope-Simpson, returning early from his holiday, grimly surveyed the number of windows in the School House – the number ran into hundreds – and set about providing covers for every one. Plywood boarding was used to black out the School Buildings; thousands of yards of curtains were deployed elsewhere. Discipline had to be strict as this Hardy notice makes clear; it refers to the School Buildings:

All blinds, ground floor included, should be put in place by the last user of each room in 2nd Lesson. Failures have already and inexcusably occurred on the 1st and 2nd floors and we have been censured by the ARP authorities. It is essential to shut the windows before putting the blinds in place.

In winter the Black Out time came during school hours. A whistle, blown by Hartshorne announced that the time had come; similarly the whistle denoted the end of Black Out in 1st Lesson. With the form rooms in constant use during the Cheltonian occupation, the atmosphere became extremely thick. Certain masters, who had a tight hold on discipline, would order the lights to be put out and the windows opened and teach in the dark for five or ten minutes – such were Kitchin and Major Pearson and Alec Binney. Finding one's way round the Site in the dark required concentration and the avoidance of unexpected obstacles like parked cars; new boys sometimes found it difficult to navigate back to their Houses after third lesson. There was much white paint to indicate obstacles like lamp posts or to point the way.

One group to whose existing difficulties the Black Out added were the Dayboys, most of whom cycled to school. Gerry Symons comments:

Living at home on The Mount there was much cycling to be done – to 1st Lesson at 7.45 am, back home for breakfast, returning for Chapel at 9.30 am. A return trip home for lunch and on occasions when higher up the school another round trip in the evening. A strong memory is of early morning cycling through rutted snow, with a weak 'black out' lamp and the street lights shaded. This was the era of double summer time in mid-winter just to add to our difficulties.

Coming from the opposite side of the town David Ormrod from London Road found similar difficulties and remembers the exhilaration of the down hill run from the Site into Coleham. During the floods his journey was extended as he had to go round by the by-pass.

Francis de Hamel has clear memories of ARP as it affected the boys. He emphasises the great fear of gas in the early days and that gas masks, encased in cardboard boxes were carried everywhere, even into Chapel, though this discipline was gradually abandoned. Emptied, the boxes could conveniently contain a picnic lunch 'with the additional merit of seemingly looking virtuous.'

A shed, a sort of tunnel barn about fifteen feet long and six feet high with a trap at one end was erected near the Armoury. Every so often we were lined up and made to enter this shed with gas masks on and then, once seated, told to take our masks off to convince us how efficient they were. The gas used in this exercise was tear-gas and I shall never forget the sudden appalling pouring from the eyes, burning in the nose and constriction of the throat, and of course the acrid pong of the gas as we blindly staggered to the exit. It was a splendid demo of the efficiency of the masks.

Also a little flat table, about eighteen inches square, mounted on a wooden pole, looking a little like an over-grown bird table, appeared alongside the Science Building. We were told it would change colour from yellow to green if mustard gas landed on it. Practical chemistry, we were told by Charlie Larkin.

Francis de Hamel also remembers the drill for using a stirrup pump.

This was a sort of bicycle pump with a big wooden handle, a foot or two of hose and spray nozzle. We had to put one end in a bucket of water, stand on a flat wire foot and pump like mad. One person did the pumping while the other lay down prone and directed the spray on to the burning bomb. (These were incendiaries). That was the idea. But they burned with intense heat, sufficient to melt steel and, once prone, it was difficult to avoid being cooked. Certainly that applied to the thermite ones supplied by the Chemistry department. They were wicked.

Yet another grand gimmick from which we suffered or were trained was a thing known as a trailer-pump. This was a sort of grand-master of the stirrup pump – sophisticated and technical – too difficult for mere amateurs like young schoolboys to understand, let alone operate. Nevertheless, once the initial esoteric over-enthusiasm by ARP Fire Wardens had worn off a bit, we, mere schoolboys, were permitted to 'play' with them. But only the monitors. For the first time in my life I got to learn the difference between males and females. Such expertise was required to tell which end of a big hose one had got hold of, and which inlet fitted which outlet. This valuable information I found useful for the rest of my life.

There were occasional practices in the House of so-called 'bomb drill' at night. The House bell rang and bedroom monitors saw to it that sleepy boys were turned out of their beds, counted to see that none was left behind, to assemble in dressing gowns in the basement, shivering and bung-eyed, probably accompanied by an out-of-temper Housemaster to await the All Clear, then to trudge back upstairs to flop into bed.

The absorption of Cheltenham College into the life of the Site was wonderfully well managed. Having got over an initial disappointment – it was said that Cheltenham Ladies College was arriving – Salopians welcomed the visitors warmly. (They were at once called 'the Chelts'). Olly Johnson remembers being told that they must be kind to the Chelts as it was not their fault that they were not Salopians. The editor of *The Salopian* waxed eloquent: 'Indeed we may almost count their presence on the Site as one of the major blessings conferred on us by a notoriously flighty providence'. He did however admit that Cheltonian daily dress was a bit bewildering at first, as the boys wore mortar boards and short gowns over sports jackets and Salopians had to suppress the urge to 'cap' them. The Chelts were equally surprised to see Salopian Sunday dress – top hat and tails. *The Salopian* firmly warns against the temptation to remove as souvenirs the tassel or the badge from the mortar boards, known as 'Collegers'.

The host school preserved to a considerable degree its usual timetable; for the Chelts it was games in the morning and work in the afternoon, not entirely a disadvantage on short winter days when the best of the weather was in the morning. For the visitors the bicycle was an essential item, for almost all the boys were billeted within cycling distance of the Site. Billets were various. Basil Oldham could not have been more delighted to welcome six Chelts which enabled him to play the Housemaster role again. But there were also some less easy relationships – 'If you wake that baby again I'll kill you!'

Owen Darrell, whose home was and is in Bermuda, had been at Cheltenham for only a year when he found himself transferred to Shrewsbury. With another boy he shared comfortable accommodation.

Our hosts were a pleasant couple in their late seventies with an elderly sister living with them. There was thus always someone to welcome us when we cycled back in the late afternoon for supper. Some of my most lasting memories were the home-made sponge layer cakes. Apparently, according to my wife, I still talk about them. The home owners had been imbued with the idea (enthusiastically adopted) that they must play their part in the war effort. It was a united Britain.

Like others of the visitors, Owen Darrell was impressed by the beauty of the Site and soon felt welcome.

The fine School Chapel was where I was once called upon to read a lesson to assembled Cheltonians and we all felt as much at home as in our own chapel. Such was our feeling of acceptance at Shrewsbury School.

The countryside too was explored.

I recall walks round the Wrekin and participating in beagling; and in the record cold winter I found myself trying to ice-skate on a beautiful bend of the nearby Severn. Much Wenlock likewise brings back memories of pleasant walks and, when again reading Housman, I began to wonder if I too could become a Shropshire Lad, on at least a non-admitted basis . . . ?

The boys in fact saw little of each other – they were always passing on the staircases and passages. Good relations were established between the Head Boys, J. D. Matthews of Shrewsbury (captain of cricket and of football, later to play cricket for Cambridge and Scotland, later still to become Senior Consultant Surgeon Physician at the Royal Infirmary at Edinburgh and Surgeon and Moderator of High Constables and Guard of Honour, Holyrood House), and P. B. C. Moore of Cheltenham (now Lord Moore of Wolvercote, GCB, CMG, former Private Secretary to the Queen and keeper of the Queen's Archives, also a rugby football international). There were two notable events involving both schools. On 11th November Cheltenham played Rugby and Shrewsbury played Bradfield; the timetable was adjusted so that Salopians could cheer for Cheltenham and Cheltonians could cheer for Shrewsbury. Both the home sides won. The Tucks run in the same month saw both schools turn out in full number; on the traditional 'gently forward' 342 couples left the School Gates on the familiar five mile odyssey. Salopians occupied the first seven places. Sixteen couples of staff also participated. A rugby match between the two schools resulted in an easy win for Cheltenham; the referee was Hardy, in his long shorts. There was in fact warfare between the schools – in the form of a field day at Attingham, when the contingents 'fought a long hour by Shrewsbury clock'.

Social contact was made through the various school societies to which the visitors were invited; and closer contact was made by some in the Sanatorium during a virulent outbreak of flu in the Lent Term. Amongst the Chelts was Lindsay Anderson, later well known in the film world, who directed the film *If . . .*, partly shot at his old school, which raised eyebrows in the turbulent Sixties. The Salopian Francis King, novelist and critic, recollects Lindsay Anderson playing Thisbe at Shrewsbury, as one of the great performances which stays in his memory.

In the Christmas holidays of 1939–40, the Headmasters Conference was held at Shrewsbury, 104 visitors being accommodated in the various Houses. There was much to discuss, particularly on the subject of entries and whether schools which had been evacuated would continue to attract sufficient boys. Hardy's own position was difficult; there were fourteen fewer boys in the Lent Term and nine masters were preparing to join up. And there were difficult questions to be answered. Should boys leave early in order to have a short time at the University before being called up and thus, as it were, stake their claim? Or was it better to complete school life and enjoy the full benefits of the last year, generally the most productive and most enjoyable? It was no wonder that parents were puzzled and uncertain.

The winter of 1939–40 was severe. In the first six weeks of the Lent term it was not possible to play football. A long freeze, a quick thaw and another freeze turned the Common into a sheet of ice. One boy put on his skates outside his House, Tombling's, and skated as far as Kingsland House. An ice hockey match between Shrewsbury and Cheltenham was played on the school cricket wicket – and won by the visitors. The Chelts enjoyed the spectacle of top-hatted and tail-coated Salopians skating on Sunday afternoons. There was no mitigation of the normal timetable. First Lesson and a cold shower started the day; bedroom windows were open at night as usual. Rowland Guy remembers his endeavours to keep warm in bed wearing a fisherman's jersey, camel hair bedsocks, OTC gloves and two extra rugs. 'Nobody actually died,' he commented. It was in this term too that rationing began to bite; bacon, sugar, butter and ham were now on the ration. The ration book had become the key to life.

With the Russian invasion of Finland, the war – though

distant – became a little more real. 'The Russian bear is clawing away at the Baltic in an attempt to reach England,' wrote the Editor of *The Salopian*. A grand Musical Fete was held in the Alington Hall to raise funds for Finland; £183 accrued.

The end of term brought news to Cheltenham that the Government would not now require their site and that they could therefore return. An immense cheer went up at the Cheltonian assembly in the Alington Hall. During the first days of the holidays they gradually packed up; the fourteen railway containers in which they had arrived were again summoned and the Shrewsbury Site knew them no more. A teak seat, with suitable inscription, was presented to the hosts and can be found beside the Alington Hall which had been the axis on which the Cheltonian world had revolved. *The Salopian* printed a quatrain *Ad Collegium Cheltoniense*:

> ite domum, socii. Fessi simul ite, Penates.
> Iam satis exsilii triste tulistis onus.
> Tempus adest; reduces votis gratamur amicis,
> prosequitur precibus nostra Sabrina suis.

2

German Invasion?

WHAT must be the most momentous term in the School's history started on 3rd May 1940, the day that the evacuation of Norway was announced after a disastrous short campaign. It might have been hoped that the School would now settle down to a more normal existence after the Chelts had left, but only a week after the boys returned Hitler unleashed his Blitzkrieg and for the next month the country held its breath as the retreat to Dunkirk took place. Of immediate consequence on the Site was the formation of the Local Defence Volunteers ('Look, Duck and Vanish') shortly to be re-named the Home Guard by Winston Churchill. Senior boys were encouraged to join – with parents' consent.

Those with a historic bent could look back to the threat from Spain in the time of Queen Elizabeth I, when in 1581 Sir Henry Sidney, Lord Warden of the Marches, reviewed the boys on the Gay Meadow – 360 strong – where 'the captains made their orisons how valiantly they would feight and defend the countrey'. Or they might recollect the formation of cadet companies to repel Boney; later to ward off the supposed threat from Napoleon III when the Rifle Volunteers were formed, of whom Captain E. B. Moser was a local member.

The K (for Kingsland) Company of the Home Guard was commanded by Tom Taylor with headquarters in the school orderly room. There were four platoons, the boys forming two of them; they were the mobile reserve mounted on their bicycles. There were two advanced headquarters in Kingsland House and in Kingsland Grange School and the task allotted to K Company in the early stages was to defend the by-pass between the roundabout at Longden Road and that at Port Hill. Locations for – largely non-existent – weapons and fields of fire were reconnoitred and trenches dug. Tom Taylor, who was excused teaching for a time, had a wider brief, to site weapon pits on all the roads radiating out from the town in which task Thomas Metcalfe, then in Severn Hill, assisted him. The strong points were either sited with a good field of fire or close but concealed near the road from where Molotov cocktails could be thrown.

Dad's Army almost automatically comes to mind when the Home Guard is mentioned but, in Shrewsbury as elsewhere, the original volunteers were in fact mainly fit men in their forties or younger men in reserved occupations. But most lacked any military background. This led to the well-trained OTC boys with Cert A acting as instructors. On the Common after tea there would be groups teaching arms drill or weapon training. Patrick Lacey remembers with embarrassment 'teaching' the use of the aiming disk to an ex-soldier who had served for twenty-one years with the KSLI. Kingston Adams, having a civilian driving licence, found himself detailed to drive Hans Pendlebury as he went about his army duties. At the first parade of the LDV Hans had turned up wearing his tin hat and carrying his .45 pistol, both survivors of the First War.

The possibility of invasion by air was thought to be strong. Accordingly all flat spaces on which aircraft or gliders might land were covered with obstacles. On the Common cricket sight screens and teak benches were placed at strategic points; later poles were erected. Later still the Bursar had the excellent idea of planting hops round the poles; but when sheep were introduced to keep the grass down they ate the hops.

Holland having been captured largely through the dropping of parachute troops, the likelihood of this form of attack was envisaged. A ridiculous rumour had swept the country that some Nazis had descended on Holland dressed as nuns with light automatics under their habits. There was, of course, no basis for this but when a boy Home Guard, on sentry duty at dusk saw a nun-like figure with flapping gown cycling towards him across the Site he was quick to challenge; it turned out to be McEachran. Another absurdity actually emanated from the Air Ministry, that if one saw a German parachutist landing with both arms held high he was not surrendering but holding two grenades. The idea of landing in unknown terrain without the use of the arms was obviously ridiculous. When the RSSH ran out into the country they were surprised to see that the little Bomere Pool had a wire across it, suspended on a buoy, in case any passing German seaplane happened to call in.

The fall of France was sensational news. It happened on a day when the Corps were rehearsing the Inspection parade. Peter Beanland recollects that the proceedings were suddenly stopped and the contingent formed into a hollow square. Tom Taylor gave the boys this extraordinary news which really did seem to bring the possibility of invasion nearer. Hartshorne was aflame with patriotic fire and kept quoting Ernest Bevin's remark, 'We're in the Final'. With his characteristic slight stutter he gave his opinion, 'They'll come within a f-f-fortnight'.

Shrewsbury was not slow in manufacturing the 'Molotov Cocktail'. Olly Johnson recounts the process:

The design was sophisticated and the manufacture skilled. The design was essentially by Taylor (physicist) and Larkin (chemist). Glass bottles were deeply engraved with vertical and radial grooves. Tom Taylor devised a precise pattern that ensured fracture on impact. The contents were petrol and engine oil mixed to a critical viscosity. A 'fuse' consisting of a piece of flannel tied to the neck of the bottle was soaked in petrol, ignited and fired at an enemy vehicle. It spread a burning goo over the tank and further cocktails could be lobbed into the flames. If the bottles were incorrectly cut with the glass-cutting wheel, there was a risk of the bottle breaking in the hand of the thrower with serious consequences if the fuse had been lit. The factory that manufactured the cocktails was in the John's Hole by the Baths. Roger Dixey, 'Hank' Darlington and I were the workforce and we made hundreds. The bottles came from the Houses and a good claret bottle was ideal. An interesting sidelight was provided into the Housemasters' cellars.

A demonstration of the cocktails was held for the benefit of visiting brass hats from the Barracks. An old Austin 12, kindly donated by Hugh Brooke and Alec Peterson, was rolled down the slope towards the Craig Fields, attacked and set on fire very satisfactorily; verisimilitude was provided by two 'Germans' – Dixey and Johnson – wearing appropriate helmets.

The OTC rifles, Lee Enfields, were valued highly after the army had lost most of its equipment at Dunkirk. Accordingly there was a 24 hour guard upon the Armoury lest a German parachutist or fifth columnist might appear. An officer and six boys every night mounted a watch, those not on duty sleeping uncomfortably in the Moser Building. There was an incident one morning when the guard were being stood down and 'easing springs', that is making sure their rifles were unloaded. Unfortunately one cartridge remained in the breech and was fired high over Oldham's, bringing an alarmed Sopwith to the window.

These Lee Enfields were soon taken away to equip the Home Guard and replaced by rifles of Italian origin which had been used at the battle of Adowa in 1896 when the Italians had sustained a remarkable defeat in Abyssinia. Bought by a German arms dealer in Hamburg, they next appeared in 1913, smuggled to Larne in Ireland to arm the Ulster Volunteers. When they came to Shrewsbury some had the Red Hand of Ulster stencilled on the butt.

Home Guard exercises were held in the surrounding countryside. Peter Beanland, being under age for the Home Guard, nevertheless was used with others as 'enemy', taken out into the country and told to try and penetrate the town defences; but, crawling through cut hay, he was 'captured'. On a similar exercise, Sandy Boyle, armed with a rattle (machine gun) and hiding in the dusk was indignant at being 'shot' by a member of his own House, Kingston Adams.

The railway station was felt to be a key target and was defended by a Home Guard company with weapon pits at strategic points, designated fields of fire and road blocks. But there was indignation when an attacking section of the OTC crept into the station on the rails behind a train; this was thought in some way to be unsporting. Later Lieutenant Stacy Colman found himself in charge of a company which consisted largely of railwaymen and devised a very detailed plan of defence, drawn out very clearly and annotated in his own fine handwriting, which still survives.

The Home Guard had a great liking for road blocks to identify German spies and agents who were thought to be arriving by sea or air. In fact the number that were rounded up was not above a dozen in the whole country and when General Alan Brooke became responsible for home defence he had all the road blocks swept away as being a hindrance to the deployment of our own troops as well as being a great irritant to normal civilian life.

In June the School once again received refugees, this time from Victoria College, Jersey, which the Germans had now occupied. Fourteen boys, the Headmaster and three staff (including one Old Salopian bearing the well known name of Salt), arrived on 21st June, all the boys being involved in public exams which they duly took. They were accommodated in Severn Hill and Oldham's and tasted the flavour of boarding school life, taking part in cricket and in swimming. Their attendance at the end of term House 'turns' in Oldham's, mostly written by the actors, gave them a glimpse of the camaraderie which a boarding House creates.

In that summer term there were the beginnings of an activity which was to expand and form the background to many boys' memories of these days – the provision of boy labour to farmers. To his great surprise, Pat Jolly found himself as the unofficial Captain of School Farming, chosen by Hardy as he held no official position in school sport.

So in June and July selected teams of older boys cycled out to Shropshire farms and did fairly backbreaking jobs such as beet singling and vegetable planting in the hot sun. I did my fair share because I felt I should set a good example. The only slight voice of discouragement was that of my Housemaster, Mr Mitford, who, I am sure, felt my time would be better employed in discussing with him such weighty matters as who were likely to be the future stars of Under 16 football in the House!

Another activity was forestry and there were two holiday

camps held at Burwarton on Lord Boyne's estate where the hard winter had wreaked havoc among the trees. The boys found that on the whole the farmers were well disposed to them and there might be tea and buns at the end of a hard afternoon. Andrew Angus recounts, with pardonable pride, that many years later Jimmy Street told him that a certain farmer had asked if he could be sent 'six boys or Gladwell and Angus'.

Amidst all this war-centred activity, the ordinary life of the School went on. It was a good year for scholarships to the Universities, mostly in classics as usual, thirteen in all. The names of John Jowett, Ian Grimble, John Champion, the Heath twins (Peter and John) and Neil Skinner are to be found amongst the awards and prizes. On the cricket field John Matthews led a fine and successful side with an exceptionally strong batting order – A. C. W. Lee, W. T. J. Rhys, M. L. Y. Ainsworth, K. A. Shearwood and the captain himself who made a century when Cheltenham, lately guests on the Site, were trounced by an innings. The cricket XI found themselves playing at unfamiliar venues – Malvern at Blenheim Palace and Felsted at Ross-on-Wye. Nor was intellectual activity overshadowed by war. Papers read to learned societies included J. G. Le Quesne on 'The Emergence of Modern Music', J. Turner on 'Oliver Cromwell', F. H. King on 'Walter de la Mare' and R. S. M. Perrin on 'Drifting Continents'. More interesting, one guesses, than a visiting bigwig addressing the whole school on 'The Uses of Coal in Wartime'.

The human cost of the war was brought home to the School as news of Old Salopian casualties in the Dunkirk evacuation were reported. Twelve Old Salopians were killed. Two DSOs were awarded, three MCs, a DFC and an AFC. Other losses were being reported in the last days of term as the Battle of Britain filled the skies. Despite the difficulties, a scaled down Speech Day took place with Sir Offley Wakeman (Chairman of the Governors) giving away the prizes. The report on the annual Inspection of the Corps was good. 'This OTC is distinctly above average. Morale is very high', wrote the Inspecting Officer, who was accompanied by Hardy in his increasingly old uniform.

There was no Henley, the course being covered with obstacles to prevent enemy landings. Bumpers did not take place except for House 3rd boats.

Ronald Marsden introduced an element of fantasy into the invasion summer, writing that he and a friend in Oldham's, John Cuckney,

decided that when the invasion happened we'd break out of school and head North. I had some maps of the area, we thought we'd fall in with a guerrilla group. We both had sheath knives and I had a knuckle duster and Cuckney a .38 revolver which he had got from his brother in the KSLI. I had a flask of sherry and we both hoarded chocolate and any rations we could get hold of – Horlicks, malted milk tablets etc. We were too young to join the Home Guard so we thought we would do our own thing.

Despite the stresses of this extraordinary Summer Term in which the sun seemed to shine every day ('good invasion weather', people said), morale remained high. Olly Johnson, then a praepostor in his last term, writes:

The first year of the war and my last at Shrewsbury was probably the happiest time of my life. Pre-war discipline had been strict but there was a dramatic change in September 1939. The odds against a long life had shortened so there was a light-hearted 'eat, drink and be merry' feeling that affected every aspect of school life. I was working for my Oxford Science Prelim and had many Private Readers, spent in the Science Bs or Moser Bs, a fair amount of time spent writing and arranging music. If I had a Private Reader in First Lesson I stayed in bed and was served tea by Cecilia, the head skivvy and occasionally she laced it with the Joe's whisky. Paul Holmes taught me and became a close friend; the gap between staff and pupils narrowed. In the LDV I drove a car and Paul Holmes and I reconnoitred outlying observation posts which were usually licensed premises.

Olly Johnson was a leading figure in the school musical world and describes one of the light hearted musicals which Toby Barnaby encouraged and organised, a man who combined very real musical talent with a sharp wit. This is Olly's description of a revue called *Seconds Out*:

Among the leading lights were Gladwell, Kelly and Dixey (and of course Olly himself). A 'pit' orchestra was assembled with support from local ladies. Miss Fry, the School House matron, played the cello. Addison and senior Band Members were enlisted. Barnaby played the piano. I conducted and wrote some of the music. I think it was the first time that Barnaby's classic *Steadies from Bevan* was sung. But the climax of the whole show was a real tear jerker. A large two-dimensional model of the School Buildings was made in the carpentry shop and it filled the back of the Alibarn stage in the final scene with lights in all the windows. Then the entire company sang 'There'll always be a Kingsland', the lights went out one by one and the last notes died in darkness. There wasn't a dry eye in the house. They were strangely emotional days.

Schoolboys do not normally feel deep emotion, but there was certainly something in the air as the summer term reached its end. As one member of staff wrote at the time, 'The usual saying of good-byes was somehow intensified. It really did seem the end of an era'. Many of the leavers would not see Shrewsbury again. Roger Dixey wrote in his diary, '29 July. Final Chapel service. Psalm 122. Abide with Me and Jerusalem. All weeping'.

Olly Johnson wrote:

The Norway shambles and defeat in France made for a grim outlook and I don't know how this was translated into a magical happy time on Kingsland but it most certainly was.

So the OTC contingent marched off to camp at Oswestry, bivouacking for a night *en route*, sustained by the Band, leaving the Site to its summer peace after a term the like of which would not be seen again. During the holidays the Alington Hall was re-decorated. Two of the painters left a message in the cornice written on a cigarette packet signed with their names. It was found thirty years later when the Hall was again decorated. The simple message was 'Balls to Hitler'.

The Band 1939. (*Seated from left*) W. H. Rhys, J. B. Hearn, M. P. Twiston Davies, Capt R. H. J. Brooke, Sgt Major W. Addison, Major V. C. Knollys, D. B. P. Haynes, R. Thicknesse, M. L. Y. Ainsworth. (J. D. Johnson in tiger skin.)

Pre-war Officers Training Corps. (*2nd left*) Major J. M. West; (*3rd left*) Major H. H. Hardy; (*right front*) Lord Bridgeman; and sundry nervous cadets.

Home-made Molotoff cocktails prove their destructive power.

Air raid shelter on Central.

Issued by the Ministry of Information in co-operation with the War Office
and the Ministry of Home Security

Beating the INVADER

A MESSAGE FROM THE PRIME MINISTER

IF invasion comes, everyone—young or old, men and women—will be eager to play their part worthily. By far the greater part of the country will not be immediately involved. Even along our coasts, the greater part will remain unaffected. But where the enemy lands, or tries to land, there will be most violent fighting. Not only will there be the battles when the enemy tries to come ashore, but afterwards there will fall upon his lodgments very heavy British counter-attacks, and all the time the lodgments will be under the heaviest attack by British bombers. The fewer civilians or non-combatants in these areas, the better—apart from essential workers who must remain. So if you are advised by the authorities to leave the place where you live, it is your duty to go elsewhere when you are told to leave. When the attack begins, it will be too late to go ; and, unless you receive definite instructions to move, your duty then will be to stay where you are. You will have to get into the safest place you can find, and stay there until the battle is over. For all of you then the order and the duty will be : " STAND FIRM ".

This also applies to people inland if any considerable number of parachutists or air-borne troops are landed in their neighbourhood. Above all, they must not cumber the roads. Like their fellow-countrymen on the coasts, they must " STAND FIRM ". The Home Guard, supported by strong mobile columns wherever the enemy's numbers require it, will immediately come to grips with the invaders, and there is little doubt will soon destroy them.

Throughout the rest of the country where there is no fighting going on and no close cannon fire or rifle fire can be heard, everyone will govern his conduct by the second great order and duty, namely, " CARRY ON ". It may easily be some weeks before the invader has been totally destroyed, that is to say, killed or captured to the last man who has landed on our shores. Meanwhile, all work must be continued to the utmost, and no time lost.

The following notes have been prepared to tell everyone in rather more detail what to do, and they should be carefully studied. Each man and woman should think out a clear plan of personal action in accordance with the general scheme.

Winston S. Churchill

Summer 1940.

1940 . Shrewsbury *v* Cheltenham ice hockey.

1940 . Lt Colman leads his Home Guard platoon.

As We Were: Sunday morning after Chapel.

Headmasters Conference:
H. H. Hardy and J. B. Bell.

Heads of School Conference:
J. D. Matthews and
P. B. C. Moore

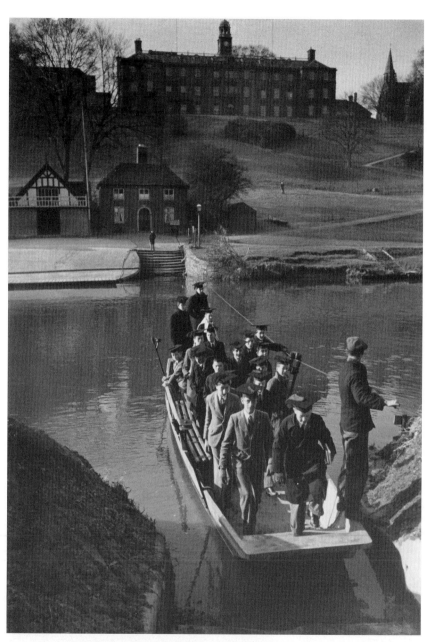

Chelts going back to their billets propelled by Fred the Ferryman.

3

Settling Down

WHEN term began in September 1940 there were 451 boys – 24 fewer than in the previous term. There was beginning to be considerable doubt about the ability of the Public Schools to continue and the Archbishop of Canterbury headed a committee to enquire and make recommendations on the matter of numbers. Shortly after this the Governing Bodies Association came into being as a co-ordinating body and to counter attacks from the Labour party, now part of the Government.

Hardy had to face the loss of eight masters who had joined up – Tom Taylor, Jack Grundy, 'Val' Hill, Peter Hawkesworth, Mike Powell, Basil Deed, Paul Holmes and Bill Winlaw; Arthur Broadbent was soon to follow. The 7th Battalion of the KSLI absorbed a number of staff and boys. In fact it began to replicate the OTC Tom Taylor was second-in-command and 'Val' Hill, Hugh Brooke and Mike Powell commanded companies; Paul Holmes was the battalion Intelligence Officer. The battalion defended the cold and windy Yorkshire beaches, before being converted to an anti-tank role.

Hardy had to try and find temporaries, which meant the old or the unfit. Some stayed for the duration, others came and went. Foremost to re-join the Salopian colours was Johnny Key who had taught at the School since 1919 and had just entered a well-earned retirement. Ian Andrews describes his form's first view of this venerable figure:

He looked really really old and his gown hooked on at the level of the elbow. He had a shuffling gait and looked like an old owl who was asleep. Most certainly he was NOT asleep. He was an excellent teacher and maintained an iron grip on the class apparently with no particular effort.

Johnny Key taught French and German. 'He would address members of the form by their names translated into dog-French', David Horton remembers. 'One boy called Hambrook became Monsieur Jambon-Rouisseau'. Another temporary, Bill Cartwright, became a familiar figure. He had a German wife and lived at Westbury, coming in to early school on a milk float. He was not an enthusiast for Hitler but was for German culture. Unfortunately his grasp of form room discipline was insecure and many boys were not keen to learn their enemy's language. However he proved to be a major figure on the agricultural scene particularly on the Home Farm, though he had his eccentricities, collecting from the ash trays in the Common Room to use the product in some mysterious beneficial way and planting nails among the vegetables in the hope of introducing more iron.

Here is a recollection by Francis de Hamel of another temporary:

A new youngish master turned up and announced he was our new form master. On that first day he clapped his hands for silence and announced in a high pitched voice that he was always to be addressed as Lieutenant-Commander. We were gobsmacked. We had never before addressed any master with a title, always 'Sir'. And Lieutenant-Commander was no big deal – we had fathers and uncles with higher rank than that. When we got rowdy he would bang his desk-top and shout, 'Order!' This having little effect, he said he would report us to the Headmaster for 'insubordinate behaviour' – an unwise move which only encouraged us. Once things had become a near riot he really did his bun. In a fury he turned to the boy next to me and squeaked, 'You, boy, take a thousand penals!' There was a stunned silence. A 'penal' consisted of transcribing a lined foolscap page – about 33 lines – of Virgil or Ovid and it took about ten or fifteen minutes to write out one penal. But now, after ten seconds of silence while we mentally digested the implications of a *thousand* penals, all hell was let loose. We cheered, laughed and banged our desks in merriment. He stormed out of the form room and soon left the school. Why had he left the Navy?

Ronald Ridout was another temporary who found the going heavy, though he was an enthusiast for modern literature and set his Remove form to read O'Neill's *Mourning Becomes Electra*. Ralph Shuffrey recalls that:

Sadly he was totally incapable of keeping order. At the end of the period we would move our desks forward so that he was surrounded and unable to leave until he had remitted any punishments awarded.

But that was not the end of Ronald Ridout's connection with education. He wrote a series of textbooks on English Language teaching which spread on an astonishing scale. You could hardly enter a school in the British Commonwealth without encountering *Ridout*. He died worth many hundred thousand pounds.

Later came men of a different calibre; one was the Revd D. B. Kittermaster, master at Harrow for much of his life and famous for his sermons, some of which were published. John Beattie recollects that 'he was a fine orator jumping up and down in the pulpit. The content was memorable and the boys were entranced'. Another fine gentleman was O. P. Churchyard, who had taught at Tonbridge and had been a friend of Hardy's in the Rifle Brigade; sadly he died in 1943.

An extraordinary incident in the 1940 Michaelmas Term is remembered by Roger Buckley, John Lingford Hughes and others. Looking out of the windows of the School Building there came into view a German bomber, a Ju88, which was flying along the line of the river at a height which seemed almost lower than the top floor of the School Buildings, so near indeed that the crew were discernible. There was no official comment on this strange – and frightening – happening. Rumour suggested that the plane was following the river, that it later turned south, flew across the Bristol Channel and either crashed or was brought down in Somerset.

1941 opened with another winter of frost, snow and flood. Certainly school life was rigorous, with rationing beginning to bite and a consequent shortage of fuel to heat the Houses. Defying the eloquence of Godfray Le Quesne, the Debating

Society refused to condemn capital punishment; and, despite the School's classical tradition, a motion that 'the new world order should be founded on the principles of the classical philosophers' was lost. There was no lacking the customary lament that the whole place was going downhill, as a correspondent in *The Salopian* complained:

The number of unprivileged cyclists is ever increasing. Non-School Firsts walk about with their coats open and wearing multi-coloured handkerchiefs in their breast pockets, while the merest doul reposes on the seats on the pier. Have you, Sir, noticed any of this slackness?

Basil Oldham, whose activities in wartime were manifold, welcomed as School Librarian six hundred manuscripts and printed books sent for safety by the Royal Society of Antiquaries from London. It was also at this time that Miss Moser died. She had a life interest in her brother's collection of water colours, which now passed to the School where a room in the Moser Building had long been designated to receive it. As regards the display of the pictures and the appropriate furnishing of the room, a long controversy lay ahead, with J. B. O. showing himself at his most combative.

Normal events took place, varied by wartime activities such as Potato Planting Week, with Hope-Simpson to the fore. The School played a rugby fixture with Gordonstoun, then near Welshpool. Bernard Dobbs describes the occasion:

When our coach turned into the long avenue, we were amazed to see boys dressed in corduroy shorts and grey polo necks being encouraged over a complete military assault course. Events were signalled not by a bell but by a bugle. Despite the over-abundance of brawn and our team's general lack of experience, we won the match easily.

In the soccer world Shrewsbury defeated Westminster by 12 – 0, a score which stands in the record books; Alan Booth scored seven. The cricketers had a fine season with five victories which came to an end only when rain stopped play during the match against Westminster on the Worcester County Ground, Shrewsbury having declared at 275 for 8. Michael Ainsworth had

a season's average of 56 and James Mackinnon of 49. Thanks to
the initiative and hospitality of Eton, there was a miniature
regatta at Henley in which the 1st VIII took part.

Speech Day brought a small gathering of parents and other
visitors. The Dean of St Paul's presented the prizes. *The Salopian*
reports that his speech was largely concerned with the New
Order after the war. It also reported that 'few parents dressed for
the play'. A chapel collection for the Lord Mayor of Liverpool's
fund to assist those bombed out of their homes realised £11. 10s.
The Missioner reported that one third of the Club members
were homeless. This Speech Day saw for the first time the mass
Physical Training display by the whole school, acting in unison
to the music of the Band. It was to become an annual feature for
the next ten years.

Bumping Races were revived at the end of term, Tombling's
being Head of the River, thus underlining their remarkable
successes in most sporting fields at this time. It is interesting that
of all the boys rowing in Bumpers only two weighed twelve stone
or more.

In general the School had sustained the first two years of war
without fundamental change. Shropshire was a comparatively
safe area. Only once was a bomb dropped on the town,
presumably at random, by a bomber on the way home. The only
interesting target at this stage was the airfield at Shawbury, a
holding station for aircraft and a Flying Training School, which
was bombed three times in 1940, with little damage resulting.
On Kingsland there were occasional Alerts when boys spent
time in the basements or ground floors of their houses and
the characteristic sound of German bombers passing overhead
on their way to Liverpool became a familiar accompaniment to
summer evenings.

'Apart from minor irritations and inconveniences, the war has
intruded very little on our lives,' wrote the editor of *The Salopian*.
Hardy, however, described the Lent Term as 'the most ex-
hausting I have ever experienced'. But his end of term reflection
for his Governors was tranquil:

I must with all of us express profound thankfulness for the undisturbed nights which have hitherto been our portion and for the general physical tranquillity vouchsafed to us, in which there has been unexpectedly little to strain the nerves of the five hundred individuals, nine tenths of them young, who constitute the School in the 388th year of its history.

As the German bombing campaign developed, on some evenings a red glow in the sky could be seen over Birmingham. One occasion which brought Shropshire to the fore – although unknown at the time – was when the boffins 'bent the beam' by which German bombers navigated, so that instead of unloading on Birmingham a heavy attack was diverted to the Long Mynd, to the great surprise of the local sheep.

Michaelmas 1941 saw the numbers sink to 440 boys – forty-four less than in 1939 – provoking speculation that some drastic re-organisation might be necessary. Alec Peterson now left the staff to take up a Government post in the psychological warfare department. Hardy was not pleased. He wrote in his report to the Governors that Peterson had been 'tempted by an offer of work in a civilian capacity at a salary much in excess of that considered adequate for men who offer their lives as subalterns'. In fact Peterson had a distinguished career and became Deputy Director of Psychological Warfare on Mountbatten's staff in the South East Asia command. Later during the Malaya emergency in the 1950s, General Templer specifically asked for him as Director-General of Information Services. Murray Senior also left to go into Intelligence. Alec Binney was under the umbrella of SOE and disappeared to do mysterious things in West Africa.

Another who disappeared at this time was the Revd Humphrey Beevor, School Chaplain, to become a Chaplain in the Navy – the prelude to a career which saw him become Editor of the *Church Times* (in which capacity he signed up the young cub reporter Edward Heath), and Bishop of the African diocese of Lebombo, finishing his working life as a Housemaster at King's School, Canterbury. He was succeeded by a distinguished classical scholar, Guy Furnivall, a man of simple yet powerful faith. Discipline in the form room in the lower regions of the

School did not, however, come easily to him. Another who was to make a considerable impression on the Salopian scene was Bandmaster Allsebrook. He succeeded CSM Addison, who will be fondly remembered by members of the Band which he really created in the years following its foundation in 1935. Allsebrook had been in the 17th/21st Lancers and at first found the transition difficult but soon established his own way, the boys rather enjoying his generally pessimistic outlook. At a time when the Band was in good shape, a friend remarked to him that at the forthcoming concert the performance should be good. 'There are times when I've been more despondent', was the reply, which was about as optimistic as he could get. Bandsmen will remember with pleasure the opportunities which wartime brought, not only in the Corps but in the form of outside engagements in the town such as War Weapons Week, Salute the Soldier Week, Wings for Victory and various fundraising events.

Until his departure in 1943 to be Music Director of the Liverpool Council of Social Service, Toby Barnaby played a major role in providing entertainment in the form of visiting lecturers and musicians. The list is impressive – Leon Goosens, Ida Haendal, Myra Hess, Eileen Joyce, Irene Kohler, Cyril Smith. The Shrewsbury Orchestral Society held their concerts in the Alington Hall as the Music Hall had been taken over by the Royal Army Pay Corps. Clifford Curzon was one of several distinguished artists who played with them under the energetic baton of Frederic Morris. The visits were not without their perils; the piano broke down twice when Myra Hess was playing; after the second time she was heard to mutter, 'Now for Beechers Brook'. Nor were the soloists without critics. It is worth quoting Toby Barnaby's critique of a performance by Ida Haendal which is typical of his wit and erudition:

Miss Haendal then played a group of solos, (a), (b) and (c). I have forgotten what their other titles were but you can look them up in the programme. The Devil, at some time in their career, seems to have come to all performers, especially violinists, and shown them all the audiences of the world in a moment of time, saying, 'All these will

29

fall down and worship you if you will only play them Tripe'. Hence (a), (b) and (c). The Tripe may be beautifully served, and subtly garnished, but it still remains fundamentally, immutably and inescapably, Tripe.

There is no novelty in this. The device is at least as old as Homer. The bard Demodocus, having reduced Odysseus to tears with Piece (a), 'The Strife of Agamemnon and Achilles', and having tried to tickle the fancy of that much enduring man with (b) 'Ares and Aphrodite' (for adults only), finally brought the house down with (c) 'The Battle of Troy', and would doubtless have obliged with further 'Selections from Homer' (arr. Demodocus) had not Alcinous applied the closure by ordering drinks all round. Even so did Miss Haendal purvey (to borrow a metaphor from heraldry) (a) The Tripe Dormant, (b) The Tripe Sinister, and (c) The Tripe Rampant. But for us (alas!) there was no worldly Alcinous.

On another somewhat less distinguished occasion, a rather elderly quartet were entertaining the School before 3rd Lesson. The music did not exactly stir the blood but, to the performers' surprised delight, enormous applause greeted their efforts and encores were both called for and played. They did not realise that every minute they played was a minute off 3rd Lesson; Hardy sat in a black cloud trying not to look at his watch.

Tony Barnaby also arranged lectures, either for the whole school or for senior boys, and secured some good speakers, among them Brigadier Sandford on Abyssinia, where he played an important role as a close friend of the Emperor, Sir Ronald Storrs, diplomat of wide experience on the Middle East of which he probably had more experience than any other Englishman, and Laurence Housman on his brother. Later in the war came the electrifying Harry Rée (OS) a major figure in the French Resistance and Quintin Hogg (later Lord Hailsham) with an exciting vision of the post war world.

George Simmons continued as before the war to produce the annual Speech Day play – 'The Late Christopher Bean', 'I Killed the Count', 'Busman's Honeymoon' and similar comedies. George with his consistent good humour and sense of fun was a much liked figure on the staff, whether he was leading a platoon in the Home Guard or attracting a boy's wandering attention in a French lesson by the despatch of a well-aimed piece of chalk. (Today no doubt this would lead to a court case.)

So the narrow school world was penetrated by instruction, information and entertainment from outside. Life was not all corps parades and planting potatoes (though Hope-Simpson did this year supervise the planting of 6000 spring cabbages with the help of six volunteers per House). The accounts of the Debating Society make interesting reading. The anti-German mood seemed to strengthen. The moral case for fighting the war had been put in a 1939 pamphlet by Cyril Alington, then Dean of Durham, entitled 'The Last Crusade', which treated the enemy as misguided and mistaken but not wholly bad.

But by 1942 a different note was heard. A motion that 'This House recommends the imposition of drastic reprisals after the war' was carried 61–23. As the editor of *The Salopian* mused:

we were fighting two years ago to make the world safe for people to live in; now the cry has changed and the watchword is revenge; we fight now it seems, to bring not safety to all men but extermination to the inhabitants of Germany.

In another issue of the magazine, the editor calls for increased effort:

Are we doing our best? Is the School on the whole pulling its weight or does slackness still hide somewhere? There is a time for play and a time for work and the battles of the empire must be fought in form room and on the Common, on the land and in our daily life.

Patriotism was indeed strong and in another debate the House agreed that 'it would welcome some sort of national service after the war'. (They certainly got it; national service stretched on for nearly twenty years after this debate).

Among the leavers at the end of the Summer Term 1941 was a group of Ridgemount boys, Tony Lee, David Beswick, Robin Guy and Paul Hawkins, who all joined the navy; Allan Gibson joined the RAF and Ken Rhodes the Army. They were soon scattered about the world and Robin Guy's father suggested that a way of keeping in touch was for letters to be sent to him and he

would copy them to all; this he did. To-day Ken Rhodes has all
41 air letter cards. Robin Guy recalls that the war provided
opportunities for unusual activities, one of which was volunteering to go down to the machine shops at the Technical
College to make small parts for munitions. With a friend,
dressed in cloth caps and overalls, they took a glass of beer at the
Old Post Office, both on their way there and back, together with
a Balkan Sobranie, and joined the factory workers. Unfortunately these endeavours came to a sudden stop when Housemaster Kitchin discovered that the machine shop had closed for
holidays some time earlier.

So the term ended and another contingent of Salopians was
almost immediately absorbed into HM Forces. Rowland Guy
wrote:

We went to Chapel for the last time and were admonished to be sober
and vigilant. Distantly could be heard the town band playing in the
Quarry – a customary accompaniment to Chapel in the summer
evenings. Suddenly we realised that our school days had disappeared
for ever as we sang 'God be with you till we meet again'. The prayer
worked for some but not others as the school war memorial sadly
testified in years to come. And so we left to join the turmoil and
excitement of late 1941.

4

Marching and Digging

NINETEEN FORTY TWO was a disastrous year for the Allies: the surrender at Singapore of more than 70,000 men, the loss of Burma and the two capital ships, *Prince of Wales* and *Repulse*; the loss of Tobruk and Rommel's advance to the Egyptian border; the continued German offensive in Russia and the siege of Stalingrad; the increasing toll of shipping by the U Boats; the disaster of the Dieppe raid. All made for general gloom.

Shrewsbury School had by now settled into its wartime guise; few boys could remember the School in peacetime. Uniform school dress had been abandoned and boys were allowed to wear 'sober coloured jackets'. How to define that expression? Bernard Dobbs was rebuked by Hardy for wearing 'a horsecloth'. The effusive Willie Court's mauve jacket was definitely ruled out. Hardy's comments on infringements were generally colourful. A boy of whose haircut he did not approve was said to look like 'a bookmaker's assistant'. (What experience can Hardy have had of bookmakers' assistants?) Top hats and tails gradually disappeared, the last person to be so equipped being Godfray Le Quesne who wore this distinguishing dress until he left in July 1942.

Hardy continually strove to keep the School as normal as possible and this was the gist of his Speech Day addresses and his termly reports to his Governors. The academic programme did suffer to some extent because of the presence of the temporary masters, but classical teaching – the main intellectual trunk of the School – maintained its customary high standard through the powerful team of Jimmy Street, Stacy Colman, Harry Dawson and Jim Pitts-Tucker with Frankie Barnes providing the classical *hors d'oeuvres* to the younger age group. The determined and deliberate teaching of David Bevan and Johnny Key successfully pushed both the willing and the less willing through the School Certificate. Appearing in various roles, though nominally teaching modern languages, Frank McEachran floated about in the timetable, scattering Spells as he went, adding his own ingredients of philosophy and literature. One form, when asked by him if they wanted to do Higher Certificate German or be educated, opted for the latter, to their great benefit. The average annual number of Oxford and Cambridge awards throughout the war numbered ten. In these mid-war years the names of Timothy Cross, Lawson, Le Quesne, Sloane-Stanley, Van Agnew, Dunce, Stinton, Treasure and James Mackinnon are amongst those which appear on the Honours Boards.

Hardy regretted the absence of 18 year olds who were now being called up earlier, as this took away much of the leadership normally provided by boys in their last year. The Universities and Services were now providing six month courses before call up which were naturally attractive. The average age of the staff was high and much was lost through the absence of energetic younger masters, though it is worth recording that the masters' fives team of Sale, Street, Phillips, Matthews, Pitts-Tucker and Colman defeated the school team – a game where guile counted as much as fitness. There was much delight when Mike Powell returned to the staff in 1942, having been placed in a low medical category which meant a desk job at Copthorne Barracks from which Hardy managed to disentangle him after months of negotiation with the War Office, who both lost the papers and then confused him with his brother. Mike Powell was then thirty-two and had had two years army experience.

The two occupations which inevitably filled many hours were the Corps and farming. David Bevan was in command and at his right hand those well remembered NCOs, RSM Evans and CSM Blud, both immaculately turned out. Evans had been awarded an MC in the First War, a rare decoration for an NCO. He seldom spoke unless spoken to but never lacked an answer to any military question, a man always to be found in the right place at the right time. Blud was a first class marksman and had a remarkable aptitude for handling weapons; he too had been decorated and held the Military Medal. He always took the Recruits squad and many will remember their first military experience under his watchful eye or their first firing of ball ammunition under his supervision.

By 1942 the First World War uniform had been replaced by battle dress. To turn out in the old uniform had required considerable effort. The green webbing – belt and braces – had to be cleaned as did the brass buttons of the jacket; then the long puttees were wound round the leg between knee and ankle. If they were too tight the blood stream suffered; if too loose they could come down on parade, trailing like the tail of a comet, and cause great embarrassment. The old Italian rifles were both long and heavy and were very unpopular; one boy remembers the whole bolt action falling off while he marched. They were to be replaced as supplies became available.

To Hardy's annoyance the name OTC was abandoned and the contingent became part of the Junior Training Corps. Hardy maintained that training officers was an exact description of what the Corps was about. Each House had a platoon with three infantry sections, consisting in theory of eight boys with rifles, a Bren gunner and a Sten gunner. In 1942 the KSLI badge was adopted, satirised irreverently as 'King Solomon's Last Issue'. The immediate object of the cadets was to pass Certificate A which showed a reasonable level of competence and was thought to assist one on the way to a commission. The exam took a whole day between nine o'clock and five at the Barracks, part of the syllabus being to drill conscripted recruits who were training at the Barracks and who were not enthusiastic.

Once or twice a term there were Field Days which were most elaborate exercises. First, fall in by House platoons, correctly dressed with packed lunch and full water bottle; then fall in by Companies; finally the whole Battalion paraded outside

Oldham's on the Common. With the Commanding Officer at the head (in pre-war days the immaculate figure of Major West, booted and spurred), the parade moved off to the music of the Band. Eyes right at the War Memorial, then down to the Kingsland Bridge, where the command 'break step' was given, the subversives in the back rank giving the counter order 'break wind' *sotto voce*. Then over St John's Hill, passing the Exchange and Mart (out of bounds) where it was said to be possible to sell your text books, and so up Pride Hill, all traffic being stopped. This was the best part of the march as Salopian citizens lined the road and the Band was at its most powerful, enjoying the resonance of the high buildings on either side. 'A' Company was in the lead (School House and Rigg's) led by the indomitable Captain Hope-Simpson who gave the impression that he had been leading 'A' Company since the Hundred Years War. On the right was the famed shop of Pelican Snelson, Cigar Importer, whose sign was so enjoyed by Neville Cardus; on the left was Morris's café, a popular venue with the boys (Chelsea buns for 2d) and then the Raven Hotel, used by many generations of parents; on past Sidoli's, another well known name (poor Dominic Sidoli was rounded up together with other aliens in the summer of 1940 and served his time in the Isle of Man) and past the Old Schools, under the stony gaze of Charles Darwin, and so to the station. Here awaited a special train which took the battalion to near-by places such as Cressage, Leaton or Leebotwood for a few hours of internecine warfare. Those with responsibility were carefully briefed as to what was meant to take place but for the PBI it was as real warfare was, a period of manning a ditch or hedge, a few impulsive movements at the double and the hopeful discharge of blank ammunition in the supposed direction of the enemy. Rowland Guy described a Field Day as 'a kind of armed picnic'. Charles Appleton found these days 'very like a real life battle – SNAFU'. Robin Jenks found the bayonet an excellent tool for opening a tin of condensed milk. So at about 3.30 a bugle was blown for the ceasefire, to be at once followed by a burst of intense firing as unused blanks were discharged. At the tea RV would be found the dependable CSM Blud with tea and buns before the train back and the march up to Kingsland. Raymond Eccleston has a good description of such a day:

One half of us climbed up a hill which we had to defend while the other half of us were to attack it. It was a filthy day, mostly raining and we ate sodden sandwiches and waited for an attack which never came. The ground sheets of the wise virgins became as blotting paper and they were as soaked as the foolish virgins who had left theirs behind to save weight. When we came to entrain again we entered the carriage full of steaming bodies and angrily asked the opposition why their attack never materialised. Equally angry they asked why we had not defended the hill. It transpired that we had defended one hill while they had attacked another! Oh, the inexpressible joy of a hot (communal) bath and the comfort of a clean, dry, warm bed. Practically the whole school was late for 1st lesson the next day.

Another Field Day recollection is that of Hal Dixon, a signaller:

In one inter-school battle we got one radio, a spare, on to the enemy net and with false orders got them to evacuate a hill before we attacked it. This was most satisfying to us in the Signals but it deprived part of our side of one of the two scheduled battles; the infantry probably had a miserable time, since battles formed the one reward for carrying the heavy rifle all day.

Most boys had Corps parades on three days in the week. It was not all drudgery as there were opportunities for senior boys to have motor cycle training; the scientists were introduced to army signalling; and the Bren gun was found to be a more effective weapon than the old Lewis gun. The Sten was also introduced; did it really only cost five shillings to produce as was rumoured? It was not a popular weapon and thought to be too capable of delivering 'friendly fire' as illustrated by John Beilby's experience:

The incident centres on a firing range on a Field Day. The weather was bad but instruction in the use of automatic weapons proceeded. Our (post Cert A) section was lined up with our fully-loaded Sten guns on safety, waiting for CSM Blud to give the order to fire. He was standing between us and the targets. Before any order could be given, a sharp burst of fire issued from the weapon of a chap next to me. Bullets hit the soft ground immediately in front of the CSM, spraying him from boots to cap badge with mud. To his credit, he stood his ground long enough to issue those expletives most likely to bring the nerve-shattering incident to an end – no one was hurt and the firing continued as planned.

Seemingly endless Corps parades might cause some grumbling but morale remained high. Boys knew well enough that the majority would soon be in the army and this was an introduction; Cert A was important. It was thought at the time that there was an advantage in volunteering instead of waiting to be conscripted, thus enabling a choice of regiment. Later in the war when Ernest Bevin had introduced coal mining into national service – every tenth conscript, it was said – volunteering could enable one to escape this fate. Raymond Eccleston went down town to a school which had been taken over by the army, in order to volunteer. He recalls:

We started off by filling in papers and squeezed ourselves behind the requisitioned desks intended for small children. The Sergeant in charge first asked who could not read and write. 'What a stupid question', I thought. Imagine my amazement when half a dozen hands went up. We were a very mixed bunch. Later we were medically examined and the rumour went round that one of our number had been turned down as being a hermaphrodite! It was an enlightening experience. Next day I was sworn in and took my oath.

Raymond Guy reflected on these days of high military endeavour:

Only we stood between the Germanic hordes and Wales though I don't think the Welsh fully appreciated their good fortune.

After the excitements, invasion fears and improvisations of 1940, the Home Guard had settled into a properly structured addendum to the regular army. David Bevan commanded 'K' Company with his three platoons led by Lieutenant Childs, Captain Simmons and Lieutenant Colman; there were between

S. S. Sopwith, Housemaster in his Oldham's Study in 1940. (Eton collars were soon to disappear.)

Off on a Field Day.

David Bevan labours
at a forestry camp.

To everyone who has or can get an allotment or garden

Owing to the shipping position we shall need every bit of food we can possibly grow at home.

Last summer many gardens had a surplus of perishable vegetables such as lettuce and cabbage. This winter those same gardens are getting short not only of keeping vegetables such as onions, carrots and other root crops, but also of fresh winter vegetables such as late cabbage, savoys and kale.

We <u>must</u> try to prevent that happening this year. Next winter is going to be a critical period.

This leaflet tells you how to crop your ground to the best advantage so as to get vegetables all the year round.

Please study it carefully and carry out the advice it contains.

MINISTER OF AGRICULTURE & FISHERIES.

Farming Supremo:
R. St J. Pitts Tucker.

A-farming we will go.

Digging for
Victory?
Break for music:
Peter Bowring,
Henry Bowring,
John Rhys

Digging for
victory at
Severn Hill.
Note air raid
shelter in
foreground.

On the Home Farm (Sanatorium in background).

RSM Joyce.

PT on Speech Day

Break PT.

Break PT.

80 and 90 boys in the ranks. The company was now a mobile reserve to the Battalion, bicycles ensuring mobility; each section had a Bren gun and held centrally were five heavy Browning machine guns under the command of Major A. H. Pearson, a noted figure of the time, who had been a machine gunner in the First War and awarded an MC. Ammunition was in short supply; each gun had two filled belts with fifteen belts in reserve. Another weapon which was handled rather gingerly was the Blacker Bombard. Francis de Hamel recalls:

We used to practice with this device for hours outside the Armoury, fitting the parts together and taking them apart again by numbers. The Bomber launched from a sort of sloping steel downpipe a large mortar bomb with fins. It gave a big bang and was lots of fun. The shell whistled through the air in a huge trajectory to land, one hoped, on the enemy a couple of hundred yards away. I enjoyed firing this thing. We demolished things on the range. Like wooden sheds. Or we pretended we had.

Home Guard parades and exercises were frequent and often wide-ranging. One exercise in 1942 went on for 48 hours; the School timetable had to be modified. Training in the countryside was made more difficult because all road signs had been removed so that map reading was of the first importance. On one practice Alert, David Bevan went to his HQ, which was the orderly room, to hear that enemy parachutists had been located in the water tower fields. On asking what initial action had been taken by the duty officer he was told that a Commando had been sent out. 'And who was in the Commando?' said Bevan. 'Mr Oldham, Fred the Ferryman and that boy from the Tech', was the answer. Of such were Commandos made.

The war to Basil Oldham was a godsend. Now fully recovered from his breakdown in 1932, he found a new lease of life in military activity. He was wanted! As Quartermaster of 'K' Company he kept the Company stores in his cellar at Little Grange in Kennedy Road. Later when cadet forces were formed from schools in the town, he became a Company commander with the rank of Major, thus combining the roles of CQMS and Officer and constantly changing his battle dress with the

MARCHING AS TO WAR

relevant badges so that he knew when to salute and when to be saluted. His town cadets soon had the status that boys in his House had occupied and he oversaw their lives in every particular, even forming a confirmation class with the confirmation service taking place in the School Chapel.

The real excitement for the Home Guard had come in September 1940, in the school holidays, when the code name CROMWELL was flashed round the country, meaning 'Invasion imminent'. David Bevan gives a graphic account of this long night as he and his adjutant, Charlie Larkin, sat in the Orderly Room having mustered the troops to their prepared positions and waiting developments. In fact the alert had been signalled because a fleet of fishing boats in the West Country had been unidentified as they returned to port; the next morning the troops stood down. The other vital code word was OLIVER, which was never used, meaning that invasion had actually occurred, the receipt of which meant setting up road blocks and other obstacles. There were 50 Molotov cocktails per block and in Woodfield Road alone were sixteen anti-tank obstacles and a large number of 'hairpins' (what were they?). How effective the Home Guard would have been is a matter for conjecture but there was no lack of effort. (David Bevan's Secret Operation Order No.1 was, 'If invasion comes, lock Hardy in the Chapel').

Looking back it really seems somewhat absurd to envisage that the German army would actually appear in Shropshire. The Germans would have had to have marched for 250 miles from the south coast, by which time the battle would long since have been lost or won. One boy, digging a weapon pit to cover the Kingsland Bridge, did wonder to himself in what possible circumstances he could actually find himself firing at Germans out of it. It was difficult to imagine why any enemy tactician should be in the least interested in Shropshire, the occupation of which would entail no military advantage save the closure of a railway station of some importance – but of no greater importance than a dozen others. However the need to be doing what was done everywhere – putting the country in a posture of defence – was paramount from the psychological point of view, however dubious the value of the actual defences. A message from the local Home Guard commander radiated the general feeling: 'All should know that the force is taking an increasingly important part in the whole plan of Imperial Defence'.

.

5

The Domestic Front

To make the boys fit to fight there was no greater fanatic than Sergeant-Major Joyce. 'What I want is the man with guts, courage and dash', he proclaimed. Raymond Eccleston remembers Joyce's approach to war:

Don't stick the bayonet in here', Joyce demonstrated, indicating his stomach, 'stick it in here', he said, indicating his throat. With that he brought out a bayonet training stick, a long bamboo pole with a canvas bobble on one end and a wire loop at the other end. Swinging this round his head , he charged at the assembled class. We fled. We fled up the ropes. We fled up the wall bars. We fled anywhere to get out of the way of this whirling dervish. Some followed behind him at what they thought was a safe distance until he turned on them and chased them. He sought to raise the blood lust of a callow youth of 14 who had no thought of even harming a fly and whose blood was thoroughly chilled by the spectacle! I served in the army for four years after leaving school but never met anyone half as bloodthirsty as Sergeant-Major Joyce.

When there was much talk of enemy parachutists, Joyce had the boys jumping from the wall bars to simulate falling from a parachute; and then even jumping from the balcony, which was really quite high, until a broken leg put an end to this particular exercise.

Physical Training was always at the forefront of Hardy's mind. It was he who had caused the gymnasium to be erected in 1938; there followed the series of PT tests – Standard, 1st Class and Special. The latter was extremely difficult and few succeeded; it carried the status of a School First.

On Speech Day there was also a Physical Training Display by

a selected squad in which the acrobatics of Micky Jones were noticeable – Hardy called them 'perilous'. Micky was in the football XI and used to enliven the half time intervals by walking round the centre circle on his hands. Another Hardy innovation was a short session of PT in the morning break, under House arrangements; it was not popular.

Boxing was a further activity which flourished under the general direction of David Bevan, himself a boxing Blue. The inter-House contests in the gym were theatrical, the ring brilliantly lit, the audience – which was large – silent and appreciative; David Bevan as referee, judges from outside the School and Major Pearson with the stop watch – three one minute rounds. 'Well fought Blue, Red the winner', announced Bevan, in his deliberate way. 'When I say, " 'Box on!' – Box on; Box on!" '. *The Salopian* commented:

The standard of fighting was high but too few people made any attempt to hit their opponents' bodies, the majority preferring bleeding noses and black eyes.

Apart from military activity another large scale wartime occupation came into being – farming. The School Site was gradually developed as different areas were dug or ploughed, the main centre being the so-called Home Farm where the Craft Centre now is. At peak output, seven tons of potatoes were grown, enough to feed the whole school for a month. Other plots were situated behind Kingsland House and on the Craig Fields; and beside the drive by Severn Hill and outside Oldham's. There was a good deal of digging by the boys to establish these plots – heavy work on clay soil. John Chavasse was heard to say that he would rather move heaven than earth. In addition to potatoes, leeks, beets, turnips and carrots were raised. Hope-Simpson, a horticulturist of great skill, and Bill Cartwright were the organisers of these plots on the Site.

Help to farmers had started in a small way in 1940 but this activity expanded enormously under the direction of Jim Pitts-Tucker. Jim was really a pacifist Christian and had much wrestling with his conscience as his friends on the staff went off

43

to join the Forces. However he really found his metier in the organisation of agricultural assistance to farmers. Every half holiday up to 150 boys went off into the countryside, some on bicycles, some picked up by farmers. The work was hard – singling beet was particularly back breaking but there was the satisfaction of being paid as well as helping the war effort. Rates varied, often 6d or 8d an hour. An afternoon's work produced a sum which would buy a pint of bitter and five Woodbines for refreshment on the way home. These half holidays were popular with some; better to be out in the country than condemned to an afternoon of second leagues. But much depended on the weather.

In the holidays all those eligible were urged to go on farming camps. The way had already been shown by forestry camps at Burwarton on the Boyne estate in 1940. An epic poem in *The Salopian* describes the joys of camping and the attendant Herculean labours:

> The youths meanwhile their weary limbs have strewn
> In the balmy sleep, nor yet expect the dawn,
> What time the drowsy god upon them smiles,
> Granting oblivion of the morrow's toils;
> When, hark! The zealous TUCKER bids them rise,
> Expelling Morpheus with his strident noise,
> Rousing the youth by stimulating din
> Of breath exhaled through instrument of tin.
> The blatant music smites the dullard ear;
> They groan, apprised that breakfast time draws near....
>
> Again, PITTS-TUCKER sounds the horrid blast,
> Urging the crew to seek with haste
> On wheeled engines borne, the sylvan groves.
> Swift down the track the legion moves....
> Here Nordic SKINNER, famed as Rover Scout,
> Plies his tough axe amidst the sylvan rout,
> Here ruddy WILLIAMSON and NASMITH small
> Do four men's work, nor seem to tire at all,
> Here clamorous DIXEY leads the Moser crew
> Here Olly JOHNSON carves the branches through.

Industrious wights! May Jove benignant smile
Upon those hours of unremitting toil!
Not soon to faithful foresters comes rest
Who labour at the Boyne's Estate behest.

In 1941 four large farming camps had been arranged by the organisational skills of Jim Pitts-Tucker. These lasted for three or four weeks and made a considerable hole in the holiday, some of which for most had already been taken up by Corps Camp. The camps were arranged according to the requirements of the Ministry of Agriculture and upwards of 250 boys worked in them, some in Shropshire, others in Gloucestershire and one – an Oldham's speciality – at Little Barrington in Oxfordshire. This was run with great efficiency by Willie Matthews while the Housemaster Sopwith flew his flag in the nearby bar of the Bay Tree, a comfortable hotel. 'I have a distaste for messing about with the soil', he is said to have admitted. Wives of staff did the cooking, daughters often came too so there was a veneer of civilisation. One camper remembers returning after a sweaty day's work to see Sallie Colman sitting in a deck chair, reading a novel, stroking the cat in her lap while a wireless played softly in the background. These camps continued until 1945, attended by an increasing number of boys and staff. Though the work was hard, mostly stooking, the atmosphere was relaxed, the discipline light and staff and boys mixed happily; boys also got to know contemporaries in other Houses whom they would not have come across on the Site.

And there were experiences and contacts – sometimes with Land Girls. David Horton recollects meeting a POW called Alphonse, whom the farmer in charge called Umflus, a courteous man who had been a lawyer. Jeffrey Lee and a friend worked for a farmer called Dan:

when the weather was unsuitable for cutting, he showed us how to harness an enormous horse and how to control it. We were sent off to a field to cart chaff. We were of course horrified but the horse was quite marvellous and never misbehaved; we carted chaff all day.

45

In other camps senior boys were taught how to drive Fordson tractors. Richard Sinnett found that farming had its compensations, being one of a group of boys who helped the Revd E. M. Cooke, Vicar of Westbury. At one time School Missioner in Everton and driver of the Old Salopian ambulance in the First War, the Vicar had been at Shrewsbury from 1897 to 1902. He had had a nephew in Oldham's and had formed an affinity with the House where he was a well-known figure: 'Cooke's yer uncle'. The result of helping him on his glebe land was, according to Richard Sinnett, very worthwhile: 'We had a wizard feed afterwards, lettuce, goose eggs and salad, bottled blackberries and gats of <u>real</u> cream and lots of creamy cakes and buns to finish with'.

Nearer home, Charles Appleton and his friend Rutledge enterprisingly rented an allotment near the Kingsland Bridge from the local Council. They sold the produce to their House and did well financially. Francis de Hamel volunteered to learn to plough. Leaving Severn Hill at 5.30 am he was taken to nearby fields in the dark before dawn to crank a reluctant Fordson tractor which supplied the motive power. Having learnt how to mark out plots, he became an accomplished ploughman. Derek Lea was shocked when, accompanying a farmer to Ludlow market where a flock of sixty sheep was purchased, he was told to take them back to the farm a couple of miles away. Mounted on his bicycle, he found that the sheep somehow knew the right road. As the war went on there were more and more POWs working in the Shropshire fields. Ian Andrews remembers that the Italians 'were very entertaining, with spectacular tales of their amorous adventures whilst our amorous adventures amounted to nil'.

Wartime was the golden age of the bicycle. Restricted to a privileged few before the war, they were now essential to the war effort. With very little traffic on the roads, boys travelled far into the countryside on the week-ends, visiting distant places in Wales, calling at pubs for the sustaining pint and seeking out farms and places where one could get food off the ration, particularly eggs. Not that food was always the object; Peter

Bowring had sisters at Moreton Hall where he and his friends migrated on Sunday afternoons

taking tea with three or four attractive budding nymphets in the headmistress's drawing room, struck speechless with pubescent passion, to whom we would write ardent letters the following week.

The distances covered by the bicycle were extraordinary. Peter Cator thought nothing of cycling to Llangollen for lunch and then back; at the end of term he cycled to Cambridge in a day. Charles Appleton measured ten thousand miles between 1941 and 1943. John Lea and David Rutherford held the London record – 169 miles in 13 hours. An additional wartime hazard was the removal of all signposts so that the Germans, having landed, would not know where they were. Philip Welch writes:

What a joy it was on Sunday afternoons in the summer, or on Ascension Day to be able to cycle towards Welshpool, naming all the pubs in German – I can only remember "Die Sieben Sterne" - over Wenlock Edge, by train to Church Stretton to climb the Long Mynd and eat tea in Carding Mill Valley.

Farming certainly added a new dimension to school life. At the end of the war the Ministry of Agriculture gave its opinion that Shrewsbury had provided more help to farmers than any other school – a pleasing reflection on the work of Jim Pitts-Tucker, his many helpers and the legion of willing (or unwilling) volunteers.

As the war years passed, the sustaining of the domestic front became more and more difficult. Boys did their own chores, domestic servants were hard to come by and often of unreliable quality. Housemaster's wives did an immense amount of work themselves. Ridgemount had a contact with a priest in Ireland who persuaded girls to come over and work; Oldham's were happy to have a stable couple, Mr and Mrs Rushworth. Ration books were of prime importance and as some foods were issued on an individual basis, each boy had his 2oz of butter per week, his 6oz of margarine, his 1oz of cheese, with sugar when available; those who did not take sugar with their tea sent their portion home to Mum to make jam.

Adolescents (they were not teenagers in those days) are always hungry. But having said that there seems general agreement that the standard of food in most Houses was pretty good considering the circumstances. The rations were supplemented as far as possible. For some time the School Shop was able to continue with 'Shop teas' (typically sausage and chips) but this gradually came to an end. Every month there was a surge of buying as the sweet ration became available. Food parcels from home kept up morale, though few were as fortunate as Rowland Guy who had a brace of pheasants sent most weeks in the season. Martin Wemyss, with a highlander friend, had a reliable source of venison, which hung in his study locker before being stewed. Kim Dodwell kept a rifle with a silencer and telescopic sights in his study which was bad news for the rabbits who used to gambol round the Smokers' Trees of an evening. One boy received an occasional orange – but his mother asked him to send back the peel (marmalade?). There were times when some dishes proved too much for the palate. In School House one table unanimously rejected cauliflower cheese only to be compelled to eat it by Dougie Saunders, Head of House. When Severn Hill rejected some very smelly herrings they were told that 'a hundred million people in the world would give their souls for a nice fresh herring'. Nor did whalemeat, sago and tripe stand much chance with the traditional schoolboy. It was found that the slit trenches outside Oldham's were fertile soil for marrows, a dish which the boys saw rather too often. Fruit appeared only in season; bananas were unknown though Philip Welch records that he was sent a banana which was so precious that he limited himself to one bite a week. Jam was rationed and each boy had a jam jar; the amount varied in quantity and in quality. Oldham's used to be given pots which bore the label 'Red Plum Stoneless' soon re-christened to 'Red Stone Plumless'. Only now can a crime committed by Donald Walker (who was captain of the Home Farm) be admitted:

The one vegetable we all loathed in Oldham's was parsnips; perhaps it was the way they were served up but they were dry, woody and quite revolting. Late one night when the new crop was just showing above the ground I stole out of the House, crept down to the shed, mixed up some strong weed killer and watered the lot! Parsnips never appeared on the menu again.

If you could get down town (wearing your 'basher' with the band in House colours), food could be bought at Morris's or Sidoli's; or, if parents came, which was not often, there was the prospect of filling meals at The Raven, The Lion or The George. And there was still available a good old stand-by in its traditional form – fish and chips wrapped in newspaper. So by various expedients, hungry youth was kept alive and indeed physically fit. No obesity in those days.

6

Hard Times

As 1942 turned into 1943 the country's morale was lifted by the victory at Alamein and by the German defeat at Stalingrad. How much did these events impinge on the lives of the boys? Some followed the war news avidly but for most the war was a backcloth against which they lived their Salopian lives which to them were wholly normal; boys accept what is without bothering to think what might be or might have been. There was no television; there might be a wireless in the House Headroom but it would not be an accompaniment to life. (The rule in School House was that you could have a wireless if you built it.) There were the truncated newspapers of the day (four sheets) but most boys did not go further than a glance at the headlines. Few looked far ahead. There was not much point in planning a career when national service stretched into an indefinite future.

As their predecessors had before them, the boys concentrated on school life with its regular routines – work, games, amusements, the social scene. Patrick Lacey remembers that the foremost event in the first year of the war was the footballing triumph of his House, Headroom, in defeating the hitherto triumphant Tombling's in both Cup and League. Richard Sinnett has the complete set of the letters to his parents ('Thank you very much for the wizard parcel') in which he speaks of his running successes:

When I get my house colours I can have a house tie, use the monitors' bath in the changing room without permission and walk under a clump of trees outside the House called the Oasis. I can also go about the

House with my coat open. I am getting my running colours (crossed chocolate horns) embroidered on to my running vest down at Afford's.

No wartime relaxation of the hierarchical and privilege-ridden society detectable here!

Mr Afford was a familiar figure, visiting each House every week to take orders for clothes, though most boys would be buying from the second hand market. Another familiar figure circulating daily in his smart Wolseley car, trilby hat and well-tailored suit was Dr Urwick, for many years MO to the School and active in councils of both town and school. An even more familiar figure disappeared in 1942. This was Fred the Ferryman who lived in the cottage by the boathouse. Fred was quite a young man and it was a long time before he was called up – much later than his age group. When investigation took place it was found that some clerk, puzzled as to what category a ferryman should be in, had marked him down as a Merchant Seaman and as such he was not of course called up.

John Moulsdale (1940–45) still possesses his diary of those years. He finds only two mentions of the war – a lecture on the campaign in Libya and the sounding of church bells to celebrate the desert victory of 1942. Otherwise the normal events of school life fill the pages:

12 Feb. Horrible cold and miserable corps parade. 15 March. Another awful corps parade – retreat from school bank to water tower. 19 June. V hot battalion parade – practice for inspection!

As may be gathered Moulsdale was not very keen on the Corps and transferred to the Air section which was run with great efficiency by the Revd L. F. Harvey (wearing his clerical collar with his RAF uniform) and Willie Matthews. Games dominate the diary entries.

14 Feb. Did five changes in the day – Form PT, Fives, Rugger and Fives again. 21 Feb. Ghastly House tow (run) over Senior Bumph Hunts course and got back late for lunch but managed a fives game after that!

Sundays provided a contrast: often he biked to Montford Bridge and bathed in the river there. On Ascension Day he 'biked to Oswestry – ate ration lunches – no luck with flicks –

walk in country, got lost, wizard tea – v sappy ride back to be in time'. And there were other recreations:

We went to the cinema fairly regularly, concealing our straw hats at point of entry. In one year my friend and I saw 8 films including *Sea Wolf* (Edward G. Robinson) after 20 minutes of very dangerous queuing.

Perhaps surprisingly John Moulsdale records that his prime relaxation was reading and that in one year he read 47 books – Buchan, Hugh Walpole, A. E. W. Mason, Du Maurier, Edgar Wallace etc. Breaking the routine was the excitement of the wedding of Pat Sale (his Housemaster's daughter) to Leslie Minford:

2 March. Big wedding day. Went to wedding then played Under 16 leagues against Rigg's; owing to . . . in goal we lost 8–2. Poor show!

Moulsdale reports the frequent rotting of Joe Whitfield in form in the expectation that he would lose his temper; the boys were seldom disappointed. John Lingford-Hughes reports an incident in the Classical Remove concerning one Cross:

He [Cross] had noticed that when Harry Dawson came into the form room he would grab the edge of the door and slam it behind him without looking and sweep to the Master's desk at the front. Just behind the door were some strategically placed coat hooks. Cross discovered that it was possible to tether one end of a thunderflash to one of these hooks and the business end to the back of the door. At the appointed time, Harry Dawson swept into the room, slammed the door and there was the most almighty explosion . . .

Apparently peace was ultimately restored. In the war Cross became an expert in jungle warfare.

From time to time the real meaning of war was brought home by casualties of family or friends. Hardy did not follow the example of Alington who, in the First War, had read out the casualties on Sunday evenings in Chapel. In accordance with his oft-repeated principle, he wanted to keep things as normal as possible and did not want to put emphasis on death. 'Such contemplation', he wrote, 'is not wholesome for the young'.

Nonetheless, with meticulous care, he personally wrote to mothers and wives of Salopians who were killed.

Three deaths particularly affected the boys: that of Mark Scott, who less than a year before had been Head of the School and was drowned while serving as an Ordinary Seaman. His brother had been killed in 1942 on his first operational flight in the RAF. James Mackinnon, Head of School and in many ways a school idol, was killed in Burma in 1944 serving with the Royal Marine Commando. He had a university scholarship awaiting him and had been an outstanding sportsman. Boys still spoke of his amazing shot from the half way line which had defeated Repton. He was School captain of cricket, fives and boxing and played at Lord's for The Rest against the Lords Schools. Timothy Cross, killed in Italy in 1944 while serving with the Rifle Brigade, was an outstanding scholar. In his last year he obtained more marks in the Higher Certificate than any other candidate in the whole country; he won the Sidney Gold Medal and a scholarship to New College, Oxford. He was in the cricket XI and an all round sportsman. When he left Hardy wrote of 'an admirable combination of scholarship and outdoor prowess'.

In the spring and summer of 1943, as the war moved to the end of its fourth year, there were signs of weariness. The work of the School continued its high standard despite some weaknesses where temporaries stood in. One of the more interesting was Bruce Montgomery, author, poet and musician. Under the name Edmund Crispin he was to write a series of detective novels, one set in a public school which, though named Castrevenford, is clearly Shrewsbury. Entitled *Love Lies Bleeding*, the tale unwinds round a Speech Day and a murder. Certain characters seem to have been based on Salopian staff, particularly McEachran and Tommy Taylor. Unfortunately Bruce Montgomery's grip over discipline was insecure and he departed for pastures new.

Outside events broke the monotony of school routine – an Empire Youth Service in the Alington Hall, support for Mrs Churchill's Aid to Russia Fund, the Corps marching round the town in a week entitled 'Salute the Soldier'. Fundraising took place to support a Prisoners Fund and thirty-three Old Salopian prisoners each received 200 cigarettes. At this time too there was some excitement as American soldiers began arriving in the county and town, with various ancillary airfields established at such places as Atcham, Montford Bridge, Cosford, Sleap and Condover. The Raven Hotel was taken over by the Americans who found the School Bank an excellent place for their amatory adventures with the local girls. Richard Gardner comments that

this sight produced alternating emotions of adolescent voyeurism and curiosity, and 'well brought up' disdain for such exhibitionistic behaviour. In Moser's we had a particularly ill-favoured Welsh maid who became pregnant by a GI. This caused a stir.

The establishment of a 30 yard range on the School Bank below Ridgemount rather curbed these activities and Home Guard patrols in that area became less interesting.

The thriving Air section of the Corps found the American arrival of great interest as they saw for the first time Thunderbolts and other modern aircraft. The boys themselves were flown in Oxfords or Avro Ansons at Shawbury. In order to establish good relations a large party was invited to see a baseball match at the Gay Meadow. The general opinion was that the spectacle was rather boring. Salopians did not stoop to the popular 'Got any gum, chum', but it was certainly true that cartons of delicious luncheon meat occasionally appeared, while there were dark whispers of how much an American would pay for a Salopian straw hat. American visitors invited to see a school football match probably found it as boring as Salopians found baseball.

School football in wartime reached a high standard. Against the traditional rivals, Repton, Malvern, Charterhouse and Bradfield, only one match was lost between 1941 and 1947. Some distinguished visitors played on the Common for army teams. Dick Groves found that in one match he never seemed to be able to get hold of the ball; he was marked by Billy Wright, later to captain England. Michael Barber records that Tommy Lawton taught him how to give a kidney punch to an opponent when jumping to head the ball from behind.

Mowing with gas power. Groundsman Len at the controls.

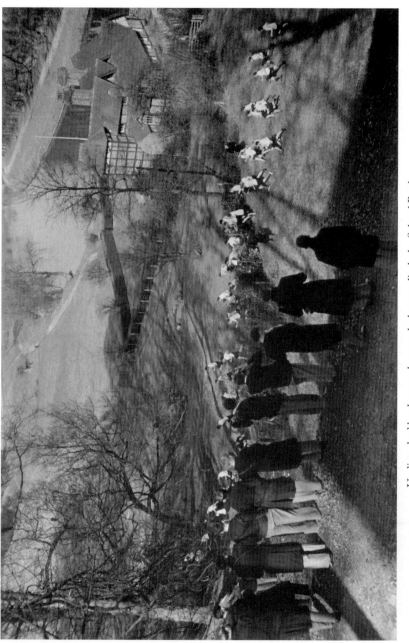

Undisturbed by the war the steeplechasers climb the School Bank . . .

. . . and negotiate the water jump.

Arthur Everard Kitchin.

J. F. Wolfenden.

No.1 Battalion Home Guards.   SECRET.
(Shropshire Zone).
                                        OPERATION ORDER No. 3
                                         (Cancelling O.O. No.2).
                                               Copy No..7....
Ref. Maps O.S. 1" to 1 m. SHEETS 60 & 61,
    and Sketch Map issued to O.C. Coys.

1. INFORMATION.
    (1) Enemy. Enemy troops may attempt to enter SHREWSBURY
            (a) on foot and possibly disguised.
            (b) by vehicles, either enemy or commandeered.
            (c) by landing from the air by plane, glider or parachute.

    (2) Own Troops.
            O.C.Troops, SHREWSBURY, commanding the combined
            forces of No.1 Battn. H.G. (less "F" Coy) :
            details from the I.T.C., K.S.L.I. : and 100
            riflemen R.A.P.C. is responsible for the defence
            of Shrewsbury.

2. INTENTION.
            (a) To deny enemy access to SHREWSBURY.
            (b) To round up and destroy enemy parachute troops.
            (c) To hold and harass a serious attack until the arrival
                of reinforcements.
            (d) To defend area allotted to "F" Coy.

3. METHOD.
    (1) DISPOSITIONS.
            (a) "A","B", "C", "D" & "E" Coys. will man the posts of
                the defensive cordon, and all ranks must understand
                that these posts are not to be vacated except by
                written orders from O.C. Troops, SHREWSBURY, or the
                Battn. Commander.
            (b) "Z" Coy. will be responsible for the defence of
                SHREWSBURY Station.
            (c) "F" & "W" Coys. will take up Battle positions
                as known to them.
            (d) Works Platoons attached to "D" Coy. will defend their
                respective buildings.
          —(e) "K" Coy. will be in reserve at The Schools,KINGSLAND.
            (f) Road blocks and barricades will be erected.
                Incoming traffic will be challenged, care being taken
                to avoid delay with legitimate traffic.
            (g) Anti-tank Hairpins will be erected. (See Appendix
                "A" attached).
                (NOTE. Sub paras. (f) and (g) above will only be put
                into operation on receipt of direct orders from
                O.C.Troops, SHREWSBURY, unless approach of hostile
                A.F.V's renders immediate barricades necessary,
                when local commanders will use their discretion).
            (h) Instructions regarding the use of the heavy
                Browning M/G's will be issued later.

A Home Guard Field Day Operation Order.

SHREWSBURY SCHOOL
PRIZE GIVING

July 1st, 1944

Speaker :-

THE RIGHT HONOURABLE AND MOST REVEREND

WILLIAM TEMPLE, P.C., D.D., D.LITT.,
LORD ARCHBISHOP OF CANTERBURY.

THE SIDNEY GOLD MEDAL—	R. F. D. Shuffrey
THE MOSS PRIZE—	R. F. D. Shuffrey
LATIN HEXAMETERS PRIZE—	R. F. D. Shuffrey
LATIN ELEGIACS PRIZE—	R. O. Marshall
	B. W. C. Knowlman
GREEK IAMBICS PRIZE—	R. F. D. Shuffrey
FLETCHER LATIN PRIZE (1943)—	
(Middle School)	I. M. O. Andrews
DUKES FRENCH PRIZES—	
Modern Side	R. E. Utiger
Classical and other Sides *Divided*	{W. E. C. Court
	{A. M. Pilch
BENTLEY GERMAN PRIZE—	R. E. Utiger
BRIGHT HISTORY PRIZE—	W. E. C. Court
Honourable Mention	K. C. Thompson
HALLAM HISTORY PRIZE—	W. E. C. Court
Honourable Mention	A. C. R. Thompson
KITSON CLARK ENGLISH LITERATURE	
PRIZE—	J. M. Barr
Proxime Accessit	R. F. D. Shuffrey
WILKINSON ENGLISH LITERATURE PRIZE—	R. T. Brain
Proxime Accesserunt	{J. M. N. Hearn
	{G. M. Hicks
HEADMASTER'S ENGLISH LITERATURE PRIZE—	C. G. Heath
Proxime Accessit	G. R. R. Treasure
Commended	D. M. Clark
WITHERS ENGLISH LITERATURE PRIZE—	A. H. P. Cornish
KITSON CLARK POETRY PRIZE—	R. F. D. Shuffrey
WOODS MEMORIAL ESSAY PRIZE—	D. O. Forshaw

1944. The Archbishop's visit: part of the Prize List.

Inspection 1943. Major Bevan conducts General Sir Bernard Paget.

At the saluting base is Major Hardy.

Inspection 1945. Lt Gen Sir Miles Dempsey takes the salute.

Home Guard activity as regards the boys diminished steadily, though the force was not 'stood down' until 1944. Once Hitler had attacked Russia in 1941, there was no possibility of invasion. But Corps parades continued to take much of boys' time – too much according to a well-argued letter in *The Salopian*. David Bevan had a particularly heavy burden to carry as commander of the Corps, company commander in the Home Guard and, from 1944, Housemaster. He reveals some sign of strain in a scorching letter to the CO at the barracks concerning the conduct of the Cert A exam:

The cadets on parade were splendidly turned out and very keen. They were examined by a Board of officers who had no sort of idea of the scope of the exam, its syllabus or its objects. They had no idea at all of the intelligence and clear objective critical minds of the examinees. The exam was conducted under no sort of method whatever. To boys accustomed to examination conditions, the exam was a complete farce. As trustees of public money (i.e. the Cert A grants per caput of those who passed), the conduct of those responsible was scandalous. As Commanding Office submitting the candidates, I felt thoroughly ashamed. I should like this complaint to be taken to the very highest level.

Was it? We shall never know. There is no reply on the file.

In 1943 Hardy decided that the time had come for radical decisions regarding Houses and Housemasters. The plain fact was that three Housemasters were, as Hardy kindly put it, 'past their best'. The numbers make this plain. Mitford in Severn Hill had 28 boys; he had been Housemaster for 18 years; Tombling had 32 boys and had been Housemaster for 14 years; Whitfield had 32 boys and had done 16 years. By contrast the energetic Alan Phillips had 40 boys and could not take all the applicants. The Governors had no power to remove a Housemaster, so persuasive steps had to be taken. Already the old system whereby a Housemaster owned his House and lived on the fee income had broken down and the School was now supporting those whose income had diminished. According to Peter Bowring, Joe Whitfield's irascibility had increased considerably, not least with his quiet and amiable wife, Megan. One of his merits, in the eyes of the boys, was that when in the pulpit he was very brief. Peter Bowring remembers one of his more memorable utterances during Evensong:

When he reached the pulpit, an amazing grappling, accompanied by much heavy breathing and reddening of face, enabled him to haul his vestments up high enough to delve into his waistcoat pocket and procure his ancient timepiece. As he held it in the palm of his hand and gazed at it, he pronounced, in measured tones, 'it is six thirty-five p.m. on Sunday the seventeenth of June nineteen hundred and forty. There is still time to repent'.

Joe was persuaded to retire and Tom and Mary Taylor moved in to initiate a wholly different regime.

A decision was made to close Tombling's, as regards living conditions the most primitive of the Houses, and Tombling and his boys moved to Severn Hill, following a brief but unsuccessful negotiation whereby Severn Hill was to have been sold to a Prep School called St Aubyn's. Tombling was not pleased about the move and later admitted that he never felt the same about his House thereafter. His boys, numbering 22, were not pleased either and, having been at the centre of affairs opposite the School gates, they now found themselves marooned. Eight of Mitford's boys remained, so with six new boys Tombling had a House of 36. Micky Jones however was transferred to Ingram's by Hardy's edict 'where he is badly needed'. So the old regime of Housemaster-Barons came to a timely end.

In Ridgemount another regime was coming to an end. Kitchin, whom the phrase 'a fine figure of a man' could not more aptly have described, was fading fast, as Parkinson's disease strengthened its hold. At first he had been able to cycle to school, though a boy in Ridgemount, Roger Leslie, was strategically placed to push him up the incline before Oldham's. A new boy, Richard Brain, was walking up to school one day when, as he recalls:

I saw in a shrubbery of the House grounds the puzzling sight of a mortar board. Going to retrieve it I found Kitch lying on the ground having fallen off his bicycle. I was much too small to help him get up, so I ran back to the House and told two monitors who simply got him up and, presumably with his insistence, put him back on his bike, started him off with a push and Kitch pedalled slowly to the School Buildings.

When cycling became impossible, he was driven in a car by the Head of House. As their Housemaster became more and more enfeebled, the boys took over. At one point the then Head of House attempted to stir things by asserting that he knew who the next Housemaster would be and that his wife was a poor cook. Both conjectures were untrue, but the rumour encouraged them to keep the Kitch regime going and continue to enjoy Ruth Kitchin's cooking. The monitors ran the House and continued the rather nonchalant humour and atmosphere which they had inherited from pre-war boys like John Bromley-Davenport, Peter Stockton (both of whom were killed) and Tim Singleton (later to be President of the Law Society). When the time came, Kitch gave a farewell party in the Ridgemount garden. That very morning he had had a fall and broken his hip but he received his guests with his usual charm although in considerable pain. When David Bevan succeeded, no adult except the matron had been on the boys' side of the House for two years.

In the summer term of 1943, General Sir Bernard Paget inspected the Corps; he had been in Churchill's from 1901 to 1905. As Commander in Chief, Home Forces, he trained the army which was to land on D Day in 1944 and was bitterly disappointed to be superseded by General Montgomery; his role was not dissimilar to that of Sir John Moore who trained the army which Wellington led.

John Lingford Hughes writes:

After the Inspection we repaired to our Houses in order to change out of our thick battle dress, and in my House at least it was the study monitor's privilege to change in his study instead of among the changing room crowd. In one such study we had been planning a restorative game of bridge and the study monitor, one Richard Heaton, had just removed his socks when there was a knock at the door and it opened to reveal the distinguished General. He said that this used to be his study and looked round appreciatively. 'Still the same old smell', he said and departed. In the stunned silence Richard Heaton's socks took on a lustre they had not previously known.

On Speech Day 1943 Hardy commented with pride on three Old Salopians in important appointments at the Universities – Francis de Hamel, President of the Cambridge University Boat Club, Tom Wotherspoon, President of the Oxford University Boat Club and Godfray Le Quesne, President of the Oxford Union. In the same term Hardy was awarded the CBE. He had been a headmaster for 25 years and three times Chairman of the Headmasters' Conference. At the end of term he dropped a bombshell in announcing his resignation, to take place a year hence. The Governors urged him to stay until the end of the war, but he shrewdly commented that at that stage Shrewsbury would be better served by a more flexible mind.

Academic results continued at a high level despite the demands on boys' time by soldiering and farming. When the Board of Education offered generous scholarships for boys to study Oriental Languages no fewer than six of the eight Salopian candidates were successful. Hardy greeted the news wryly. The boys had done brilliantly but, as they left early, there was a gap in the fee income and in Hardy's estimation, a loss of at least four university scholarships. At the other end of the scale, he was deeply upset by seven boys who cheated in the School Certificate exam – 'the most painful occurrence I have had in ten years'. Raymond Eccleston was one of the leavers at the end of the 1943 summer term and writes a fitting requiem to his Salopian years:

A few days before the end of term my friends and I sat out on the pier one beautiful summer evening and looked out over the Common. We reflected on our time at Shrewsbury and the education we had had which extended far beyond the classroom. We contemplated the future without enthusiasm. We savoured our last moments at Shrewsbury as if they were gold dust slipping between fingers. Four of us still remain today. We have been firm friends ever since, even though we only see one another every few years when we meet at Shrewsbury, now with increasing difficulty, and inspect the Site to see how the present generation is looking after our precious place. On our latest visit this year (2003) the Site looked as well as ever. Floreat Salopia!

7

Change in Command

IN the summer holidays of 1943 the Corps broke new ground in going to camp at Linley Hall, some 20 miles from the Site. It was the property of Admiral Sir James Startin who had entered the Navy in 1869 and had a most distinguished career. Now in his nineties he welcomed the contingent and took a close interest in the proceedings. An advance guard went by bicycle (in full kit) and everyone else marched; the boys slept in tents on paliasses and had the run of the Hall grounds, including the lake where the Admiral kept a boat. At church parade on Sunday he appeared dressed in the uniform of an Elder Brother of Trinity House, sat on a stool throughout and declaimed the lesson by heart – 'Put on the whole armour of God . . .' The camp was a strenuous experience and ended with an assault course under Corndon Hill which included the firing of live rounds. The camp was repeated the next year. It being the Admiral's birthday, his boat on the lake was dressed overall. He died at the age of 93.

In the Michaelmas Term the boys numbered 433 – a sharp decline of 18 from the Summer Term. To assemble the School was no simple matter. Nearly all came by train, trunks having been sent by PLA (Passenger Luggage in Advance). The timing of trains was uncertain and they were always full, generally, it seemed, of sleeping members of HM Forces; many journeys were spent standing in the corridor. John Moulsdale remembers leaving Reading at 2.35 am and arriving at Shrewsbury at 2.30 am. The blackout complicated matters as there was often un-certainty as to which station the train was pulling into. Yet no one seemed deterred by distance; boys came, for example, from

Ireland and the Isle of Man. Michael Wood's experience speaks for itself:

I remember my first day at Shrewsbury in January 1940 as one of the most frightening of my life. I was late starting on the train from London and it soon got dark. I was only 13 and had no idea how far it was. There were no names on the stations and the others in the carriage seemed to be asleep. I kept jumping out on to the platform to see where we were and jumping in again just as the train moved off. Eventually I got out at Shrewsbury and went outside the station. Everyone disappeared and I could see nothing in the black out. I wandered about for a bit and then back to the station. At last another train came in and I found someone from Rigg's who showed me the door of Moser's.

The term showed changes in the body politic. David Bevan was in Ridgemount and his first term is dramatically described in his book *Recollections*: a new boy ran away, the cook left and the Matron went mad; Tombling began his exile in Severn Hill; Tom Taylor moved into Churchill's and instituted a rigorously efficient regime, not liked by all. John Lingford Hughes, a monitor, remembers that one of Major Taylor's first acts was

to inform the senior members that upon obtaining command of a company in the Army, his first act was to reduce a number of sergeants to the ranks and impose stricter discipline. Having guaranteed the total hostility of the senior men in the House, he just had to wait till we all left.

Another incident made John Lingford Hughes himself less than popular; his bedroom was having a rather noisy mill,

when the Housemaster appeared at the door and said that if we brought down the ceiling of Matron's room (which was underneath), it would be on my head. Upon his departure, we speculated about this curious proposition in physics.

The old guard of Housemasters soldiered on – Street, Sopwith and Hope-Simpson, and the popular and wonderfully ineffective Dicky Sale. The latter was still umpiring, although increasingly deaf, and had a system of signals from the square leg umpire when there was an appeal for caught at the wicket. Geoffrey Powell recounts the long-standing argument between

Dicky Sale and Desmond Clark who frequently asked to visit the town to buy birthday presents for female relations. Dicky kept a (disputed) note of the extraordinary number of Clark grandmothers. ('My good owl . . . ')

The winter of 1943-44 was a very hard one, as wartime winters always seemed to be. But the weather did not break the School's routine – cold showers in the morning, physical training in the morning break (discarding jackets) and on the mornings when there was no PT Hardy still insisted that boys were turned out of form rooms into the open air. The shortage of fuel meant that the old-fashioned heating systems provided minimum heat. It was hardly possible even to get warm in a bath as the Government had laid down that baths should not be more than five inches deep; and in most Houses bath water was shared with others on a relay system. Water left in jugs or bowls froze overnight. The ingenious John Gorst made an electric water heater out of carbon rods taken from dry cell torch batteries, thus manu-facturing for himself a hot water bottle.

In general school discipline held up well in wartime conditions. The black out of course made it easy to slip out of the House unnoticed and go to one of the town's four cinemas, to be temporarily transported by the beauty of Vivien Leigh or Rita Hayworth; easy also to slip into a carefully chosen pub for a quiet pint. Girls hardly existed. When two members of Tombling's struck up acquaintance with girls who walked by the House on their way to the Radbrook College, they were invited to tea; but on attempting to enter the Radbrook boarding house the boys were apprehended and given a rocket by the Headmistress which they never forgot. Although the Debating Society might heavily defeat a motion that 'The growing independence of women is a menace to society', yet the presence of females on the Site was not recognised until the 1950s when a Ladies Lavatory was constructed in the Alington Hall. (A watershed indeed.) Thinking of school days, Kingston Adams records:

My decision to remain in the army after the war was to some extent a result of my time spent at Shrewsbury and particularly the last year – such a splendid sense of service and discipline had been instilled during my five years, learning to obey orders when a junior boy and later how to give them, that it seemed natural for me to continue in the life to which I had become used and practise what I learned at Shrewsbury.

In many ways those were innocent days. No drugs, no difficult tangles with girlfriends, no constant TV advertisements encouraging consumption and dictating fashions. It was virtually impossible for any boy to be obese. Life was very insular, which had advantages and disadvantages. Parents were seldom seen; there were neither half terms nor weekend breaks. The Michaelmas Term plodded on for twelve weeks and with summer camps the holidays spent at home diminished. Contact was maintained by much letter writing; most felt that the weekly letter was a necessary link, especially when fathers were absent on war service. Boys were remarkably incurious about their friends' parents and their occupations and the war was a great leveller so far as wealth and possessions were concerned.

In his last year Hardy strove hard to sustain high standards. At Christmas he wrote to his Governors (with typical phraseology):

I hope that Governors will believe that their present overseer, though worse than sexagenarian, has a natural and very particular anxiety not to let the works of the School run down in what is presumably his last year of being responsible for the winding of them.

Before the end of the Michaelmas Term 1943, speculation as to the identity of the next Headmaster was ended with the announcement that J. F. Wolfenden, then Headmaster of Uppingham, had been appointed. The Governors had, for once, stirred themselves to action, prodded by a comparatively new Governor, Duncan Norman. The story of the appointment is told elsewhere. There was a strong Old Salopian lobby pushing for the appointment of an Old Salopian to revive what was conceived to be the Salopian spirit of pre-Hardy days but the Governors decided otherwise, turning to a young man of 37 who already had a feel for the corridors of Whitehall in his work to found the Air Cadet movement, for which he was temporarily seconded from Uppingham. He was also about to become the

Chairman of the Headmasters' Conference. Still greater fame awaited him when he became a household name after chairing the report on homosexuality.

Hardy's last term, the summer of 1944, was an eventful one with the eyes of the whole country on the Normandy landings. For some time a section of the Shrewsbury bypass had been closed to traffic and became an enormous park for military vehicles; then one day they all vanished and all knew that D Day was near. Hardy's last Speech Day was distinguished in having as principal guest William Temple, Archbishop of Canterbury, with whom Hardy had sat in the Sixth Form at Rugby. The Archbishop presented the prizes and preached the next day. Sadly Hardy's last days were not without controversy. At a meeting of Governors with Wolfenden at which he was not present, it was decided that the Headmaster should return to School House and that Kingsland House should again become a boarding house. Hardy was astonished and hurt. Needless to say, Wolfenden, when in office, saw what a hopelessly unpractical scheme this was and no more was heard of it, but it soured Hardy's last term so far as his Governors were concerned. He was retiring on a pension of £610 a year. Hardy later wrote, 'That is not an extravagant provision for a man who has been for three years Chairman of the Headmasters' Conference and has some repute in the scholastic world'.

Hardy could be brusque and insensitive; he was never a popular figure nor did he wish to be. But to most Salopians he was seen to lead the school with vigour and determination as he met the many puzzling wartime demands. His early work had laid the administrative foundations of the School and money was found to build the Science Building and the Gymnasium. At Speech Day he might well look round and see with satisfaction two of his creations – the School Band and the Physical Training Display. Many Old Salopians owed much to him as he followed their careers and gave helpful advice, for he was not unconnected with the corridors of power. Many, too, will remember with gratitude his encouragement to boys to get out and enjoy the Shropshire countryside through country expeditions and the use of bicycles. On a Sunday afternoon he loved to walk over the Shropshire hills.

> For your large hearted wisdom did present
> New liberties, new music, much beside,
> Granting to scholars, sometimes mewed and pent
> The freedom of the Shropshire countryside.

Hardy's wartime philosophy, to which he adhered tenaciously, was expressed in a 1941 report to his Governors; it is also an excellent example of his prose style:

And so we go on our apparently rather normal way, with not a few makeshifts at various points, perhaps and fortunately not too obvious, and sometimes wondering how long this comparatively even tenor can be maintained, but thankful that it has been possible so long as it has, and continually hoping that those whom fierce ordeals await, when they reach the age of 19, may arrive at that crisis with bodies fit and minds not unduly disturbed; and that even the youngest, whom crisis may overtake long before that age, may yet have been in some measure made ready to meet it the more undauntedly that their schooldays were till then providentially as normal and tranquil as can be looked for in the most tense period of their nation's history.

8

The End of the Affair

WITH the beginning of the Michaelmas Term 1944, there was a keen sense of anticipation concerning the characteristics of the new Headmaster, not however shared by the editors of *The Salopian*, who made no mention at all in their columns of the new arrival. Richard Gardner reports 'a big difference in atmosphere' while Richard Sinnett wrote to his parents that:

We are all very pleased with Mr Wolfenden. He has introduced no new ideas so far. He is very nice and greets you with a broad smile. He treats the praepostors as friends whom he might have known all his life.

Richard Hicks in the Classical Upper VIth recalls that 'in form, when he was there, he was bright, incisive and fun'.

It was immediately obvious that this was a very different man from his predecessor. He was forthcoming in human relationships, urbane, confident and possessed of a remarkable quickness of mind. John Lingford Hughes describes the first time that he addressed the School in the Alington Hall:

He spoke, among other things, of feelings of humility standing before us in such a venerable and distinguished school. This was a novelty to us, since whatever qualities we might ascribe to our former Headmaster, humility was definitely not one of them. I believe that by the end of his speech he had the boys cautiously on his side, but not all of the masters.

Wolfenden was very sensitive about coughing in Chapel; he read the lessons with feeling and carefully constructed emphases.

66

In one service, when someone coughed, he stopped for a few seconds, on the second instance he stopped for a very long time and stared at the offender and when it happened a third time, he slammed the Bible shut.

So recollects Martin Plumptre. On another subject he surprised the boys by talking quite freely on sex, a subject which was largely taboo as far as the staff was concerned. Michael Valentine remembers Dick Sale gingerly touching on the subject when addressing new boys: 'You will all be aware of the dangers of self abuse'. They didn't know what this was but when they discovered they tended to discount the dangers.

Wolfenden was a great communicator. He instituted weekly praepostors' meetings and in wide-ranging discussions the boys felt that they were playing a real part in running the School. A new Headmaster's notice board outside the School Building was in constant use. The final sentence at the end of one notice is said to have read 'You should not be reading this now'. It was remarkable that Wolfenden so quickly obtained a grip on the School – it was said that he knew the name of every boy – considering his many absences in London on either Government or Headmasters' Conference business; he was Chairman of the latter body. Hartshorne, the School porter, who had danced attendance on Hardy, now found that he had become chauffeur to his successor, continually going to the station and often meeting the midnight train from Euston which arrived around 6 am. At the end of his first term Wolfenden publicly denied the rumour that he was also headmaster of another school. Salopians now appreciated the joke that Uppingham's leaving present had been a first class season ticket between London and Shrewsbury.

To general surprise the School was full in the Michaelmas Term – 491 boys. With the end of the war expected, most Public Schools found that there was a wave of entries. The last winter of the war lived up to expectations with remarkable low temperatures; the river froze and brave (and foolhardy) boys tried the ice. Martin Plumptre was one who also recollects that the School House urinals froze and the chemists were busy working out the freezing point of urine. Not being used to the Salopian tradition, Wolfenden cancelled 1st Lesson for some weeks. To convey some warmth to English hearts, HH The Thakore Sahib of Palitana sent a gift to the School of £500, to mark his Silver Jubilee. He had been a popular boy in the School House during the First World War, a brilliant cricketer and fives player whose various turbans added colour to the field. His grateful subjects erected a life size marble statue to mark the event. In the Second War, Salopians wandering in India found warm hospitality at his court. Despite the freeze, the ironically named Double Summer time still persisted which meant daylight long persisting into what should have been night. As Wolfenden said, 'Boys like cows, find Double Summer Time very trying but for different reasons'.

One of the Headmaster's main responsibilities was engaging staff to replace not only the temporaries but also a handful of time-honoured men who were moving off to Headmasterships – Jim Pitts-Tucker, L. F. Harvey, Murray Senior, Alec Peterson, Charlie Larkin and Basil Deed; while Frank McCarthy moved to Oxford as Chaplain of Balliol. Another who would be much missed was Major A. H. Pearson ('Pearcrack'). His eccentricities were many and much relished; he wore the same jacket and trousers through the war and was said to have made them last by unpicking the seams and re-sewing. He would not start a teaching period without checking that all the desks were aligned in straight lines and windows open the 'standard amount'. It was compulsory to start writing on a piece of penal (paper) three lines above the first printed line to save paper. His methods of teaching were highly original, his grip on discipline tight. Misdemeanours meant coming in ten minutes early before 1st Lesson. He had organised – and participated – in the cross country running and the athletics for many years. He was rumoured to have been a gifted all-round sportsman in his Cambridge days. It is worth repeating a wholly apocryphal story told of his younger days. He was threatened by a thug in the East End one day but reacted quickly by squaring up to him with the classical boxing stance, saying 'Boxing Blue'. The thug then ran for it but Pearson ran easily along side him, saying 'Running Blue'. In despair the thug dived into the Thames only for Pearson to do the same and swim alongside him - 'Swimming Blue'. Not only was he to be missed at the School but also in Everton at the Mission; he had led countless boys in ascents of the Breiddens during the 'Mish' visits. To them he was the 'Mad Major'.

VE Day came on what should have been the first day of the Summer Term but as it was declared a public holiday, the boys did not come back – except one. The proclamation of the holiday having been somewhat delayed, Brian Hutton (Lord Hutton), a new boy, had already started from Ireland. His first task at his new school was to help carry beer for a party improvised by David and Hilary Bevan in Ridgemount where a bonfire was lit. Those present stood on the terrace and looked over the town where every light was lit – a sight not seen since 1939. To the Corps Inspection that year came General Sir Miles Dempsey, commanding the 2nd Army, who flew over from Germany. He had been in Chance's from 1911–14 and captain of an outstanding cricket XI which included Palitana. His next posting was as C-in-C South-East Asia after Lord Mountbatten. The reality of the war was brought home to members of the Air Section of the Corps who were flown in a Lancaster bomber over the devastated Ruhr. VJ Day came in the holidays when many boys were on the last of the harvest camps. Richard Brain was on a camp in Gloucestershire:

15 August was a complete holiday from farm work for all; from our camp we went in the evening to Westonbirt School, at the invitation of the Headmistress presumably, to a celebration and dancing on the lawns there, with a local band; the school girls were on holiday but numerous girls from Tetbury and around arrived. Dancing like that was a new experience.

The victory of the Labour party in the General Election raised some anxieties about the future of the Public Schools, although the Fleming Report had already been accepted whereby the schools agreed to accept up to 25% of their intake from Local

Authorities, a figure never attained, although a number of most successful boys came to Shrewsbury via this channel. Hugh Davies remembers a visit of two or three Labour MPs. Lunching at Head Table in the School House, one of the female MPs said to Ben Davies (Hugh's brother) 'What's your name?' 'Davies'. 'And yours?' 'Jones'. 'And yours?' 'Smith'. 'Oh come on! Think I was born yesterday?' For all the sound and fury, nothing was done about the Public Schools until years later when Harold Wilson took the time-honoured course of postponement by appointing a Royal Commission. It took a mass of evidence and a Report was slowly gurgitated. No one ever took the slightest notice of it; Lord Annan, one of its members, afterwards said that of all the committees he had ever sat on, the Public Schools Commission had been the biggest waste of time.

So the war ended. To camp at Kinmel Park went the Corps; while there they heard the news of the atomic bombs. According to Joe Hambrook, all turned to Hal Dixon, a science scholar, 'who became a kind of instant Einstein (or maybe Oppen-heimer), asking him for explanations of nuclear fission and the mysteries of the first atomic bomb'. To farming camps up and down the country went, for the last time, some 200 boys. The Site, on which it was thought five years ago that the Germans might land, resumed its drowsy end-of-summer atmosphere as the ground staff prepared for the first term of peace.

Shrewsbury had been very fortunate compared with other schools which had been seriously disrupted either by the enemy or by having to move. Despite the somewhat frenzied activity of 1940, there was never any likelihood of the war actually reaching Shropshire in any form. So the wheels continued to turn although the effort required to keep them moving was considerable. Most boys saw the war as a continuing backdrop to life on Kingsland but one which affected them little save those who had fathers or brothers engaged in conflict. The centre of life was on Kingsland and the usual school activities were all-absorbing. Certainly the war made for a greater sense of togetherness as boys mingled in military or farming activities and camps, where the staff were discovered to be quite human and where masters' wives and daughters also played their part. Boarding life was more isolated than usual with parents seldom if ever seen during term time, more emphasis being put on the social unit of the Houses where, despite the traditional hierarchical structure, there was perhaps more camaraderie than in pre-war days. Corporal punishment remained but was seldom used in most Houses. (One boy being offered the alternative of 3 strokes with a slipper or 13 with a toothbrush chose the latter; he regretted it.) Public opinion condemned any sort of bullying. In Houses like Ingram's, Churchill's or Ridgemount where the grip of the Housemaster was lax, the senior boys showed much initiative in taking responsibility themselves.

One comment on the wartime scene from the viewpoint of 2004: had the Health and Safety police then been active, how greatly would the boys have been limited in their activities! Living conditions would have been condemned by today's standards (boys sharing baths!); the risks inherent in military activity – firing live rounds, driving vehicles; the possible dangers in the activities connected with farming; adventures on the frozen river; unsupervised parties on the Shropshire hills; river bathing in summer with no authority present – all these and more would today be forbidden.

The years immediately after the war saw a continuation of wartime austerity; rationing, if anything, became tighter; bread was rationed for the first time in 1947. The hoped-for amelioration in living conditions did not occur while the biggest freeze of all ushered in 1947 during which year the Severn reached a record flood level with the water head high in the School boathouse. While materially things remained the same, there was a surge of energy in the School following the arrival of Wolfenden's new appointments to the staff and the final disappearance of the temporaries. So arrived on the scene Ken Chew, Harry Forster, Arnold Hagger, John Woodroffe, Basil Saint, Felix Ewing, Peter Knight, Donald Scott, David Brown and Reginald Harwood, with others to follow.

Just when it seemed that worries about the number of boys in the School had ceased and Hardy's pessimism on this subject seemed to be false, a new and major worry arose. During the war, the Governors, Headmaster and Bursar had thought it unwise to raise the fees in order not to deter potential parents. But now, with inflation increasing, it was clear that the only way to balance the books was a large-scale increase. The full boarding fee had remained at £180 pa since 1921; in 1947 it was raised to £236 and the prophets of woe foretold an inevitable shortage of boys. Every effort was made to run the school more economically and to increase the numbers by using every available space to house pupils, some of whom lived with members of the staff for their first term or two. In fact the prophets were quite wrong and for the next decade or more there were more applicants than places.

Thus Shrewsbury settled down to the Wolfenden age – though it was only to last six years. By the time he left in 1950, the air raid shelters had disappeared, there were sweets in the Shop and the boys were back in blue suits – an outward sign of a return to pre-war life. Salopians of the 1930s would find that there was not much change in the lives of their successors in the 1950s. Change did come indeed in the maelstrom of the 1960s; but by that time the war was but a distant memory.

Appendix

As the reader will have seen, this book, as I noted in my Preface, is largely based on the memories of Old Salopians. One contribution, from J. P. Williams (O 1941–43), was such a delightful essay in its own right that I have included it in full.

'My recollections of Shrewsbury during the War are those of a refugee from a state of madness who unexpectedly finds himself in a haven of eccentric sanity.

'An unusual chain of events led my brother Hugh and I to Shrewsbury in the spring of 1941. In September 1939, when mass evacuation was the order of the day, our South London day-school decided to retreat to a grim, rat-infested hell-hole on the far south-west coast of Cornwall. Effective schooling virtually ceased and survival became the main preoccupation of boys and teachers alike. Majestic seascapes, lashed into frenzied animation by unrelenting gales, did nothing to relieve the general squalor and discomfort which were beginning to cause sickness and physical distress among the forty wretches crammed into a house designed for ten people. When we arrived home for Christmas, looking like a couple of ragamuffins, we were not surprised to hear that there would be no going back, and that places had been found for us elsewhere – at Dulwich College.

'After one short term at Dulwich disruption again set in. France had been overrun by the Germans, who now threatened this country with air attack and invasion. I shall never forget the sight of exhausted soldiers returning from Dunkirk in a seemingly endless procession of trains, which travelled slowly past the College grounds at the very end of May and in early June 1940. There was a feeling of impending catastrophe in the air, and when the Battle of Britain began in July it was decided that Hugh and I would leave London for Mother's family home at Cressage (eight miles south-east of Shrewsbury), while Father stayed near his work at the Admiralty.

'For six months we grew like weeds in an abandoned garden, while our future education was being considered. To pass away the time I tried my hand at coarse fishing in the Severn, learnt how to identify and to catalogue plants and animals of the local countryside and discovered Eternity embedded in the Here-and-Now. More than anything I wanted to join up and fight the Germans who were busily devastating the part of London in which I had grown up. On the night of 18th September 1940 they had all but destroyed our Blackheath home, and looters had stolen everything not wrecked by bomb-blast. In the same attack friends had been killed, and my two canaries were buried beneath the rubble of their foster home.

'In January 1941, a few weeks before my fifteenth birthday, Hugh and I were summoned to Kingsland House to sit for an extempore Common Entrance examination. I recall being at a very low ebb as I grappled with questions any thirteen-year-old should have sailed through. I felt smothered by external events, and the idea of starting all over again numbed my senses.

'Shortly after the ordeal by Common Entrance Hugh and I learnt that we had passed the test and that we were to be translated as 'new scum' to Oldham's Hall. We were to spend a term or two in the third form, under the benign control of the School Chaplain, and future bishop of Lebombo, the Reverend Humphrey Beevor.

'Shielded from reality by our entertainingly urbane Head of House, Godfray Le Quesne, Oldham's Hall became for me a home from home, where even someone condemned to penal servitude under the 'doul' system might reinvent himself as an ironic observer of low life. I felt like the Mock Turtle in *Alice in Wonderland*, such was my understanding of his Ambition, Distraction Uglification and Derision.

'Thanks to our enigmatic Housemaster, S. S. Sopwith, who presided over us with the sanguine frugality of a ring-master, oddballs like me were nurtured as if they were desirable in any well-ordered society. My appointment to the job of Hall constable gave me the chance to observe – and to boss about – the low life to which, for so long, I had been attached. No sooner had I settled into the job than, out of the blue, I was elevated to the utterly preposterous House Captaincy of Farming! What a joke that was to become as my dream of dominion over the weeds of this world became clogged in the mud of *malentendu*. I had applauded the S'with when he said, 'If there's one thing I can't abide, it's mucking about with the earth.' But suddenly I felt ensnared in a surreal world where playing-cards were painting cabbages bright yellow for ease of identification in the dark. I needed help, so I sought advice from the legendary Cartwright, Salopia's authority on all matters agricultural – but it was to no avail. 'There's a man in Dusseldorf I hate,' was all he would say.

'Odd frames from *Salopian Days: The Movie* come to mind; RSM Joyce shouting 'Up the wall-bars go!' Pearcrack screaming 'Windows open standard amount!' Cuddy Mitford hurling books out of the window as a reward for inattention; eggs boiling merrily in the glue-pot during an art period in Top Schools; the Tucks Run; Bumpers in the eye of a dry-bob; 1st XI cricket viewed from afar; the thrill of a first-rate fives tournament; and, not least, Sunday musical evenings at the home of Johnny Johnson and his crooning Jack Russell.

'Two memorable sequences from the *movie* survive in the mind's eye. The first is of Frank McEachran (Kek), Shrewsbury's own March Hare, taking us on a conducted tour of his private, irreverently surreal world, as we sat, hands clasped behind our backs, soaking up wisdom of ages, from the Greek classics to the modern poets. A thought-provoking quotation from Rainer Maria Rilke has journeyed with me down the years:

> Ist es möglich, dasz die ganze Weltgeschichte
> miszverstanden worden ist?......Ja, es ist möglich.

Also a couplet from the *Eclogue for Christmas* by Louis MacNeice comes to mind:

And not till the Goths again come swarming down the hill
Will cease the clangour of the electric drill.

'The other sequence relates to an afternoon on Unky Cooke's
"farm" at Westbury. If Kek was Shrewsbury's March Hare, then
surely Unky was the Mad Hatter.

'One of my duties as HCF was to organise parties of boys to
help local farmers with time-consuming jobs like sugar-beet
singling; but there was another task from which I would never
willingly exclude myself – that of helping the Reverend Cooke
on his Rectory farm. This covert operation involved Unky
collecting three or four of us from Oldham's Hall in his battered
old 1920s Rolls-Royce tourer (which became a hen-house after
dark), driving like a bat out of hell down narrow country lanes to
his crumbling Georgian rectory, and setting us to work with
flash-hooks. After a few desultory swipes at half-dead stinging-
nettles we would be invited indoors for a slap-up tea of crumpets,
fried eggs and home-made rhubarb jam, swilled down with a fair
quantity of elderberry wine. The feast was accompanied by a
hundred decibels of Wagnerian grand opera, blasted at us
through the gigantic papier-mache horn of Unky's wind-up
Ginn gramophone. The afternoon ended with a hair-raising
dash for home, and with luck another tea.

'The nine terms I spent at Shrewsbury transformed my
outlook on life by giving me an independent turn of mind and an
ability to see the funny side of things. Athletically and
academically I was no great shakes, but in the end I had learnt
how to go on learning. I thought of Kingsland as a very special
place, guarded symbolically from a hostile world by the Toll
Bridge, which in one great leap spanned Salopia's *Rubicon*.

'In September 1943 I volunteered for service in the Royal
Marines, and in January the following year I set off for
Lympstone with a copy of *Endymion* in my pocket and a dagger
between my teeth.

'Floreat Salopia!'

Roll of Honour

INTRODUCTION

AFTER the Great War, the Old Salopian Club published a *Roll of Service 1914–1918* (Wilding & Son Ltd, 1921). It contains a list of all Old Salopians who had served during the war, with obituaries of most of those who died. It also contains statistics concerning other casualties, such as those wounded. No similar list was produced after the Second World War, although there is in the School Library a Roll of Honour book, giving some information about those who died. The Commonwealth War Graves Commission (CWGC) cemetery registers contain additional information, from which it has now been possible to produce a more detailed Roll. This new Roll also contains the names of some individuals who are not in any other School list. In this the 60th anniversary year of the end of the war, this compilation will, it is hoped, fill a gap in the records of the School.

The Great War *Roll of Service* records that 321 Old Salopians lost their lives. This Roll of Honour contains 238 names, a number the size of which came as a surprise to the compiler. It includes a few individuals who died after the war and for reasons unconnected with it. They have been included as they are on the School War Memorial.

The obituaries of many of those who died were printed in *The Salopian*. These sometimes contain details of the circumstances of an individual's death. The School Library and the compiler of this Roll hold a record of these obituaries.

Some information has been obtained from the internet. Such information has only been included when it is believed to be accurate. Information about ships in which individuals died can be obtained by typing the name of the ship into an internet search-engine such as Google. Short histories of most Royal Air Force squadrons can be found on the Ministry of Defence website <www.raf.mod.uk/history/sqn_hist.html>.

The CWGC cemetery and memorial registers give details of each individual who died between 3 September 1939 and 31 December 1947. In addition to the information contained in this Roll, most register entries give the individual's service number, the names and address of his next-of-kin (normally his parents) and the location of the grave in the cemetery. This information is obtainable either from the CWGC headquarters, or on their internet website, <www.cwgc.org>.

A list of abbreviations is at the end of this Roll.

The casualties, listed by Service, rank, Army by corps and place of burial, are:

SERVICE

Royal Navy (including Fleet Air Arm – 5)	22
Royal Marines	2
Army	132
Royal Air Force	78
Merchant Navy	1
Civilians	3
TOTAL	238

RANK

Major-General	1
Brigadier	1
Air Commodore	1
Lieutenant-Colonel	4
Wing Commander	3
Lieutenant Commander	1
Major	23
Squadron Leader	5
Captain (Army)	44
Lieutenant (Navy)	4
Lieutenant (Marines)	1
Flight Lieutenant	15
Sub-Lieutenant	11

Lieutenant (Army)	33
Flying Officer	19
2nd Lieutenant (Army)	10
2nd Lieutenant (Marines)	1
Pilot Officer	19
Chaplain (Army)	1
Warrant Officer (Army)	1
Sergeant (Army)	2
Sergeant (RAF)	14
Junior NCOs and Other Ranks (all services)	20

ARMY BY CORPS

Commands and Staff	2
Royal Armoured Corps	12
Royal Artillery	35
Royal Engineers	6
Royal Corps of Signals	3
Infantry	68
Royal Army Chaplains Department	1
Royal Army Medical Corps	1
Intelligence Corps	2
Royal Pioneer Corps	1
General Service Corps	1
TOTAL	132

PLACE OF BURIAL

Of the 238 who died throughout the world, the details of only three are not known. 178 are buried in known and recorded graves. Those with no known grave are remembered on memorials in countries abroad and at home. The United Kingdom memorials contain the names of men who died at sea, or in or over countries with no memorial, particularly Germany. Of the thirty remembered in the United Kingdom, fifteen are airmen named on the Runnymede Memorial and nine are sailors on the Portsmouth and Plymouth memorials. The totals by country are:

Country	Buried	No Grave	Total
Algeria	2		2
Bangladesh	1		1
Belgium	8		8
Burma	4	8	12

Country	Buried	No Grave	Total
Crete	1		1
Egypt	11	5	16
Ethiopia	1		1
France	23	2	25
Germany	12		12
Gibraltar	1		1
Greece		1	1
Hong Kong	3	1	4
Holland	6		6
India	7		7
Israel	2		2
Italy	19	1	20
Japan	1		1
Kenya	2		2
Libya	4		4
Madagascar	1		1
Malta		1	1
Norway	1		1
Singapore	2	7	9
Somalia		1	1
Tunisia	9	1	10
Zimbabwe	1		1
United Kingdom	55	30	85
Details not known	1	2	3
TOTALS	178	60	238

ROLL OF HONOUR

Adams. Flying Officer Brian Adams, RAFVR. School House 1928–32. Killed 6 February 1945, aged 31. Buried in Athlone Cemetery, Bulawayo, Zimbabwe.

Alers-Hankey. Pilot Officer Nigel Clinton Alers-Hankey, RAFVR. Moser's 1925–28. Killed in action 11 June 1941, serving with 82 Squadron, Bomber Command, aged 29. Runnymede Memorial – no known grave.

Alexander. Major Malcolm George Fletcher Alexander, The Buffs (Royal East Kent Regiment). School House 1922–27. Killed in action 4 October 1943, serving with the 2nd Battalion The Lancashire Fusiliers, aged 34. Buried in Sangro River War Cemetery, Italy.

Almond. Sub-Lieutenant (A) Eric Roy Almond, RNVR, Fleet Air Arm. School House 1937–40. Killed 3 October 1943 in a flying accident, serving in HMS *Daedalus*,[1] aged 20. Buried in St Cuthbert's Churchyard, Lytham, Lancashire.

Ambler. Captain Philip Ambler, 5th Battalion 7th Rajput Regiment, Indian Army. Rigg's 1924–28. Killed in action 19 December 1941, aged 30. Buried in Stanley Military Cemetery, Hong Kong.

Andreae. Flying Officer Christopher John Drake Andreae, RAFVR. Churchill's 1930–35. Killed in action 15 August 1940 over the English Channel, serving with 64 Squadron, Fighter Command, aged 23. Runnymede Memorial – no known grave.

Anthony. Lieutenant Patrick Vaughan Anthony, The Somerset Light Infantry and The Northamptonshire Regiment. Churchill's 1928–33. Killed in action 15 June 1943, aged 28. Buried in Medjez-el-Bab War Cemetery, Tunisia.

Ashburner. Private Michael John Ashburner, The Royal Warwickshire Regiment. Ingram's 1938–42. Killed in action 20 January 1944, serving with the 7th Battalion The Oxfordshire and Buckinghamshire Light Infantry, aged 19. Buried in Minturno War Cemetery, Italy.

Ashby. Lieutenant John Grover Ashby, Royal Artillery. Ingram's 1936–41. Died of typhoid 24 January 1944, serving with 142 Field Regiment, aged 20. Buried in Caserta War Cemetery, Italy.

Atkinson. Pilot Officer Harold Derrick Atkinson DFC, RAF. Ridgemount 1932–37. Killed in action 25 August 1940 over Dorset, serving with 213

---

[1] HMS *Daedalus* was a Royal Naval Air Station at Lee-on-Solent, Hampshire.

Squadron, Fighter Command, aged 22. Buried in Market Weighton Cemetery, Yorkshire.

Bagott. 2nd Lieutenant William Hugh Pearman Bagott, The King's Shropshire Light Infantry. School House 1932–37. Killed 28 November 1940 in a firearms accident, serving with the 2nd Battalion The Herefordshire Regiment, aged 22. Buried in St Mary's Churchyard, Kings Winford, Dudley.

Bailey. 2nd Lieutenant Andrew John Hamilton Bailey, 1st Battalion The King's Own Yorkshire Light Infantry. Chance's 1932–36. Killed in action between 26 and 28 April 1940, aged 21. Buried in Kvam Churchyard, Norway.

Bain. Captain John Donald Stuart Bain, Royal Artillery. Moser's 1917–21. Died of wounds 8 December 1940, after serving with 68 Anti-Tank Regiment, aged 37. Buried in Catterick Military Cemetery, Yorkshire.

Baines. Major Richard Gough Talbot Baines, 1st Battalion The Hampshire Regiment. School House 1927–32. Killed in action 6 June 1944, aged 30. Buried in Bayeux War Cemetery, Normandy.

Balfour. Lieutenant William James Balfour, RNR. School House 1920–24. Died 15 January 1943, serving in HMS *Philoctetes*,[2] aged 36. Commemorated in Arnos Vale Crematorium, Bristol.

Barber. Flying Officer John Stuart Barber, RAFVR. Tombling's 1936–40. Killed in action 22 October 1943 in a raid over Germany, serving with 77 Squadron, Bomber Command, aged 21. Buried in Hanover War Cemetery.

Barnard. Flying Officer Anthony Edward Buchanan Barnard, RAFVR. Chance's 1935–39. Killed 13 April 1943, serving with 489 (RNZAF) Squadron, Coastal Command, aged 21. Runnymede Memorial – no known grave.

Barr. Sub-Lieutenant (A) Robert Geoffrey Barr, RNVR, Fleet Air Arm. School House 1937–41. Killed 23 March 1944 in a flying accident, serving in HMS *Daedalus*,[3] aged 20. Buried in St John's Churchyard, Roundhay, Leeds.

Barton. Sergeant Pilot Henry Harvey Molyneux Barton, RAFVR. Rigg's 1934–39. Killed in action 15 August 1941, serving with 150 Squadron, Bomber Command, aged 20. Buried in Leeuwarden General Cemetery, Holland.

Bell. Flying Officer Andrew George Henry Bell, RAF. Ridgemount 1928–32. Killed 31 August 1939 in a flying accident on patrol off Norway, aged 25. No known grave.

---

[2] HMS *Philoctetes* was a destroyer depot ship, which survived the war.
[3] HMS *Daedalus* was a Royal Naval Air Station at Lee-on-Solent, Hampshire.

Birch. Lieutenant Robert Massy Birch, 1st Battalion The Rifle Brigade. Dayboys 1938–42. Killed in action 28 July 1944, aged 20. Buried in Banneville-la-Campagne War Cemetery, Normandy.

Blagg. Lieutenant Peter Henry Blagg, 1st Battalion The Royal Welch Fusiliers. Ingram's 1932–37. Killed in action 18 March 1943 at Donbaik, Burma aged 24. Rangoon Memorial – no known grave.

Blakeway. Lieutenant Roger Charles Blakeway, Royal Engineers. School House 1918–22. Killed in action 29 May 1940 aboard HMS *Grafton*,[4] serving with 671 General Construction Company, aged 36. Dunkirk Memorial – no known grave.

Bland. Pilot Officer George Roxberry Bland, RAFVR. Moser's 1935–40. Killed in action 16 April 1942 off Cherbourg, serving with 234 Squadron, Fighter Command, aged 20. Runnymede Memorial – no known grave.

Bland. Major William Fraser Bland, Royal Artillery. Moser's 1924–26. Killed in action 12 February 1942, serving with 5 Field Regiment, aged 34. Singapore Memorial – no known grave.

Bone. Flight Sergeant Anthony Bone, RAFVR. Churchill's 1939–43. Killed 18 March 1946 in an air accident over Rutland, aged 20. Buried in St Andrew's Churchyard, Whitchurch, Devon.

Bone. Flight Lieutenant John Bone, RAFVR. Churchill's 1935–41. Killed in action 3 May 1945 over Kiel, serving with 3 (Fighter) Squadron, aged 22. Buried in Kiel War Cemetery, Germany.

Booth. Flying Officer Kenneth Stanley Booth, RAFVR. Tombling's 1928–32. Killed 22 February 1942, serving with 16 Squadron, aged 27. Commemorated in Plymouth City Crematorium.

Borrett. Major Allen Cotton James Borrett, 1st/5th Battalion The Queen's Royal Regiment. Tombling's 1933–37. Killed in action 16 June 1944, aged 24. Buried in Bayeux War Cemetery, Normandy.

Boult. 2nd Lieutenant Reginald Herbert Boult, Royal Artillery. Rigg's 1934–38. Killed in action 25 January 1942, serving with 135 Field Regiment, aged 21. Singapore Memorial – no known grave.

Bowen. Flight Lieutenant Charles Earle Bowen, RAF. Oldham's 1929–32. Killed in action 1 October 1940 off the Isle of Wight, serving with 607 Squadron, Fighter Command, aged 24. Runnymede Memorial – no known grave.

Bowring. Flying Officer Norman Harvey Bowring, RAFVR. Churchill's 1933–38. Killed in action 4 December 1943, serving with 405 (RCAF) Squadron, Bomber Command, aged 23. Buried in Berlin War Cemetery.

Boyes. Flight Lieutenant Arthur Singleton Boyes, RAFVR. School

---

[4] The destroyer HMS *Grafton* was sunk in the English Channel by the German submarine U–62 during the Dunkirk evacuation.

House 1935–38. Killed in action 24 April 1944, serving with No 5 (Army Co-operation) Squadron, aged 24. Buried in Taukkyan War Cemetery, Rangoon, Burma.

Bradley. Wing Commander Terence Patrick Armstrong Bradley DSO DFC, RAF. Ridgemount 1931–34. Killed 10 April 1945 in an air accident, serving with 27 Squadron, aged 28. Buried in Chittagong War Cemetery, Bangladesh.

Bromley-Davenport. Captain John Bromley-Davenport, The Cheshire Regiment. Ridgemount 1933–38. Killed in action 2 November 1944, serving with the 1st Battalion The Manchester Regiment, aged 24. Buried in Leopoldsburg War Cemetery, Belgium.

Brotherton. Major Eric John Roderick Brotherton MC, 2nd Battalion The Royal Tank Regiment. Chance's 1929–34. Died of wounds 13 September 1944, aged 28. Buried in Coriano Ridge War Cemetery, Italy.

Bruce. Pilot Officer James Chisholm Bruce, Malayan Volunteer Air Force. Moore's 1921–26. Died 30 November 1942 in Mitsushima prisoner-of-war camp, Tokyo, aged 35. Buried in Yokohama War Cemetery, Japan.

Bulmer. Flight Lieutenant Edward Charles Bulmer, RAFVR. School House 1921–25. Killed 1 June 1944, aged 37. Buried in Hereford Cemetery.

Bulmer. Captain Oscar Theodore Bulmer, The King's Shropshire Light Infantry. Churchill's 1927–30. Killed in action 9 September 1944, serving with the 1st Battalion The Herefordshire Regiment, aged 31. Buried in Geel War Cemetery, Antwerp Province, Belgium.

Burne. Captain Roger Sambrooke Burne, Royal Artillery. Ridgemount 1932–36. Killed in action 3 August 1944, serving with 61 Field Regiment, aged 26. Buried in Ryes War Cemetery, Normandy.

Burt. Leading Aircraftsman Ronald Douglas Burt, RAFVR. Chance's 1934–38. Killed in action 20 April 1941, aged 20. Buried in St Mary's Churchyard, Knighton, Radnor.

Byrde. Captain Richard George De Fer Byrde, 1st Battalion The Welch Regiment. School House 1928–33. Killed in action 27 May 1941, aged 26. Buried in Suda Bay War Cemetery, Crete.

Carrick. Captain Michael Howard Carrick MC, Royal Artillery. Moser's 1934–38. Killed in action 27 June 1944, serving with 121 Medium Regiment, aged 24. Buried in Bayeux War Cemetery, Normandy.

Carter. Air Commodore Guy Lloyd Carter DSO AFC, RAF. School House 1915–17. Killed 18 July 1944, serving with HQ Balkan Air Force, aged 44. Buried in Bari War Cemetery, Italy.

Cave. Lieutenant George Charles Montagu Major Cave, The Devonshire Regiment. School House 1934–39. Killed in action 14 July 1943, serving with No. 3 Commando, aged 22. Buried in Catania War Cemetery, Sicily.

Chaine-Nickson. Lieutenant Michael Henry Chaine-Nickson, 2nd Battalion The Irish Guards. School House 1932–35. Killed in action 27 July 1944, aged 25. Buried in Ranville War Cemetery, Normandy.

Chant. Leading Aircraftman Richard Anthony Chant, RAFVR. Rigg's 1931–35. Killed 2 December 1940 in a night-flying accident, aged 23. Buried in St Peter's Churchyard, Stoke-upon-Tern, Shropshire.

Chant. Flying Officer William Morton Chant, RAFVR. Dayboys 1937–39. Killed in action 3 June 1944, serving with 158 Squadron, Bomber Command, aged 21. Buried in St-Désir War Cemetery, Normandy.

Clapham. Flight Lieutenant William Roy Clapham, RAF. School House 1924–28. Killed in action 28 May 1940 over Dunkirk, serving with 16 Squadron, aged 29. Buried in Longuenesse Cemetery, St-Omer, Pas-de-Calais, France.

Clark. Major Francis William Clark, The Argyll and Sutherland Highlanders. School House 1925–30. Died of wounds between 3 and 6 February 1944, serving with No. 9 Commando, aged 31. Cassino Memorial, Italy – no known grave.

Clark. 2nd Lieutenant Neil Blake Clark, Irish Guards. Tombling's 1939–44. Killed 17 January 1946 in a grenade accident, aged 19. Buried in Maghera Churchyard, Northern Ireland.

Clark. Sub-Lieutenant Thomas Roderick Jackson Clark, RNVR. Ingram's 1938–43. Killed in action 6 December 1944 in HMS *Bullen*,[5] aged 20. Chatham Memorial – no known grave.

Clarkson. Captain Charles Kenneth Clarkson, Royal Corps of Signals. School House 1930–34. Killed 15 February 1944, serving with 56th Divisional Signals Regiment, aged 27. Buried in Anzio War Cemetery, Italy.

Clayton. Lieutenant Arthur Edmondston Clayton, Hong Kong and Singapore Royal Artillery. Tombling's 1930–33. Killed in action 25 December 1941, serving with 1st Hong Kong Regiment, aged 25. Sai Wan Memorial, Hong Kong – no known grave.

Clegg-Hill. Major The Honourable Frederick Raymond Clegg-Hill, 4th Battalion The King's Shropshire Light Infantry. Oldham's 1924–28. Killed in action 13 April 1945, aged 35. Buried in Becklingen War Cemetery, Soltau, Germany.

Clover. Private Joseph Alexander Clover, The Royal Natal Carbineers. Rigg's 1930–35. Shot and killed 1 November 1942 on his third attempt to

---

[5] The frigate HMS *Bullen* was torpedoed and sunk by the German submarine U–775 off Strathy Point, northern Scotland.

escape from a prisoner-of-war camp, aged 26. Buried in Tripoli War Cemetery, Libya.

Clover. Lieutenant Commander (S) John Hugh Peterson Clover, RN (Retired). Moore's 1921–25. Died 14 April 1948, aged 40.

Cochrane. Captain Joseph Brian Cochrane, Royal Engineers. Baker's/Moore's 1916–21. Died 26 September 1945, aged 43. Buried in Madras War Cemetery, India.

Coe. Lance Corporal William Charles Coe, 3rd (East African) Reconnaissance Regiment. Chance's 1921–24. Killed in action 20 July 1940, aged 33. Buried in Nairobi War Cemetery, Kenya.

Coleman. Lance Bombardier John Coleman, Royal Artillery. Tombling's 1934–39. Killed in action 28 May 1940, serving with 69 Medium Regiment, aged 19. Buried in Wormhoudt Cemetery, Pas-de-Calais, France.

Colmore. Sergeant Reginald Thomas Blayney Colmore, Intelligence Corps, Ingram's 1929–34. Killed 27 August 1941, serving with 18 Field Security Section, aged 26. Buried in St Mary's Churchyard, Studham, Bedfordshire.

Colvile. Captain Philip Antony Fiennes Colvile, 1st Battalion The Oxfordshire and Buckinghamshire Light Infantry. School House 1932–36. Killed in action 16 July 1944, aged 26. Buried in Brouay War Cemetery, Normandy.

Comins. Captain (QM) Colin Frederick Innes Comins, Royal Artillery. Rigg's 1918–22. Died 14 April 1942 whilst a prisoner-of-war, after serving with 122 Field Regiment, aged 38. Buried in Kranji War Cemetery, Singapore.

Cooke. Wing Commander Humphrey Desmond Cooke, RAF. Oldham's 1927–31. Killed in action 26 June 1942 over Bremen, serving with 206 Squadron, aged 28. Buried in Hamburg War Cemetery.

Cosgrave. Lieutenant Henry Alexander Cosgrave, The Royal Tank Regiment. Rigg's 1933–38. Killed in action 25 October 1942, serving with HQ 7th Armoured Division, aged 22. Buried in El Alamein War Cemetery, Egypt.

Cosgrave. Sergeant Pilot Robert Gerald Cosgrave, RAF. Rigg's 1935–39. Killed 13 June 1941 in an air accident over Wales, aged 19. Commemorated in Golders Green Crematorium, London.

Cross. Lieutenant The Honourable Richmond Gilfrid Cross MBE, Royal Engineers. Ingram's 1935–40. Killed in action 13 May 1944, serving with 578 Field Company, aged 22. Buried in Cassino War Cemetery, Italy.

Cross. Lieutenant Timothy Oliver Kynaston Cross, 1st Battalion The Rifle Brigade. Ridgemount 1937–42. Killed in action 15 November 1944, aged 20. Buried in Mierlo War Cemetery, North Brabant, Holland.

Crowley. Lieutenant Humphrey William Yates Crowley, Royal Artillery. Ridgemount 1933–38. Killed in action 27 March 1945, serving with 132 Field Regiment, aged 25. Buried in Faenza War Cemetery, Italy.

Darbishire. Squadron Leader Charles Frances Darbishire, RAF. Ridgemount 1930–34. Killed in action 11 December 1941 in Libya, aged 25. Alamein Memorial, Egypt – no known grave.

Davies. Second Engineer Noel Gordon Davies, Merchant Navy. Oldham's 1923–29. Killed in action 13 September 1942 on S.S. *Stone Street*,[6] aged 32. Tower Hill Memorial, London – no known grave.

Davies-Cooke. Flying Officer Paul John Davies-Cooke, RAF. Churchill's 1930–35. Killed in action 27 September 1940 over Kent, serving with 72 Squadron, Fighter Command, aged 23. Buried in St John's Churchyard, Rhydymwyn, Flint.

Deuchar. Lieutenant James Derek Deuchar, The King's Own Scottish Borderers. School House 1921–25. Died 23 June 1940, aged 33. Buried in Corbridge Cemetery, Northumberland.

Distin. Lieutenant James Wardlaw Distin, Royal Corps of Signals. Chance's 1935–39. Killed 29 April 1943, aged 22. Buried in Enfidaville War Cemetery, Tunisia.

Douglass. Major William James Douglass, 1st Battalion The Manchester Regiment. Chance's 1922–26. Died of wounds 17 February 1942, aged 33. Buried in Kranji War Cemetery, Singapore.

Dubois. Sergeant John Dubois, RAF. Dayboys 1935–36. Died 2 January 1945, serving with 100 Squadron, Bomber Command, aged 24. Runnymede Memorial – no known grave.

Dunch. Bombardier Edward Hugh MacLagen Dunch, Royal Artillery. Moser's 1938–43. Died at sea 13 October 1947, aged 22.

Eccles-Holmes. Captain James Francis Eccles-Holmes, Indian Army. Rigg's 1912–15. Died 12 November 1939 after an operation in hospital, aged 41.

Eden-Smith. Sub-Lieutenant Waller Eden-Smith, RNVR. School House 1921–25. Killed in action 20 February 1945 in HMS *Vervain*,[7] aged 38. Portsmouth Memorial – no known grave.

Edwards. Pilot Officer William Hotchkiss Edwards, RAFVR. Dayboys 1932–36. Killed 12 March 1941, serving with 502 Squadron, Coastal Command, aged 22. Buried in Shrewsbury General Cemetery.

Evans. Major Eric Glyn Evans, Royal Artillery. Churchill's 1931–35. Killed

---

[6] S.S. *Stone Street*, in convoy ON–127, was sunk by the German submarine U–594 in the western Atlantic, east of Newfoundland.

[7] The corvette HMS *Vervain* was torpedoed and sunk in St George's Channel by the German submarine U–1276.

in action 26 April 1943, serving with 146 Field Regiment, aged 25. Buried in Enfidaville War Cemetery, Tunisia.

Evans. Captain William Lees Evans, Royal Artillery. School House 1929–33. Killed in action 8 February 1941, serving with 68 Medium Regiment, aged 25. Buried in Keren War Cemetery, Ethiopia.

Everett. Gunner John Huskisson Everett, Royal Artillery. Oldham's 1931–32. Killed in action 21 April 1943, serving with 67 Field Regiment, aged 24. Buried in Medjez-el-Bab War Cemetery, Tunisia.

Fisher. Pilot Officer John Norman Fisher, RAFVR. School House 1933–37. Killed in action 9 April 1941, serving with 9 Squadron, Bomber Command, aged 22. Buried in Reichswald War Cemetery, Kleve (Cleves), Germany.

Forgan. Captain John Keith Forgan, 6th Battalion The Cheshire Regiment. Rigg's 1935–38. Killed in action 18 September 1944, aged 23. Buried in Coriano Ridge War Cemetery, Italy.

Foster-Pegg. Lieutenant Timothy George Foster-Pegg, Royal Artillery. Ridgemount 1931–34. Died 4 August 1942, aged 25. Buried in Delhi War Cemetery, India.

Gage. Pilot Officer Douglas Hugh Gage, RAFVR. Rigg's 1931–35. Killed in action 6 June 1941 off the south coast, serving with 91 Squadron, Fighter Command, aged 23. Runnymede Memorial – no known grave.

Gale. Lieutenant Anthony Gale, Royal Marines. Chance's 1934–39. Killed in action 7 June 1944, serving with No. 45 Commando, aged 23. Buried in Tilly-sur-Seulles War Cemetery, Normandy.

Gallop. Lieutenant Michael Powell Gallop, RNVR. Ridgemount 1927–31. Killed in action 4 June 1942 in HMS *Cocker*,[8] aged 28. Lowestoft Naval Memorial, Suffolk – no known grave.

Gamble. Captain Edward Moore Gamble, Royal Army Medical Corps. Rigg's 1920–22. Died 26 December 1943. Buried in Kirkee War Cemetery, Poona, India.

Gardner. Lieutenant Nigel Drake Turville Gardner, 3rd Battalion The Coldstream Guards. Moser's 1936–41. Killed in action 22 July 1944, aged 21. Buried in Florence War Cemetery, Italy.

Gibbon Scott. Sergeant Huntley Robert Gibbon Scott, 8th King's Royal Irish Hussars. Oldham's 1937–41. Killed in action 30 March 1945, aged 22. Buried in Reichswald War Cemetery, Kleve (Cleves), Germany.

Gibson. Captain Ian Grant Gibson, 4th Battalion The Welch Regiment. Moser's 1936–38. Killed 12 August 1943 in a training accident, aged 21. Buried in Lewes Cemetery, Sussex.

---

[8] The former whaler HMS *Cocker* was torpedoed and sunk by the German submarine U–331 in the Mediterranean, off the Libyan/Egyptian coast.

Gibson-Smith. Captain Richard Fox Gibson-Smith, 4th Battalion, 1st King George V's Own Gurkha Rifles (The Malaun Regiment). Rigg's 1936–41. Killed in action 7 May 1944, aged 21. Rangoon Memorial, Burma – no known grave.

Giles. Captain Foster Abney Giles, 8th Punjab Regiment. School House 1927–29. Killed in action 16 December 1941, aged 28. Singapore Memorial – no known grave.

Giles. Gunner Kenneth Giles, Royal Artillery. Rigg's 1933–37. Died of wounds 21 June 1942, serving with 67 Medium Regiment, aged 22. Buried in Knightsbridge War Cemetery, Acroma, Libya.

Gillson. Lieutenant-Colonel Godfrey Anthony Gillson, The King's Own Scottish Borderers. Oldham's 1922–27. Killed 3 March 1944 in an aircraft loss between Calcutta and Colombo, aged 35. Rangoon Memorial, Burma – no known grave.

Glover. Flying Officer Alan Otto Glover, RAF. Moser's 1931–34. Killed in action 29 October 1939, serving with 607 Squadron, Fighter Command, aged 21. Buried in St Lawrence's Churchyard, Frodsham, Cheshire.

Glover. Sub-Lieutenant Alexander John Glover, RNVR. Moser's 1933–37. Killed in action 29 May 1940 in HMS *Gracie Fields*,[9] aged 21. Portsmouth Memorial – no known grave.

Goodbody. Captain William James Perry Goodbody, 3rd County of London Yeomanry. School House 1920–24. Died of wounds 29 May 1942, aged 36. Buried in Tobruk War Cemetery, Libya.

Goodwin. Flying Officer Henry MacDonald Goodwin, Auxiliary Air Force. Rigg's 1929–32. Killed in action 14 August 1940 off the Dorset coast, serving with 609 Squadron, Fighter Command, aged 25. Buried in St Cassian's Churchyard, Chaddesley Corbett, Worcestershire.

Gray. Sub-Lieutenant (A) John Edward Gray, RNVR, Fleet Air Arm. Ingram's 1937–42. Killed 30 May 1945 on a night-flying exercise off the East African coast, serving with 827 Squadron in HMS *Colossus*, aged 21. Lee-on-Solent Memorial – no known grave.

Greenhous. Lieutenant Guy William Norman Greenhous, The King's Shropshire Light Infantry. Dayboys 1934–37. Killed in action 28 January 1944, serving with the 1st Battalion The Sierra Leone Regiment, aged 23. Rangoon Memorial, Burma – no known grave.

Greenwood. John Edwin Greenwood. Ridgemount 1917–22. Killed 4 September 1940 in an air raid on the Vickers Armstrong Works, Weybridge, Surrey, aged 35.

Gregg. Flying Officer John Francis FitzGerald Gregg, RAFVR. School

---

[9] The minesweeper HMS *Gracie Fields* was sunk by German aircraft off Dunkirk, during the evacuation of the British Expeditionary Force.

House 1917–21. Died 29 November 1943 whilst a prisoner-of-war, aged 40. Singapore Memorial – no known grave.

Grundy. Sergeant Pilot Alan Peter James Grundy, RAFVR. Ingram's 1933–38. Killed in action 26 August 1941, serving with 106 Squadron, Bomber Command, aged 21. Runnymede Memorial – no known grave.

Hackett. Squadron Leader Charles Desmond Hackett, RAF. Churchill's 1929–33. Killed 4 April 1941, serving with 27 Squadron, aged 27. Singapore Memorial – no known grave.

Haden. Lieutenant Walter Cameron Haden, 6th Battalion The Grenadier Guards. Dayboys 1922–25. Killed in action 17 March 1943, aged 36. Buried in Sfax War Cemetery, Tunisia.

Hamilton. Major Donald George Hamilton MC, 1st Battalion The King's Shropshire Light Infantry. School House 1928–32. Killed 15 February 1942, aged 26. Buried in All Saints Old Churchyard, Churchill, Oxfordshire.

Harris. Gunner John Corbett Harris, Royal Artillery. Moore's 1918–20. Killed in action 28 October 1942, serving with 30 Light Anti-Aircraft Regiment, aged 38. Buried in El Alamein War Cemetery, Egypt.

Harrison. Captain Michael George Harrison, 2nd Battalion The Royal Welch Fusiliers. School House 1930–35. Killed in action 5 May 1942, aged 25. Buried in Diego Suarez War Cemetery, Madagascar.

Hart. Flight Lieutenant Edward Chichester Hart, RAFVR. Moser's 1931–35. Killed in action 15 September 1943, serving with 138 (Special Duties) Squadron,[10] aged 25. Runnymede Memorial – no known grave.

Harvey. Flying Officer Alexander Muir Harvey, RAFVR. Ingram's 1934–38. Killed in action 20 January 1942, serving with 49 Squadron, Bomber Command, aged 21. Buried in Noorddijk General Cemetery, Groningen, Holland.

Hellyer. Pilot Officer Denis Hellyer, RAFVR. Moser's 1931–35. Killed in action 20 May 1942, serving with 156 Squadron, Bomber Command, aged 25. Buried in Hargnies Cemetery, Ardennes, Belgium.

Hibbert. Flying Officer Nowell Percy Hibbert DFC, RAFVR. Oldham's 1936–41. Killed in action 29 January 1945 in a raid on Stuttgart, serving with 156 (Pathfinder) Squadron, Bomber Command, aged 21. Buried in Durnbach War Cemetery, Bad Tölz, Bavaria.

Hillary. Flight Lieutenant Richard Hope Hillary, RAFVR. Churchill's 1931–37. Killed 8 January 1943 in an air accident,[11] aged 23. Commemorated in Golders Green Crematorium, London.

[10] 138 (Special Duties) Squadron worked with the Special Operations Executive (SOE).
[11] Hillary, author of *The Last Enemy*, was serving with 54 Operational Training Unit, at RAF Charterhall, Berwickshire. See Michael Charlesworth, *Two of the Few*, Greenbank Press 2003, Chapter VI for the circumstances of his death.

Hingley. Lieutenant Gerald Bertram Hingley, 7th Battalion The Worcestershire Regiment. Chance's 1925–30. Killed in action 20 May 1940, aged 28. Buried in Bruyelle War Cemetery, Antoing, Tournai, Belgium.

Hoare. Lieutenant Ian Lowcock Hoare, Royal Engineers. Ingram's 1929–34. Killed 15 April 1942 in a bomb explosion, serving with 22 Bomb Disposal Company, aged 25. Buried in Norwich Cemetery.

Holdsworth. Flight Lieutenant Richard William Gilbert Holdsworth, RAFVR. School House 1924–30. Killed in action 30 April 1942, serving with 502 Squadron, Coastal Command, aged 31. Buried in Wolvercote Cemetery, Oxfordshire.

Horlick. Lieutenant Gerald Peter Horlick, RN. Churchill's 1935–39. Killed in action 14 March 1943 in HMS *Thunderbolt*,[12] aged 21. Portsmouth Memorial – no known grave.

Hulton-Harrop. Pilot Officer Montagu Leslie Hulton-Harrop, RAF. Dayboys 1928–29. Accidentally killed 6 September 1939, serving with 56 Squadron, Fighter Command, aged 26. Buried in St Andrew's Churchyard, North Weald Bassett, Essex.[13]

Hunt. Sub-Lieutenant Peter James Hunt, RNVR. Chance's 1938–42. Killed 22 April 1944, serving in HMS *Varbel*,[14] aged 19. Portsmouth Memorial – no known grave.

Hyde. Captain Gustavus Patrick Rochfort Hyde, Irish Guards. Rigg's 1920–24. Died 12 July 1945, aged 39. Buried in Brookwood Military Cemetery, Surrey.

Irvine. Pilot Officer James Melville Dundas Irvine, RAF. Tombling's 1932–36. Killed 24 May 1940 in an air accident, serving with 106 Squadron, Bomber Command, aged 21. Buried in London Road Cemetery, Coventry.

Ives. Captain James Ives, Royal Artillery. Ingram's 1918–22. Died 6 January 1944, serving with 142 Heavy Anti-Aircraft Regiment, aged 39. Buried in Yeadon Cemetery, Yorkshire.

James. Flight Lieutenant Clement Hugh Lawton James, RAFVR. Ingram's 1934–39. Killed 11 March 1944, serving with 97 Squadron, Bomber Command, aged 23. Buried in St Laurence Churchyard, Walton-upon-Trent, Staffordshire.

Jarmain. Major William John Fletcher Jarmain, Royal Artillery. Dayboys

---

[12] The submarine HMS *Thunderbolt* (formerly *Thetis*) was sunk on 14 March 1943 in the Messina Strait, Sicily by the Italian corvette *Cicogna*.
[13] Hulton-Harrop was accidentally shot down by another fighter aircraft, before proper identification.
[14] HMS *Varbel* was the shore establishment for midget submarines at The Kyles of Bute Hydropathic Hotel, Port Bannatyne, Rothesay, Scotland.

1925–29. Killed in action 26 June 1944, serving with 61 Anti-Tank Regiment, aged 33. Buried in Ranville War Cemetery, Normandy.

Johnson. Major Richard Victor Guy Neville Johnson MC, 1st Battalion The Gloucestershire Regiment. School House 1929–33. Killed in action 19 April 1942, aged 27. Rangoon Memorial, Burma – no known grave.

Johnston. Lieutenant David Kenneth Johnston, The Durham Light Infantry. Ingram's 1934–39. Killed in action 24 March 1945, serving with the 12th (Airborne) Battalion The Devonshire Regiment, aged 24. Buried in Reichswald War Cemetery, Kleve (Cleves), Germany.

Jonas. Flight Lieutenant Adrian Conway Jonas, RAFVR. Rigg's 1931–34. Killed 28 August 1944, aged 26. Buried in Chorleywood Road Cemetery, Hertfordshire.

Jones. Private Derek Stanley Fletcher Jones, Pioneer Corps. Rigg's 1926–29. Killed 16 September 1940 in a road accident, aged 27. Buried in Birkdale Cemetery, Southport, Lancashire.

Keitley. 2nd Lieutenant John Bernard Humby Keitley, 2nd Battalion The Manchester Regiment. Churchill's 1932–37. Killed in action 27 May 1940, aged 21. Dunkirk Memorial – no known grave.

Kempton. Ordinary Signalman Sylvius Lawrence Kempton, RNVR. Moser's 1936–37. Killed in action 24 May 1941 in HMS *Hood*,[15] aged 19. Portsmouth Memorial – no known grave.

King. Squadron Leader Terence Sidney Raymond King, RAF. Rigg's 1925–27. Killed in action 10 March 1944, serving with 90 Squadron, Bomber Command, aged 32. Buried in Brazey-en-Plaine Cemetery, Dijon, Côte-d'Or, France.

Knighton. Flying Officer Francis Sale Knighton, RAFVR. School House 1936–41. Killed 7 March 1944 over the Mediterranean, serving with 500 Squadron, aged 21. Malta Memorial – no known grave.

Lander. Gunner John Gerald Heath Lander, Hong Kong Volunteer Defence Corps. School House 1921–26. Killed in action 25 December 1941, aged 34. Buried in Sai Wan Cemetery, Hong Kong.

Langford-James. Sergeant John Clough Langford-James, RAFVR. Moser's 1925–27. Killed in action 10 May 1942, serving with 353 Squadron, aged 30. Buried in Delhi War Cemetery, India.

Lee. Major John Stephen Grosvenor Lee, 1st Battalion The King's Shropshire Light Infantry. Oldham's 1932–37. Killed in action 8 February 1944, aged 24. Buried in Beachhead War Cemetery, Anzio, Italy.

Lloyd. Captain Geoffrey Walter Lloyd MC, Royal Artillery. School House

---

[15] The battleship HMS *Hood* was sunk off Greenland by the German battleship *Bismarck*.

1931–35. Killed in action 21 January 1945, serving with 160 Field Regiment, aged 27. Rangoon Memorial, Burma – no known grave.

Lloyd. Major-General Wilfrid Lewis Lloyd CBE DSO and bar MC. Dayboys and Oldham's 1910–13. Killed 22 January 1944 in a motor accident whilst commanding 10th Indian Division, aged 47. Buried in Heliopolis War Cemetery, Egypt.

Lock. Lieutenant Malcolm Edward Lock, 1st (Armoured) Battalion The Coldstream Guards. Ridgemount 1935–40. Killed in action 9 March 1945, aged 23. Buried in Reichswald War Cemetery, Kleve (Cleves), Germany.

Long. Lance Bombardier Geoffrey Reuben Long, Royal Artillery. Dayboys 1935–38. Killed in action 7 October 1943, serving with 64 Field Regiment, aged 22. Buried in Naples War Cemetery, Italy.

Loram. Captain John Scott Loram MC, Royal Artillery. Moser's 1935–36. Killed in action 14 April 1943, serving with 132 Field Regiment, aged 22. Buried in Medjez-el-Bab War Cemetery, Tunisia.

Lunt. 2nd Lieutenant Donald Howard Lunt, 7th Battalion The Worcestershire Regiment. Whitfield's 1931–36. Died of wounds between 22 and 25 May 1940, aged 22. Buried in Wormhoudt Cemetery, Pas-de-Calais, France.

MacConnell. 2nd Lieutenant John Laird MacConnell, Royal Artillery. Ridgemount 1931–36. Died 17 April 1944, serving with 16 Light Anti-Aircraft Regiment, aged 26. Buried in Helensburgh Cemetery, Dumbarton, Scotland.

Mackinnon. 2nd Lieutenant James Mackinnon, Royal Marines. Tombling's 1937–42. Died of wounds 14 March 1944, serving with No. 44 Commando, aged 19. Buried in Taukkyan War Cemetery, Rangoon, Burma.

Macleod. Pilot Officer Norman Macleod, RAFVR. Tombling's 1936–40. Killed 5 August 1942, aged 20. Buried in West Kilbride Cemetery, Ayrshire, Scotland.

Malley. Lieutenant Wilfred Lucking Malley, 40th Battalion The Royal Tank Regiment. Rigg's 1921–26. Killed in action 31 October 1942, aged 34. Buried in El Alamein War Cemetery, Egypt.

Manly. Lieutenant-Colonel Lawrence Arthur Manly MC, 2nd Battalion The Lancashire Fusiliers. Moser's 1913–16. Killed in action 25 November 1942, aged 43. Buried in Oued Zarga War Cemetery, Tunisia.

Mather. Lieutenant Alfred Leigh Mather, 2nd Battalion The Cheshire Regiment. Moser's 1932–37. Killed 8 October 1942, aged 23. Buried in El Alamein War Cemetery, Egypt.

Mauchlen. Pilot Officer Douglas Clark Mauchlen, RAFVR. Chance's 1935–38. Killed 30 August 1941, serving with 38 (Bomber) Squadron, aged 20. Buried in Tripoli War Cemetery, Libya.

McHarg. Major Kenneth Willis McHarg, 1st/6th Battalion The Duke of Wellington's Regiment. Moser's 1928–32. Killed in action 16 June 1944, aged 29. Buried in Hottot-les-Bagues War Cemetery, Normandy.

Miller. Flight Lieutenant Kenneth MacIver Miller, RAF. School House 1928–32. Killed in action 3 November 1942, serving with 73 (Fighter) Squadron, aged 28. Buried in El Alamein War Cemetery, Egypt.

Mills. Squadron Leader Anthony Alan Frank Mills, RAFVR. Ingram's 1930–33. Killed in action 1 January 1945, serving with 115 Squadron, Bomber Command, aged 28. Buried in Leopoldsburg War Cemetery, Belgium.

Milward. 2nd Lieutenant Peter Charles Sutherland Milward, 2nd Battalion The Duke of Cornwall's Light Infantry. Dayboys 1934–37. Died of wounds 16 December 1939, aged 20. Buried in Beuvry Cemetery, Pas-de-Calais, France.

Mitchell. 2nd Lieutenant Geoffrey Andrew Mitchell, 4th/7th Royal Dragoon Guards. Rigg's 1937–40. Killed in action 10 June 1944, aged 20. Buried in Tilly-sur-Seulles War Cemetery, Normandy.

Mitchell. Captain Kenneth Amyot Mitchell, Royal Artillery. Rigg's 1933–38. Died of wounds 18 August 1942 whilst a prisoner-of-war, after serving with 157 Field Regiment, aged 22. Buried in Naples War Cemetery, Italy.

Mosley. Captain Michael Henry Mosley MC, 2nd Battalion The Rifle Brigade. Ridgemount 1926–31. Killed in action 2 November 1942, aged 30. Buried in El Alamein War Cemetery, Egypt.

Mossman. Captain Frederick George Mossman, Royal Artillery. Oldham's 1929–33. Died 20 June 1945, aged 29. Buried in Ramleh War Cemetery, Israel.

Muir. Captain Harold Michael Muir, The 2nd Royal Gloucestershire Hussars. Moser's 1932–36. Killed in action 6 June 1942, aged 24. Alamein Memorial, Egypt – no known grave.

Negus. Squadron Leader Michael Negus DFC, RAF. Oldham's 1933–35. Killed 7 April 1944, serving with 605 (Intruder) Squadron, Fighter Command, aged 23. Runnymede Memorial – no known grave.

Norman. Sub-Lieutenant (A) Owen Duncan Norman, RNVR, Fleet Air Arm. Rigg's 1936–40. Killed in action 12 October 1942, serving in HMS *Daedalus*,[16] aged 20. Lee-on-Solent Memorial – no known grave.[17]

Oldham. Lieutenant Donald Curzon Oldham, 1st Battalion The Rifle Brigade. Ridgemount 1935–39. Died of wounds 9 September 1942, aged 21. Buried in Heliopolis War Cemetery, Cairo, Egypt.

---

[16] HMS *Daedalus* was a Royal Naval Air Station at Lee-on-Solent, Hampshire.

[17] The Memorial Room extension to Rigg's Hall, built in 1947, and now the library, was funded by his parents in his memory.

Oldham. Lieutenant-Colonel Wilfrid Henry Burd Oldham DSO MC, 1st Battalion, 4th Prince of Wales's Own Gurkha Rifles. Oldham's 1923–28. Killed in action 16 June 1944, aged 34. Rangoon Memorial, Burma – no known grave.

Openshaw. Sergeant Oliver Ormrod Openshaw, RAFVR. School House 1934–37. Killed 8 February 1943, aged 23. Buried in St Garmon Churchyard, Llanfechain, Powys.

Ord. Sub-Lieutenant Craven Basil Ord, RNVR. Moser's 1932–36. Killed 29 October 1940 in a bomb disposal accident, serving in HMS *President*, aged 22. Buried in Shotley Royal Naval Cemetery, Suffolk.[18]

Ormrod. Captain Oliver Pim Ormrod, Royal Artillery. School House 1929–33. Died 22 October 1942, aged 26. Buried in Alexandria War Memorial Cemetery, Egypt.

Owen Hughes. Captain John Conway Owen Hughes, Royal Artillery. Ingram's 1929–34. Died 26 July 1942 whilst a prisoner-of-war, after serving with 25 Field Regiment, aged 26. Buried in Caserta War Cemetery, Italy.

Peacock. Sergeant Pilot Ernest Ronald Peacock, RAFVR. Chance's 1935–40. Killed 17 May 1941 in an air training accident in Scotland, aged 19. Runnymede Memorial – no known grave.

Pease. Lieutenant Rupert Llewellyn Pease, Federated Malay States Volunteers. Oldham's 1918–22. Died 12 July 1945 whilst a prisoner-of-war in Changi Internment Camp, Singapore, aged 39. Malaya Civilian Memorial – no known grave.

Pendlebury. Captain Henry Maurice Pendlebury, Federated Malay States Volunteers. Dayboys 1908–12. Died 22 September 1945 in hospital in Bangalore, India, after 3½ years' captivity in Singapore, aged 51.

Phillips. Wing Commander Anthony Dockray Phillips DSO DFC, RAF. Moser's 1932–35. Killed in action 4 July 1944, serving with 248 Squadron, Fighter Command, aged 26. Buried in Bénodet Cemetery, Finistère, France.

Pilkington. Ordinary Coder Brian Pilkington, RNVR. Moser's 1938–41. Killed in action 7 January 1944 in HMS *Tweed*,[19] aged 19. Portsmouth Memorial – no known grave.

Platt. Principal Secretary Robert Paus Platt OBE, Colonial Service. Moser's 1919–23. Killed 22 July 1946 in the King David Hotel, Jerusalem bomb explosion, aged 41. Buried in Jerusalem.

Plowden. Major Humphrey Roger Plowden, 17th Lancers. Sergeant's

---

[18] A paten and chalice were presented to the School Chapel in his memory.

[19] The frigate HMS *Tweed* was torpedoed and sunk by the German submarine U-305 south-west of Ireland.

1905–06. Died 11 February 1942, aged 52. Buried in Plowden Churchyard, Shropshire.

Pooley. Major John Bertram Vaughan Pooley MC, Royal Artillery. Ridgemount 1932–37. Killed in action 7 June 1944, serving with No. 3 Commando, aged 25. Buried in Bayeux War Cemetery, Normandy.

Porter. Pilot Officer Anthony Richard Porter, RAFVR. Oldham's 1935–39. Killed in action 6 December 1941, serving with 451 (RAAF) Squadron, aged 20. Alamein Memorial, Egypt – no known grave.

Pudsey. Flight Lieutenant Edward Estil Pudsey, RAFVR. Tombling's 1934–39. Killed in action 15 November 1943, serving with 264 Squadron, Fighter Command, aged 23. Buried in Clichy Cemetery, Paris.

Pullen. Pilot Officer Geoffrey Hiram Standeford Pullen, RAFVR. Rigg's 1930–33. Killed in action 17 June 1941, serving with 405 (RCAF) Squadron, Bomber Command, aged 25. Runnymede Memorial – no known grave.

Pullin. Captain Denis Herbert Pullin, Royal Artillery. Dayboys 1921–25. Killed in action 14 June 1944, serving with 127 Field Regiment, aged 37. Buried in Hermanville War Cemetery, Normandy.

Quinn. The Reverend Joseph Edward Gough Quinn MC, Royal Army Chaplains' Department. School House 1927–32. Killed in action 23 September 1943, aged 29. Buried in Salerno War Cemetery, Italy.[20]

Ractivand. Demetrius Ractivand MC. Rigg's 1912–15. Killed April 1941, when a ship on which he was being evacuated from Greece was bombed in Piraeus harbour.

Rafter. Flying Officer Charles William Arthur Haughton Rafter, RAF. School House 1932–35. Killed 11 October 1940 in an aircraft accident over Suffolk, serving with 214 Squadron, Bomber Command, aged 22. Buried in St Peter's Churchyard, Harborne, Birmingham.

Rafter. Pilot Officer William Pearse Haughton Rafter, RAF. School House 1935–36. Killed 29 November 1940 on operations over Kent, serving with 603 Squadron, Fighter Command, aged 19. Buried in St Peter's Churchyard, Harborne, Birmingham.

Raikes. Captain Marcus Hamilton Raikes, The Border Regiment. School House 1903–07. Died 13 December 1942, aged 53. Buried in Bledington Cemetery, Gloucestershire.

Randall. Sergeant Arthur Bernard Randall, RAFVR. Oldham's 1940–42. Killed in action 28 April 1944, serving with 434 (RCAF) Squadron, Bomber Command, aged 19. Buried in Heverlee War Cemetery, Louvain, Belgium.

Ray. Sergeant Stephen Curnick Ray, RAFVR. Rigg's 1935–38. Killed 29

---

[20] The Quinn History Prize was endowed in his memory by his father.

96

October 1941 on operations over the Mediterranean, serving with 148 (Bomber) Squadron, aged 20. Alamein Memorial, Egypt – no known grave.

Rée. Lieutenant Edward Anton Rée, The Royal Sussex Regiment. School House 1914–19. Died 19 March 1949 at Seaford, Sussex from hardships sustained whilst a prisoner-of-war.

Rée. Warrant Officer Class II Eric Lionel Rée, Intelligence Corps. School House 1920–24. Accidentally killed 21 November 1943, aged 37. Buried in Dely Ibrahim War Cemetery, Algeria.

Richards. Lieutenant John Morgan Richards, Royal Engineers, Ridgemount 1920–22. Killed 30 November 1944 in a motor accident, aged 38. Buried in Imphal War Cemetery, Manipur, India.

Roberts. Flight Lieutenant Egerton James Ashurst Roberts, RAFVR. School House 1916–19. Killed 12 July 1942, serving with the RAF Regiment, aged 40. Buried in Kinloss Abbey Cemetery, Grampian, Scotland.

Roberts. Captain George Richard Gorton Roberts, Royal Artillery. Tombling's 1928–33. Killed 13 or 14 April 1942 in a demonstration accident at Warminster, serving with 1 Light Anti-Aircraft Regiment, aged 27. Buried in Guilsfield Cemetery, Welshpool, Powys.

Robinson. Flying Officer John Stewart Robinson, RAFVR. Rigg's 1934–36. Killed in action 14 February 1942, serving with 62 Squadron, aged 21. Singapore Memorial – no known grave.

Robson-Scott. Sergeant Gunner Thomas Robson-Scott, RAFVR. Moser's 1936–40. Killed in action 12 December 1941, serving with 106 Squadron, Bomber Command, aged 19. Buried in Reichswald War Cemetery, Kleve (Cleves), Germany.

Rodier. Sub-Lieutenant Mark Fleming Rodier, RNVR. Ingram's 1930–35. Killed in action 28 March 1942 in the St-Nazaire raid in command of HM Motor Launch 177,[21] aged 24. Plymouth Memorial – no known grave.

Ronald. Major Alexander Scott Ronald, The King's Royal Rifle Corps. Rigg's 1923–28. Killed in action 8 November 1942, serving with No. 6 Commando, aged 33. Buried in Dely Ibrahim War Cemetery, Algeria.

Room. Lieutenant Robert Douglas Room, The Royal Irish Fusiliers. Oldham's 1934–39. Died 17 July 1945, aged 25.

Rugg. Captain Reginald Francis Rugg, The Queen's Royal Regiment.

[21] Rodier was in command of HM Motor Launch 177 during Operation Chariot – the St-Nazaire raid, for which he was posthumously mentioned in despatches. See James Dorrian, *Storming St Nazaire*, Leo Cooper 1998 (ISBN 0 85052 419 9), and C. E. Lucas Phillips, *The Greatest Raid of All*, Heinemann 1958, especially pages 177–8 and 230–1 for his part in the operation, and the circumstances of his death.

School House 1905–09. Died 21 May 1944, aged 52. Commemorated in the South London Crematorium.

Scholefield. Sub-Lieutenant (A) Lewis Ernest Hall Scholefield, RNVR. Chance's 1930–31. Killed 18 November 1940 in a flying accident off Northern Ireland, whilst attached to 502 Squadron, Coastal Command RAF, aged 24. Buried in St Thomas's Churchyard, Friarmere, Yorkshire.

Sclater. Major Robert Oakes Sclater, The York and Lancaster Regiment. Moser's 1923–27. Died 1 December 1943, aged 34. Commemorated in Glasgow Crematorium.

Scott. Pilot Officer Alec Maxtone Wright Scott, RAFVR. Rigg's 1925–30. Killed 2 January 1941 during test flying, serving with 605 Squadron, Fighter Command, aged 29. Buried in St Mary's Churchyard, Black Bourton, Oxfordshire.[22]

Scott. Ordinary Seaman Mark Scott, RNVR. School House 1935–41. Killed in action 17 January 1942 in HMS *Matabele*,[23] aged 19. Plymouth Memorial – no known grave.

Scott. Pilot Officer Michael Andrew Scott, RAFVR. School House 1929–33. Killed 24 May 1941 on operations over the North Sea, serving with 110 Squadron, Bomber Command, aged 25. Runnymede Memorial – no known grave.

Shakespear. Major Richard Harry Baird Shakespear, 2nd Battalion The Royal Scots Fusiliers. School House 1930–35. Killed 23 July 1943, aged 26. Buried in Catania War Cemetery, Sicily.

Shakespeare. Lieutenant William Shakespeare, RNVR. Moser's 1924–27. Killed 4 August 1943, serving in HM Motor Minesweeper 87, aged 32. Buried in St Just-in-Roseland Churchyard, Cornwall.

Shepherd. Ordinary Seaman Lambert Charles Shepherd, RN. Oldham's 1925–29. Killed in action 24 May 1941 in HMS *Hood*,[24] aged 30. Portsmouth Memorial – no known grave.

Shorting. Trooper Herbert John Shorting, 3rd County of London Yeomanry. Moser's 1920–25. Killed in action 6 July 1942, aged 35. Buried in El Alamein War Cemetery, Egypt.

Sinton. Flying Officer Arthur Buckby Sinton, RAFVR. Ingram's 1928–33. Killed 26 June 1943, serving with 515 Squadron, aged 28. Runnymede Memorial – no known grave.

[22] A new House Rugby Football Cup was presented in his memory by his parents, Dr and Mrs Scott.
[23] The destroyer HMS *Matabele* was torpedoed and sunk by the German submarine U-454 in the Barents Sea off Murmansk, on escort duty with Russia convoy PQ-8.
[24] The battleship HMS *Hood* was sunk off Greenland by the German battleship *Bismarck*.

Smith. 2nd Lieutenant George Brian Smith, The Northern Rhodesia Regiment. Rigg's 1919–23. Killed in action 18 August 1940, aged 34. Hargeisa Memorial, Somalia – no known grave.

Smith. Flight Lieutenant Richard Marcus Smith DFC, RAFVR. Ingram's 1930–34. Killed 30 November 1942, serving with 7 Squadron, Bomber Command, aged 26. Buried in Pécy Cemetery, Seine-et-Marne, France.

Spicer. Flight Lieutenant John Frederick Spicer, RAFVR. Tombling's 1932–36. Killed 16 June 1942 on operations over the Mediterranean, serving with 2 Photographic Reconnaissance Unit, aged 24. Alamein Memorial, Egypt – no known grave.

Steel. Major Peter Crawford Steel, 2nd Battalion The King's Shropshire Light Infantry. Ridgemount 1927–32. Killed in action 6 June 1944, aged 30. Buried in Ranville War Cemetery, Normandy.

Steele. Lieutenant William Trevor Steele, The Middlesex Regiment and Royal Artillery. Rigg's 1927–31. Killed 8 December 1941, serving with 60 Searchlight Regiment, aged 27. Buried in St Margaret's Churchyard, Hopton, Suffolk.

Stockton. Captain John Samuel Stockton, 1st Battalion The Scots Guards. Ridgemount 1932–37. Killed in action 27 April 1943, aged 24. Buried in Massicault War Cemetery, Tunisia.

Stockton. Lieutenant Peter Astley Stockton, The King's Regiment (Liverpool). Ridgemount 1934–39. Killed in action 23 April 1944, serving with the 2nd Battalion The Durham Light Infantry, aged 23. Rangoon Memorial, Burma – no known grave.

Stone. Sergeant Navigator David Campbell Stone, RAFVR. Chance's 1936–40. Killed in action 25 May 1943, serving with 100 Squadron, Bomber Command, aged 21. Buried in Jonkerbos War Cemetery, Nijmegen, Holland.

Strasser. Pilot Officer George Antony Strasser, RAFVR. Churchill's 1927–32. Killed in action 26 July 1942, serving with 114 Squadron, Bomber Command, aged 28. Buried in Becklingen War Cemetery, Soltau, Germany.

Sutcliffe. Captain Henry Sutcliffe, 5th Regiment The Reconnaissance Corps. Rigg's 1932–36. Killed in action 20 July 1943, aged 24. Buried in Catania War Cemetery, Sicily.

Sutherin. Flying Officer John Garnet Sutherin, RAFVR. School House 1937–41. Killed 26 August 1944, aged 21. Buried in St Dunstan's Churchyard, Cheam, Surrey.

Sutton. Captain Stephen Paul Sutton, Royal Artillery. Ridgemount 1925–30. Killed in action 17 June 1943, aged 31. Brookwood Memorial, Surrey – no known grave.

Swettenham. Major Kilner Swettenham, The Highland Light Infantry. School House 1924–28. Killed in action 4 September 1944, aged 34. Buried in Bruyelle War Cemetery, Antoing, Tournai, Belgium.

Symons. Lieutenant Terence Richard Symons, 5th Battalion The Coldstream Guards. Rigg's 1938–43. Killed in action 20 February 1945, aged 20. Buried in Mook War Cemetery, Nijmegen, Holland.

Tait. Leading Airman Graham Richard Danson Tait, RN, Fleet Air Arm. Ingram's 1934–38. Killed 10 December 1940 in a flying accident, serving in HMS *Daedalus*,[25] aged 20. Buried in St Albans Cemetery, Hertfordshire.

Thompson. Captain Robert Thompson, 5th Battalion The Coldstream Guards. School House 1926–30. Killed in action 5 January 1945, aged 33. Buried in Geel War Cemetery, Antwerp Province, Belgium.

Thornycroft. Lieutenant Charles Grey Mytton Thornycroft, Royal Engineers. Oldham's 1929–33. Killed in action 26 April 1943, serving with 144 Field Park Squadron, aged 28. Buried in Massicault War Cemetery, Tunisia.

Tynte. Lieutenant-Colonel Richard Mervyn Hardress Tynte (formerly Waller), The Cameronians (Scottish Rifles). Rigg's 1920–24. Died of wounds 10 March 1942, whilst in command of the 2nd Battalion The King's Own Yorkshire Light Infantry, aged 35. Buried in Rangoon War Cemetery, Burma.

Vaisey. Sergeant Pilot John Roland Maddison Vaisey, RAFVR. Oldham's 1930–34. Killed 30 September 1941 on operations over Germany, serving with 58 Squadron, Bomber Command, aged 25. Runnymede Memorial – no known grave.

Vickers. Major John Vickers, Royal Corps of Signals. Churchill's 1918–23. Died 8 March 1943, whilst a prisoner-of-war, aged 38. Buried in Sai Wan War Cemetery, Hong Kong.

Wales. Sergeant Pilot James Fyfe Wales, RAFVR. Moser's 1933–38. Killed 2 March 1940 in a training accident, aged 20. Buried in Eastfield Cemetery, Peterborough.

Weaver. Major John Yardley Weaver MC, Indian Army Remount Department. Moore's 1906–08. Died 15 November 1941, aged 50. Buried in Taukkyan War Cemetery, Rangoon, Burma.

White. Able Seaman Samuel Graham White, RNVR. Churchill's 1939–44. Died 5 April 1946, serving in HMS *Jackdaw*,[26] aged 19. Buried in Flaybrick Hill Cemetery, Birkenhead.

Whiteley. Brigadier John Percival Whiteley OBE TD MP, late Royal

[25] HMS *Daedalus* was a Royal Naval Air Station at Lee-on-Solent, Hampshire.
[26] HMS *Jackdaw* was a Royal Naval Air Station at Crail, Fife, Scotland.

Artillery. Moser's 1911–15. Killed 4 July 1943 in an air accident off Gibraltar,[27] aged 45. Buried in Gibraltar North Front Cemetery.

Williamson. Captain Arthur John Williamson, 2nd Battalion The Sherwood Foresters. School House 1924–28. Killed in action 31 January 1944, aged 33. Buried in Anzio War Cemetery, Italy.

Williamson. Captain Thomas McDowall Williamson, General List. Moore's 1921–26. Died 22 August 1944, serving with HQ 11th (East African) Division, aged 36. Buried in Imphal War Cemetery, Manipur, India.

Willington. Captain Frederick Willington, The West Yorkshire Regiment. Dayboys 1918–20. Died 15 October 1942, serving with the King's African Rifles. Buried in Mbaraki Cemetery, Mombasa, Kenya.

Wilson. Captain Daniel Martin Wilson MC, Royal Artillery. Moser's 1920–25. Killed in action 6 April 1943, serving with 64 Medium Regiment, aged 36. Medjez-el-Bab Memorial, Tunisia – no known grave.

Winbolt. Pilot Officer Leonard James Winbolt, RAF. Chance's 1932–36. Killed in action 17 February 1941, serving with 37 (Bomber) Squadron, aged 22. Buried in Cairo War Memorial Cemetery, Egypt.

Wood. Captain William Angus Wood MC, Royal Artillery. Rigg's 1928–33. Killed in action 25 September 1944, serving with 124 Field Regiment, aged 29. Buried in Arnhem Oosterbeek War Cemetery, Holland.

---

[27] This was the Liberator aircraft of General Sikorski, the Polish Prime Minister in exile and Commander-in-Chief, who, together with all on board except the pilot, was killed in a crash into the sea off Gibraltar.

ABBREVIATIONS

(A)	(Air) – after a naval rank
AFC	Air Force Cross
CBE	Commander of the Order of the British Empire
DFC	Distinguished Flying Cross
DSO	Companion of the Distinguished Service Order
MBE	Member of the Order of the British Empire
MC	Military Cross
OBE	Officer of the Order of the British Empire
RAAF	Royal Australian Air Force
RAFVR	Royal Air Force Volunteer Reserve
RCAF	Royal Canadian Air Force
RNR	Royal Naval Reserve
RNVR	Royal Naval Volunteer Reserve
RNZAF	Royal New Zealand Air Force
TD	Territorial Efficiency Decoration